IDENTITY, EQUITY AND SOCIAL JUSTICE IN ASIA PACIFIC EDUCATION

IDENTITY, EQUITY AND SOCIAL JUSTICE IN ASIA PACIFIC EDUCATION

Edited by Raqib Chowdhury & Lilly K. Yazdanpanah

MONASH University Publishing

CONTENTS

LOCAL EPISTEMOLOGIES IN UNDERSTANDING SOCIAL JUSTICE

Raqib Chowdhury and Lilly K. Yazdanpanah

> In a perfect world, social justice is not a relevant consideration. If in all possible respects people are identical in their qualities, relationships and material prosperity then fair treatment would accrue to all. Quite what such a world would look like remains uncertain, and whether it would constitute a human life worth living is problematic, but these considerations, fortunately, are immaterial to determining how social justice gains its purchase. Clearly, when people are equal and treated equally then questions of social justice do not arise.
>
> Clark 2006, 275

I

While contemporary research has showcased numerous studies on the transformative themes of equity, inclusiveness, access, identity and social justice in education contexts, these studies have been predominantly framed, explored and understood through 'Western' understandings, which have often failed to sufficiently problematise these themes in the settings of developing or underdeveloped countries, such as those in the Asia Pacific region. Indeed, some studies have indicated the insufficiency of Western discourses in understanding how these themes are enacted under conditions markedly different from the developed West. This has necessitated research that recognises the relevance of alternative understandings and one, in part, that makes reference to a wide range of contextual and cultural perspectives available in the literature from the Asia Pacific region – a growing reaction, one could say, to the predominance of Western social theories employed in these studies. Education's connection to social justice (or, perhaps, the other way round) is inevitable – because of how it produces learners' social and cultural identities in an increasingly multicultural milieu. Education is a rich setting in which the spatio-temporal dimensions of social justice issues are enacted on a daily basis.

This book is a response to the need for recognition of and movement towards understandings that reference the wide range of contextual and cultural perspectives available in the Asia Pacific region in relation to educational enactments of social justice. While frequently featuring as a key concept in both policy and practice, social justice is pragmatically problematic in that it is often constructed variably by educators, policy makers and other vested interest groups to their own advantages. Our understanding of social justice is foundational upon our understanding of who we are – our identities. Understanding identity is thus crucial in problematising how educational realities are conceptualised, constructed and played out, and indeed how our educational selves are manifested in our different roles as teachers and learners. Contemporary research is generally in favour of conceptualising identity as fluid or, as Hall points out, 'points of temporary attachment to the subject positions which discursive practices construct for us' (Hall 1996, 6), and this is generally how identity has been framed in the chapters of this book.

II

As European colonisers established their power over nations in Asia, Africa, and the Americas throughout the 17th to early 20th centuries, they used the masking excuse of educating and civilising the natives as a reason for their exploitation, hence making education a colonial raison d'être. Legally consolidated through administration, education was turned into a non-aggressive suppression of the natives and what Gramsci (1971) calls 'domination by consent'. The colonial education system then normalised the imperial knowledge as legitimate and an apparatus to delegitimise other ways of knowing that had been practised by the 'natives' throughout centuries. This knowledge created a frame of reference that represented the colonised identity and their knowledge as inferior and the Western knowledge system and identity as superior (Rizvi et al. 2006).

As such, education has historically played an important role in creating and maintaining domination through the colonised knowledge system where local knowledge was misapprehended and distorted, leading to the alienation of the locals from their identities and instigating social inequalities that helped the colonisers maintain their power to further dominate (Akena 2012). Through learning the language of the masters and being educated through their textbooks, the colonised nations were, and we believe to a certain extent still are, indoctrinated into the hegemonic system of Western knowledge (Rizvi et al. 2006). Their colonised identities are shaped in this manner and affect the ways they understand themselves, the Other, and the world (Young 2003). Education thus became one of the most powerful discourses of colonialism and postcolonialism.

Like elsewhere, education in Asia Pacific countries is being continuously transformed by globalisation of the economy, diasporic communities transcending national boundaries, as well as an increasingly faster pace of technological innovation – all of which offer new and unique challenges. Most economies within the region have flourished due to increased regional capital flow, trade, and other forms of economic and political interaction. The Asia Pacific also has rich and unique traditions, which create cultural diversity as well as common challenges, including obstacles of language and geographical separation. In part, educational institutes are increasingly feeling the pressure to prepare their learners as job-ready, employable graduates and active members of the citizenry.

In such a melting pot of interactions, how are educational practices in regard to equity, identity and social justice informed by perspectives rooted in local frameworks of understanding? How are education systems around the world (and in this case, in the Asia Pacific region) informed by scholarly understandings of social justice – what is fair, equitable and democratically produced and consumed? How, in this process, are our identities shaped and reshaped as we enact education across time and space?

This book's interest lies in understanding how we, as educators, discuss and address equity, identity and social justice in the context of Asia Pacific countries and how these issues are problematised through ongoing dialogue with dominant Western academic discourses in the form of empirical research. The chapters in this book engage in theoretical debates on the various issues and how these are understood and acted out by people across socioeconomic class, gender and learning opportunities. Contributors in this book speak from a blend of cultural spaces, each within their own specific educational contexts.

Some chapters address how the notion of equity is understood, communicated and implemented into specific educational contexts, while others reflect on how educational systems impact on, wound and construct identities. A number of chapters have also explored how education can have an impact by transforming itself in a wider context. All sections touch on diversity, challenges, the connection between theory and practice, and new ideas beyond what is known in Western bodies of academic knowledge.

III

In drawing all these themes together into a coherent whole, the book has drawn inspiration from a number of contemporary titles, as it has at the same time sought to distinguish itself from these titles. Johnson's *A Twenty-First Century Approach to Teaching Social Justice: Educating for Both Advocacy and Action* emphasises marginalised groups such as women, people of colour, queers, working class/poor individuals, and disabled people as well as people from the LGBTIQ community and religious minorities. This book is written with the purpose of raising awareness of social justice issues with undergraduate and graduate students rather than for a wider audience including policy makers. Nygreen's 2013 book *These Kids: Identity, Agency, and Social Justice at a Last Chance High School* is a study based on a youth-led participatory action research project in a California high school, centred on a group of students who are 'left behind' because of the deep barriers that educational discourses have created and sustained. Nygreen's main argument is that social justice in education is 'impossible' today precisely because of how we talk about it – a theme this book picks up and extends further (see, for example, Chapter Two).

Johnson and Parry's edited volume *Fostering Social Justice Through Qualitative Inquiry: A Methodological Guide* (2015), although designed as a textbook, is based on a number of theories and case studies that discuss how major qualitative methodologies are employed to create social justice in both the process and as products of qualitative research. The book is structured and 'tightly organised' so that it can be used for a course of study, rather than as an illustrative study of social justice issues across a range of settings. Similarly, Perumal's 2007 book *Identity, Diversity and Teaching for Social Justice* is a primer reader to understand personal and professional nuances of teachers' lives through a consideration of the personal, cultural and political implications of language teaching, within educational contexts. It also addresses how such considerations affect curricular decisions which are essentially political constructs which have compromised neutrality in multiple ways.

Pliner and Banks's *Teaching, Learning and Intersecting Identities in Higher Education* (2012) similarly focuses on the classroom – with references to teaching and learning processes (pedagogical strategies and methods for classroom practice), rather than on policies and practices at large and broader social settings. It also examines teaching and learning as integrated and synergistic practices and analyses the institutional power dynamics between scholars and students.

An earlier but well-known title is Vincent's 2003 *Social Justice, Education and Identity*, on how identities are enacted within the education setting, and especially how the education system, through its practices, is implicated in the realisation of just or unjust social outcomes. In particular, the authors examine the ways in which the identities of individuals and groups are formed and transformed across educational institutes with emphasis on the themes of class, ethnicity, gender, sexuality and (dis)ability.

Finally, Zuniga, Lopez and Ford's 2013 edited title *Intergroup Dialogue: Engaging Difference, Social Identities and Social Justice* addresses how to engage social identities through the processes of communication, critical reflection and collaborative action across social and cultural divides, with emphasis on higher education, school and community settings and the learning that takes place through dialogue among these groups.

Instead of reaching out, often through well-entrenched Western epistemologies, to address the greater populations of the industrialised West, a social justice approach to education allows spaces within which the needs of the deprived and marginalised are addressed more efficiently. Academic scholars find themselves camped on the binary of either vouching for a provision of enhanced opportunities for equality or equal access to educational affordances, or rather to measure equity through educational outcomes. This book takes a balanced view in that it looks at educational equity through the agenda of both sides. So while policy-level equity provision has been understood through the interests of policy makers, learners on the other hand (and on the receiving end), have also been acknowledged as agents with rich knowledge and a clear sense of what is most beneficial for them and for the society at large in empowering them as active and vocal agents of their own aspirations. As James (2012) explained:

> Critical to the work of educators who take a social justice and equity approach to teaching is their understanding – which they will pass on to their students – of the societal or structural roots and causes of the inequity and resultant social conditions and problems that they and

their students encounter in their daily lives. Within this framework, students learn to make the connections between their privileges … and come to understand the reasons for their struggles and social conditions.

Such an approach allows the various stakeholders of education to build new relationships and offer ownership to all in the construction of policies, pedagogies, the curriculum and the entire process of teaching and learning.

IV

Arguing that Bourdieu's Western-based cultural capital framework does not reflect the realities of child-rearing practices of non-Western Iraqi migrant mothers in Australia, Al-Deen and Windle present an extension to the theory. They propose that in today's globalised world where mothers transition between different cultural contexts, it is more relevant to look at cultural capital from the point of view of transnationalism, multilingualism, colonialism, ethnicity, religion and ideology. They conclude that cultural capital originates from ideology and culture rather than as a strategy for investment.

In Chapter Three, Giri traces the status of English language teaching (ELT) in Nepal back to its beginning when English was the language of power and had perpetuated sociolinguistic divides as well as social and educational inequalities. He urgently calls for ELT practitioners and policy makers to rigorously examine the role of English language education in today's Nepalese society and to determine whether and how it may have established neo-colonial divides.

In Chapter Four, Fernandes, Khan, Lavanya and Thenabadu present a cross-comparative analysis of the education of women in Bangladesh, India, Pakistan and Sri Lanka against the shared history of colonisation of these countries. The authors argue that since the colonial period, when boys and men were educated to correspond and transact with the British colonisers, there has been a significant difference in numbers between men and women in receiving formal education. This imbalance is still present as a result of what the authors call the 3Ps of Poverty, Patriarchy and the Politics of Culture and Caste, with poverty being the strongest contributor to such inequality. The authors suggest solutions to challenge the state of women's education by unlocking the patriarchal and postcolonial hierarchies of power.

In Chapter Five, a critical analysis of two English language textbooks used in Pakistani schools leads Ali to call for an epistemological shift to de-colonise educational resources by breaking the dichotomies of native-English hegemony versus the non-native English speaking Other that are evident in the teaching of culture in English language textbooks in Pakistan. This can be attained through maintaining a balance between the local and global teaching of English where non-native English language learners are recognised as multi-competent users of English. She also emphasises the importance of promoting a global and local (or 'glocal') view of English to distance ELT from concepts of coloniality. It is through providing a balance between the local and global that English language learners can be prepared to collaborate in a global society.

In Chapter Six, Shokouhi and Fard-Kashani look at the ways in which the Persian pronoun for 'I', /mæn/, is used as a marker of power in the Persian language to represent identity. The significantly higher use of the pronoun by the males in the study compared to the females shows that males are more strongly positioned to represent their identity role in the male-dominated Iranian society, despite years of living in Australia.

In Chapter Seven, Kong argues that as a response to globalisation and internationalisation of universities, Australian universities have opened their doors to a surge of non-English speaking background (NESB) international students without sufficiently supporting them. She presents an in-depth qualitative study of how five Asian postgraduate international students negotiated their identities during their studies at an Australian university. The study calls for a need to holistically support international students both in and outside the classroom by effectively responding to their emotional and language competency needs on a continual basis.

Matsunaga in Chapter Eight, looking at transnational teacher identity, demonstrates how teachers living and working in culturally and linguistically different contexts construct their professional identities initially through learning to negotiate power and emotions and then through the narratives they use to make sense of their position in the new context.

In Chapter Nine, Hanh and Thanh present a qualitative analysis of how the power distance between teachers and students can directly contribute to inequalities of relationships between students and teachers and distributions of learning opportunities for students within classrooms. To respond to this matter, rather than importing contextually irrelevant Western methods of ELT, the authors propose implementing a culturally appropriate pedagogy where such cultural features are taken into consideration so that the power gap between students and teachers is closed.

In Chapter Ten, Liyanage explains how, due to globalisation, the engagement of international donor organisations as well as local structural adjustment policies, education in Kiribati has undergone significant changes. English is now the medium of instruction at schools and an important employability factor. However, the Kiribati people's strong attachment to their local community values remains at odds with the use of English in the classroom. Liyanage argues that, rather than being imposed, changes need to be sensitive to the local culture and the educational traditions of the people in Kiribati, starting from the curriculum and a teacher education system that reflects such sensitivity.

In Chapter Eleven, Kim explains how government funding, measured against university rankings and graduate employability, is instrumental in the sustainability of Korean universities. This situation has resulted in an inequitable loop where the wealthy have monopolised the good universities, causing social-class division. As a response to this issue the government has introduced the *Three-No's* policy that prevents universities from admitting students based on entrance exams, high schools and donations. In a qualitative interview with university deans, Kim demonstrates that the policy has further complicated matters and given rise to a tension between the desire of the people for equity on one hand and the desire of the government for inducing competition-based reforms on the other.

V

This book offers a collection of studies about equality and justice, fairness and equity – all in relation to education, teaching and learning while also making references to contemporary understandings of scholarly debates and conceptualisations within the broader socioeconomic contexts lying beyond, but inevitably connected to academia. In doing so, it offers fresh understandings of how these themes are relevant to educational research and practice.

It is hoped that together this collection will facilitate a more nuanced understanding of the relevance of these themes and allow future researchers to apply new frameworks of understanding of how these are relevant to our educational practices today. It is also hoped that this collection will trigger critically informed perspectives on the implications of our new understandings of the structural and socioeconomic causes of inequality to inform our practices.

With the rise of globalisation, there is a growing tendency to 'decentre and diversify knowledge production' in light of 'representations [of] lived realities and meanings of the people' from diverse cultures and nations (Chen 2010, vii). Together the chapters critically look at how educational, social, economic and cultural practices in regard to equity, identity and social justice are informed by perspectives rooted in and often endorsed by theories originating locally. In an age of increased awareness of who we are and how we are positioned in the multiple discourses available around us, the book's primary interest lies in understanding how we, as educators, discuss and address the changed scenario of educational provision in terms of access and participation.

References

Akena, F.A. (2012). Critical analysis of the production of Western knowledge and its implications for Indigenous knowledge and decolonization. *Journal of Black Studies*, 43(6), 599-619.

Chen K.H. (2010). *Asia as method: Towards deimperialization*. Durham, NC: Duke University Press.

Clark, J.A. (2006). Social justice and education: New and continuing themes. *British Journal of Educational Studies*, 54(3), 272-287.

Dimitriadis, G., and Kamberelis, G. (2006). *Theory for education*. New York: Routledge.

Gramsci, A. (1971). *Selections from the Prison Notebooks of Antonio Gramsci*. Translated by Q. Hoare and G.N. Smith. New York: International Publishers.

Hall, S. (1996). Introduction: Who needs identity? In S. Hall and P. Du Gay (eds.), *Questions of cultural identity*. London: Sage.

James, C.E. (2012). Equity, social justice and the inclusive classroom. *Research for Teachers*, July 2012. Retrieved 17 May 2017 from http://oere.oise.utoronto.ca/wp-content/uploads/2012/11/+Research-for-Teachers-Number-10-Equity-Social-Justice-and-the-Inclusive-Classroom.pdf

McLeod, J., and Thomson, R. (2009). *Researching social change: Qualitative approaches*. London: Sage.

Rizvi, F., Lingard, B., and Lavia, J. (2006). Postcolonialism and education: Negotiating a contested terrain. *Pedagogy, Culture & Society*, 14(3), 249-262.

Vincent, C. (2003). *Social justice, education and identity*. London: Routledge Famler.

Young, R. (2003). *Postcolonialism: A very short introduction*. Oxford: Oxford University Press.

CHAPTER 2

CHALLENGES IN CONCEPTUALISING EDUCATIONAL INEQUALITIES IN THE CONTEXT OF MIGRATION

Working with Western and Islamic Conceptions of Motherhood

Taghreed Jamal Al-Deen & Joel Windle

Abstract

This paper contributes to our understanding of educational inequalities by problematising and extending the influential theoretical framework developed by French sociologist Pierre Bourdieu. We argue that migrant mothers present particular characteristics that are not easily recognised within the framework as a result of their transition between societies, involving changes in social position and cultural capital. We seek to extend the theoretical resources developed by Bourdieu by identifying the importance of ideologies of motherhood, and how these shape the interpretations and reactions of mothers when confronted with different kinds of educational settings and opportunities for developing educational strategies. Based on a study of Iraqi mothers in Australia, we show how their practices and understandings are shaped by cultural and economic contexts. Their experiences of motherhood vary based on how they are positioned in relation to intensive mothering and Islamic conceptions of motherhood. The findings suggest that the traditional relationship between parental engagement with children's education and cultural capital differs in the case of migrant mothers, requiring a rethinking of the theoretical repertoire used to understand educational inequalities in the context of cultural diversity.

Keywords: motherhood, migration, Islam, ideology, cultural capital

Introduction

A large body of literature demonstrates that the educational advantages enjoyed by families from socially privileged groups are connected to childrearing practices, conceived of as developing cultural capital (e.g., Bourdieu and Passeron 1990; Lareau 2008; Reay 1999). Yet current social constructions of motherhood in this literature often do not reflect the realities of non-Western mothers, particularly in the context of migration, who are constructed as 'Other' (Bhopal 1998). In changing social and cultural circumstances, the question of what it means to be a mother and a migrant deserves attention within studies of educational inequality. To ignore this question is to further marginalise migrant populations.

This chapter discusses a number of limitations in the influential cultural capital model (Bourdieu 1977, 1986; Bourdieu and Passeron 1990) as it relates to the role of mothers. First, we suggest the model is based on a Western conception of motherhood that is not necessarily shared in other cultures, in this case the Iraqi Islamic culture. The framework of French sociologist Pierre Bourdieu admits variation in mothering practices over time and between different status groups, but pays little attention to contact or movement between societies. Issues of transnationalism, multilingualism, colonialism, race and religion are almost entirely absent. Important differences in conceptions of motherhood that are related to these issues are therefore underplayed or unrecognised. This allows an implicit normative model of neoliberal, middle-class motherhood to emerge in educational research. The model of 'successful' mothering is judged by effective preparation for, and engagement with, formal schooling in Western nations – sometimes termed 'intensive mothering'. Increasingly, such schooling is 'marketised', placing demands on mothers to be strategic choosers as well as closely monitoring academic progress. Mothers, like some of the Iraqi participants in our study, who instead focus on moral codes, religious instruction and Arabic literacy education, therefore appear to be neglectful, inefficient or incompetent in their mothering when the cultural capital model is applied.

The chapter begins with a review of sociological studies of motherhood in relation to educational inequality, before showing how Islamic conceptions of motherhood diverge from the kinds of practices and interpretations focused on in Western frameworks. We then briefly discuss how competing conceptions of motherhood are managed in the context of migration from Iraq to Australia, and how these are influenced both by cultural frameworks and the institutional conditions of neoliberal schooling.

Motherhood and Educational Inequality

Child-rearing practices, and motherhood in particular, came into the sights of research on educational inequality through the original analysis Bourdieu developed as an attempt to move beyond explanations founded almost exclusively on economic relationships. Bourdieu criticised the explanations of differences in academic achievement advanced by his contemporaries and argued that:

> They neglect to relate scholastic investment strategies to the whole set of educational strategies and to the system of reproduction strategies, they inevitably, by a necessary paradox, let slip the best hidden and socially most determinant educational investment, namely, the domestic transmission of cultural capital. Their studies of the relationship between academic ability and academic investment show that they are unaware that ability or talent is itself the product of an investment of time and cultural capital … scholastic yield from educational action depends on the cultural capital previously invested by the family. (Bourdieu 1986, 244)

Bourdieu used the term 'reproduction' to describe the phenomenon by which advantaged social groups possess, and have better access to, institutional resources which, in turn, reaffirm and consolidate, their advantaged position in society (Bourdieu 1977, 487). It is noteworthy, in this formulation, that changes or maintenance of position are always conceived of as within a kind of closed society, insulated from other worlds of social positions and strategies that processes of migration traverse.

In this analysis, cultural capital is the key mechanism for such reproduction of advantage, and the role of mothers in primary socialisation is central (Bourdieu 1986). Parents' cultural capital, as it relates to education, exists in three forms: personal dispositions, attitudes and knowledge gained from educational experience; connections to education-related objects (e.g., books, computers, academic credentials); and connections to educational institutions (e.g., schools, universities, libraries, etc.) (Grenfell and James 1998). Cultural capital entails a collection of cultural dispositions and these dispositions are 'the product of a process of (conscious and unconscious) cultivation' (Brubaker 2004, 41). For example, Bourdieu argued that attending the theatre and visiting art galleries and museums, as well as family discussions about such cultural and aesthetic forms, are practices that are both socially restricted and construct tastes and reference points that offer scholastic advantage. Bourdieu's own empirical work in France tended to support the hypothesis, and studies in the US have also pointed to the influence of cultural activities such as music lessons on academic success (Dumais 2002).

Bourdieu (1986) argued that people possess cultural capital to varying degrees and that it shapes parents' engagement in the education of their children, explaining the differences in educational experiences between groups of children:

> The notion of cultural capital … is a theoretical hypothesis which made it possible to explain the unequal scholastic achievement of children originating from the different social classes by relating academic success, the specific profits which children from the different classes and class fractions can obtain in the academic market, to the distribution of cultural capital between the classes and class fractions. (p. 243)

This quotation not only shows that cultural capital is conceived of as something that may not be directly measurable ('a theoretical hypothesis'), but also that differentiation is conceived of primarily in terms of social class, rather than cultural, religious or ethnic groupings. Bourdieu's use of the term 'academic market' is an attempt to relativise the value of both academic knowledge and knowledge cultivated in the home. There is nothing inherently better about the family practices of particular groups, merely a closer alignment with the kinds of knowledge that has currency in formal schooling. This is important to remember, and saves Bourdieu's theory from irrelevance when other social and symbolic boundaries, beyond social class, are to be considered.

This relativism is further advanced by the concept of *habitus*. Unlike cultural capital (to be judged by value in markets such as schooling), everybody has a habitus, which can be conceived of both at individual and collective levels. Habitus can be thought of as a set of principles that guide actions and beliefs, whether or not this contributes to social advantage. Cultural capital is the product of the recognition of the educational aspects of the family's habitus in the practices and values of the educational system within which the family interacts (Lee and Bowen 2006). According to Horvat (2003), when a parent's habitus is aligned with what is valued by the institution they interact with and when that habitus assists parents to navigate that system to obtain their desired goals, it becomes embodied cultural capital. Working class families do not lack 'culture' in this perspective, but cultivate tastes and practices that are considered to be vulgar, incorrect or irrelevant by schools and teachers.

It is possible to see that Bourdieu's framework is potentially open to a wider definition of social groupings, although it is an open question as to how cultural capital and habitus may be transferable from one society to another. To date, most of the applications of Bourdieu's framework have kept the original focus on social class in Western societies, and have identified a range of processes through which mothers help to reproduce social advantages and disadvantages (Lamont and Lareau 1988; Lareau 2003; Lareau and Horvat 1999; Reay 1998a, 1998b, 1999). The role that parents – particularly mothers – play in their children's education has often been shown to be an important factor in children's general school success (Lareau 2008; Vincent 2010).

Studies in some Western settings (e.g., Griffith and Smith 2005; Reay 1995, 1998a, 1998b, 1999) suggest that mothers are more involved not only with their children's day-to-day care but also their education than fathers. These studies further examine the interplay of gender and class during the process of involvement in education. Griffith and Smith's (2005) study in Canada shows that the smooth operation of the school and children's education requires time and energy from the mothers that many working class and/or single mothers cannot afford. Similarly, Reay's (1995; 1998a; 1998b, 1999) studies in the UK confirm that middle class mothers have appropriate cultural resources and usually carry a sense of certainty and legitimacy when dealing with their children's school. Other scholars have similarly highlighted gendered and classed issues associated with supporting children's education (Crozier 2001; Lareau 2003; Standing 1999a, 1999b). Their work also explains how poor, working-class, single mothers endure emotional as well as material and cultural inequalities in doing educational care work. Moreover, they explore inequalities in mothers' access to, and activation of, capitals with respect to the production of efforts to support the education of their children. Certainly, migrant mothers confront many of the same issues as non-migrant, working-class mothers (Blackledge 2001). However, some middle-class migrants bring with them a history of high status and legitimacy in dealing with educational institutions, and these 'advantages' may either carry through or lose value in relation to a new academic market – a question our study seeks to answer.

Until now, the study of migrant mothers as a distinct category, in relation to their involvement in children's education, has not received much attention. Within the very limited literature, it is reported that migrant mothers encounter difficulties participating effectively in educational activities. These difficulties includ linguistic and cultural barriers, lack of knowledge of the education system, feelings of discrimination, and limited school support (Blackledge 2001; Chao 1996; Shannon 1996; Sohn and Wang 2006). In Bourdieu's framework, outlooks and practices are shaped by material conditions and social position, making it possible to include consideration of the influence of some of the specific barriers faced by migrant women. However, in the case of migrants (and arguably in society, more generally), responses are not shaped merely by one's social location and possibilities, but by the previously developed beliefs and ideologies used to interpret these. In the case of migrants, it is clear that these interpretive and ideological frameworks are not merely the product of current circumstances, since they were constructed, over time, in another society. But it is arguable that Bourdieu also underestimates the power of overarching interpretative frameworks relative to the direct influence of material conditions.

Ideologies of Motherhood and Mothering

With its focus on resources and the expenditure of labour through investment strategies, some of the work inspired by Bourdieu's framework leaves to one side questions of the ideological construction of motherhood, and hence a source of cultural variations in responses to different forms of advantage or adversity. This is in keeping with Bourdieu's own privileging of material conditions and social position as shaping outlooks, over ideological or discursive ('propaganda') influences (Bourdieu and Wacquant 1992). Of course, most theories of ideology also connect this construct to the maintenance, or disruption, of a social order based on material conditions. This is, we argue, one of the missing ingredients that is needed in order to bring migrant mothers into the analysis of educational inequalities.

Motherhood, as McMahon (1995, 158) suggests, plays 'a symbolic role in integrating issues of individual identity, moral choice and social commitment in the women's lives'. According to Chodorow (1989), motherhood is entwined with notions of femininity: since a woman, as a female, has the capacity to conceive, gestate, give birth and lactate, the role of motherhood is seen by society as central to a woman's identity (Arendell 2000). However,

McMahon (1995) suggests there is no universal ideal of motherhood, nor a unitary model of mothering, with activities and understandings shaped by cultural, historical and economic contexts. The experiences of motherhood vary according to class structure and family forms (Hays 1996; Lupton 2000; McMahon 1995), race (Collins 1994), ethnicity (Bhopal 1998; Liam 1999; Liamputtong 2001, 2006; Liamputtong and Naksook 2003) and religion (Sered 1996). For example, Bhopal's (1998) study on South Asian women living in East London showed that women perceive motherhood as a natural result of an arranged marriage related to the importance of bearing male children in order to continue the ancestral line and to enhance the family pride and honour. Women are judged as good or bad mothers, she argues, through this social construction of motherhood.

Religion can also be another factor that affects experiences of motherhood in ways that are largely missing from the literature on educational inequalities, especially those based in Western societies. Religions address issues of motherhood in ways such as telling women 'how many children to have, when, and with whom; religion may tell women that infertility is a punishment from the gods; and religions may tell women how to raise and educate their children. Cross-culturally, religions interpret the experiences of motherhood' (Sered 1996, 72).

Even though existing literature on motherhood has provided a rich understanding of motherhood and mothers' personal experiences, it has largely been examined from a Western cultural perspective. The ideology of motherhood is entwined with idealised notions of the white, Western, middle-class, nuclear family (Arendell 2000). The experiences of mothers outside this image, such as poor mothers and mothers from different racial, ethnic and religious backgrounds, have been largely excluded.

The dominant motherhood ideology in Western society, particularly in North America, is that of intensive mothering, which may be thought of, in Bourdieusian terms, as a strategy for building cultural capital in the next generation (Lareau 2003, 2008). Intensive mothering – as an ideology of 'child-rearing guidelines' – encompasses the view that child-rearing should be 'expert-guided, emotionally absorbing, labour intensive and financially expensive' (Hays 1996, 69). It also assumes that children require one primary caregiver: that is, the biological or social mother. The ideology of intensive mothering therefore defines women and promotes standards by which they are judged (Arendell 1999). Arendell further argues that no mother can safely or continually live up to the intensive mothering ideology, which is an idealised construct. According to Arendell (2000), a variety of deviancy discourses derive from this ideological construct of mothering, aimed differentially at mothers who do not follow this script. Targets of these discourses are mothers who do not conform to the normative narrative of white, middle-class, heterosexual marriage followed by the birth of healthy children and full-time devoted motherhood: including welfare mothers, single mothers, immigrant mothers, lesbian mothers, birth mothers, adoptive mothers, mothers who break contractual agreements or assert their autonomy in the process of utilising reproductive technologies and mothers of children with disabilities. Even those mothers who disagree with and/or do not conform to the ideology of intensive mothering are still affected by it. They are judged by others according to how closely their practices fit the ideology and position themselves in relation to it (Arendell 2000).

A danger faced by research on educational inequalities that brush over the ideological dimensions of motherhood is to celebrate 'concerted cultivation' as the best form of parenting – as it appears to be the most successful and effective. 'Effective' is a term used in evaluating mothers' practices that can easily be understood as 'good' or 'valuable'. As such, a certain set of practices, most common amongst socially dominant groups, such as tutoring, music lessons, homework monitoring, etc., is valued above others. In order to overcome this problem, it is important to relate effectiveness to the values and practices that are recognised ideologically and institutionally. Practices are not, of themselves, effective or good – they gain purchase only relative to the school system and ideological context. Advantages accrue from enacting the types of participation most valued by the school or most strongly associated with academic achievement. Parents from different ethnic backgrounds may show different types of connections because they differ in relation to dispositions, perceptions and attitudes towards education (i.e., their habitus). However, their own self-perception is shaped in important ways by the dominant Western, middle-class norm, and their distance from it. In our study, some mothers felt inadequate and experienced feelings of shame, partly as a result of their perceived inability to fulfill roles based on pre-migration models, but also to participate in activities such as strategic school choice, connected to motherhood in the neoliberal Australian education market.

Study Methodology

The chapter draws on a study of the participation of Iraqi migrant mothers in the education of their primary and secondary children. The project involved semi-structured interviews with 25 Muslim Iraqi women with school-aged children in Melbourne, Australia. The analysis focused on drawing out strategies and practices related to education, and connecting these both to the institutional conditions of schooling in Australia, and the kinds of material and symbolic resources that mothers were able to draw on and construct in their efforts (Jamal Al-deen and Windle 2015). Our work was grounded in a Bourdieusian theoretical framework; however, we found that this provided limited attention to a number of influences, particularly the interrelation between educational practices and religious, cultural and social values and beliefs formed prior to migration. This is a case study, and the findings are not intended to be generalisable.

The study employed a qualitative approach, which allows for an in-depth exploration of participants' experiences, perceptions and beliefs. The purposive sample was recruited through community associations: (1) the Muslim Iraqi community in the northern suburbs of the Australian city of Melbourne; (2) an Arab Iraqi community association located in a south-eastern suburb in Melbourne; and (3) three Iraqi ethnic schools located in north-west, east and south-east areas of Melbourne. In total, 25 mothers were recruited, with all but three being interviewed at least twice. Data was collected through audio-taped, face-to-face, semi-structured interviews conducted in Arabic, the participants' as well as the first author's native language.

The majority of participants lived in areas with a relatively high population of migrants and low socioeconomic status (Al-Khudairi 2005). All of the mothers had children enrolled in public and/or private (including Islamic) primary and/or secondary schools in 2010. All had resided in Australia for a minimum of two years and held permanent resident visas or were Australian citizens. These mothers came from different parts of Iraq, mainly from the south and centre. The women and/or their husbands and children were forced out of their country by war, life-threatening situations and intolerable living conditions. Among these women, only two were in paid employment, although some of them were tertiary educated and had jobs in Iraq. Seven of them held Bachelor degrees, four held TAFE (technical and further education) diplomas, three had completed secondary school, and the remaining eleven had at most incomplete secondary school studies.

Findings

Intensification of Motherhood as a Religiously-defined Social Role

The interplay of material conditions and ideological standards of motherhood is made clear by the experience of unemployment amongst the participants. Virtually all of the mothers were without paid employment. Some mothers belonged to the middle or upper-middle class in Iraq but, once they migrated to Australia, this group usually encountered difficulties in employment, thus affecting their class status and intensifying the importance of mothering as part of their social identity and self-perception. Even those mothers in paid employment considered this to be secondary to their mothering duties, and something they could easily forego without losing status or self-regard.

The mothers in the study cited religious texts, including the Qur'an and hadith (the sayings of the Prophet), to explain the centrality of motherhood to their lives. In Islam, motherhood is considered as a blessing from God to human beings. There are several verses in the Holy Qur'an that mention the significance of motherhood (Kausar 2006). In Islamic texts, mothers are to be shown utmost respect and veneration. The Qur'an and the hadith state explicitly that children are to respect their parents, especially their mothers. In one well known hadith, it is stated that mothers are deserving of the kindest of companionship, even before fathers. In several hadith, the nursing mother is described as performing moral work that deserves divine reward. One of the Prophetic Hadith states that: 'when a mother nurses, she receives for every mouthful of milk and for every suck, the reward of one good deed. And if she is kept awake by her child at night, she receives the reward of one who frees seventy slaves for the sake of Allah' (Schleifer 1996, 53). The Qur'an indicates that a Muslim ought to revere one's mother because a mother 'Beareth him in weakness upon weakness, and his weaning is in two years' (The Qur'an 31:14).

Of course, there is no uniform set of Islamic mothering practices, or interpretations of religious texts on mothering. The feminist[1] approach taken by some Muslim scholars such as Amina Wadud (1999), Leila Ahmed (1992) and Fatima Mernissi (1987) is based on the modernist exhortation to

---

1   Rules of the Qur'an were interpreted in a more patriarchal way by Islamic law (Keddie 1990; Ahmed 1992). In general, later practice was more patriarchal than the Qur'anic text affirms. This gives some basis to modern feminists and reformers who want to return to and reinterpret the Qur'an. They argue that it is not so much Islam which is oppressive to women but the way in which it has been interpreted in Muslim societies.

ignore medieval fiqh (Islamic jurisprudence) and to return to the pure Islam of the Qur'an through ijtihad (personal interpretation of Qur'an). Wadud (1999), in her book about the Qur'an, attacks the suggestion that bringing up a child is decreed a role exclusive to women. The development of modern interpretations of the Qur'an by the abovementioned feminists does not mean that in presenting these interpretations, these authors explicitly contest the ideology of motherhood that is reinforced by religious and cultural traditions: even Muslim women who are successful in social and political arenas are careful to represent themselves in ways that suggest they are not radically challenging traditional gender roles. Traditional religio-cultural ideals regarding the family and mothers' roles are still valued and respected, although, in actual practice, they are interpreted and lived in new ways (Mernissi 1987).

The centrality of motherhood to participants' lives, therefore, is explained by them in relation to religious traditions, but these on their own are not the sole explanation. Indeed, it is possible to imagine them following the same religious texts, but performing a different kind of mothering if they were successful in entering paid employment. At the same time, the experience of motherhood is intensified by the surrounding ideological pressures of intensive mothering, as a standard against which they are measured. Their cultural capital, mobilised in educational efforts, therefore becomes more important to self-definition and self-evaluation as 'good' mothers. Some indeed adopted and embraced intensive mothering. For other mothers unable to maintain their cultural capital in the transition to Australian society, at least with regard to the academic market, the intensification of their roles as mothers became a source of tension.

Feelings of Shame and Inadequacy

Through unemployment, and the underemployment or precarious paid work undertaken by their husbands, some of the women in the study lost their social status relative to their lives in Iraq. However, many also experienced a loss of cultural capital. In particular, a loss of knowledge of the workings of the education system placed some participants in a vulnerable position in which they experienced acute anxiety. The focus of this anxiety was connected to cultural and religious framings about the 'good mother'. Perceived failure to be able to effectively support children's education provided a threat to mothers' sense of self-worth. As Heba (unemployed, diploma of children's service, husband is a taxi driver, Bachelor degree in Arts) noted:

> Back home I used to help my kids with their homework … If you
> ask me a question about any of their school subjects, I would tell
> you on which page you can find the answer. Now I feel frustrated
> because I haven't been doing my role as I used to … Everything has
> become vague. I almost know nothing about the curriculum … I feel,
> sometimes, I am not a good mother as I used to be in Iraq.

In the marketised Melbourne education system, choosing the 'right' school appears as another important task for intensive mothering (Windle 2015). Participants heard, often from within the Iraqi community, of 'good schools' and mothers who had been successful in gaining a place for their children in such schools. When they were unable to gain places for their children in 'good schools', due to distance from the mainly working-class neighbourhoods in which they lived, inability to pay fees, or academic entry tests applied to applicants, they experienced the similar kinds of feelings of inadequacy experienced by others unable to live up to the ideological standard of intensive mothering.

However, their definitions of a good school, and fears about sending their children to a 'bad school', also bear the traces of Iraqi and Islamic ideas about morality and virtue. Evaluations of schools and student populations often focused on the perceived morality of students (including Iraqi students), and the moral restraints provided by the schools. This was most important in relation to daughters. Participants see it as a mother's duty to bring children up in a 'proper' manner and deal with all their problems. A child's behaviour, particularly girls', is considered to reflect the way their mothers (not fathers) raise them. The family's economic status depends on the father, so the social status and wealth derives from him, while the aspect of 'shame' derives from the mother (Al-Khayyat 1990). An Iraqi proverb states *albint tala alla umha*, which means the daughter takes after her mother morally: the purity of the daughter reflects that of her mother. The phenomenon of honour and shame permeates Iraqi society and so women's and girls' lives are greatly affected by the importance placed on moral reputation.

Alternative Forms of Mothering

Some mothers focused on guiding their children's education in ways that were not connected to formal schooling. This was mainly due to their own limited education and sense that they were unable to provide support with school work. These efforts included teaching literacy in Arabic, and lessons on morals and ethics. Nedhal (unemployed, Grade 6 equivalent, husband was a taxi driver, Year 12 equivalent) stated:

> It is my full responsibility to make sure that they learn Arabic … My daughters are doing really well at Arabic. They can read and write. They can read Qur'an and they learnt many surah [chapters of the Quran] by heart. I teach them Arabic almost every day at home. Many Iraqi mothers from the community always say to me: you should be proud of your daughters because they can read Qur'an. Not many kids here know how to read Qur'an.

Again, the interplay of material conditions and ideological frameworks is evident in this case. Nedhal is effectively excluded from enacting intensive motherhood, in fact she is so far removed from its criteria for value that she does not even attempt some of the practices that mothers like Heba do (such as homework support). Instead, she redefines her role as a mother in ways that allow her to experience success and satisfaction in fulfilling family and religious duties – by teaching Arabic literacy and religious knowledge. This gives her a sense of pride that would not be available were she judged against the ideology of intensive mothering, or even a different interpretation of her obligations under Islam. Further, her approach places her in a position in which her inattention to formal schooling could see her judged as merely lacking in cultural capital if a conventional Bourdieusian analysis were adopted. Bringing in an analysis of motherhood ideology allows for a reinterpretation of the value of her educational efforts as related to a different scale of value (a non-academic educational market).

Forging Norms of Motherhood under Shifting Cultural and Institutional Circumstances

The findings presented above confirm other research suggesting that the process of migrating to a new region has profound effects on individual psychology and family structure and dynamics (Tummala-Narra 2004), which we connect to changes in social position and cultural capital. Iraqi women in Australia have moved to a land where they become 'different' and an ethnic minority, bringing a *habitus* that guides a distinctive set of reactions to new material conditions. Their language, their faith, their traditions and rituals all cease to be the norm and many face downward social mobility. Further, they lose the social structures that supported their mothering values and they encounter a new social field in which these orientations are questioned (Ochocka and Janzen 2008).

The amplification of the importance of mothering that occurs through the process of migration intensifies the emotional burden mothers face in attempting to guide their children's education, in the case of Iraqi mothers in Australia. For mothers who maintain the capital (cultural, linguistic and economic) that enables them to navigate the marketised Australian education system in a way they feel is effective, their efforts are rewarded with a sense of themselves as 'good mothers'. This sense is likely to be different from that experienced by non-migrant mothers from other cultural and religious backgrounds, and its implications for family dynamics are also distinctive – due to the ideological complex outlined above. For those who feel they are unable to effectively engage with this new educational terrain, the frustrations extend to a religious and cultural crisis of motherhood. It is essential, therefore, to consider the family–school relationship not merely in terms of resources or capital, but in relation to the interpretative frames that different groups of parents bring with them, and the formative ideological contexts in which these are forged.

A major risk faced by the cultural capital framework is to measure all families against a normative ideal of the 'successful' family. Practices of concerted cultivation and strategic investment in navigating marketised schooling can be taken as something to which all families should aspire. It is important, therefore, to remind ourselves that concerted cultivation is not merely a strategy of educational investment that appears to pay off, but an ideology. It is principally an ideology of motherhood, with mothers assigned the primary role in child-rearing and schooling within a normative, Western model of the nuclear family. Other ideological framings emerge from other histories and cultural settings. The Islamic model of motherhood provides a distinctive set of rationales and duties for mothers, particularly in relation to education and for migrant mothers. However, education may be interpreted in different ways – from formal schooling, to the preservation of cultural heritage to the development of morals. Rather than dismissing Iraqi mothers who grant their children autonomy in schooling and focus on literacy in Arabic as inadequate or ineffective (or 'bad mothers'), we need to recognise that they are enacting a different form of mothering. This form of mothering is, of course, shaped by material circumstances and social location (particularly of exclusion from involvement in formal schooling for some participants), but the ideological and cultural dimensions cannot be ignored.

References

Ahmed, L. (1992). *Women and gender in Islam*. New Haven, CT: Yale University Press.

Al-Khayyat, S. (1990). *Honour and shame: Women in modern Iraq*. London: Saqi Books.

Arendell, T. (1999). *Hegemonic motherhood: Deviancy discourses and employed mother's accounts of out-of-school time issues* (Report No. 9, 1-30). Berkeley: Centre for Working Families, University of California.

Arendell. T. (2000). Conceiving and investigating motherhood: The decade's scholarship. *Journal of Marriage and the Family, 62*(4), 1192–1207.

Bell, S.E. (2004). Intensive performances of mothering: A sociological perspective. *Qualitative Research, 4*(1), 45-75.

Bhopal, K. (1998). South Asian women in East London: Motherhood and social support. *Women's Studies International Forum, 21*(5), 485-492.

Blackledge, A. (2001). The wrong sort of capital? Bangladeshi women and their children's schooling in Birmingham, U.K. *International Journal of Bilingualism, 5*(3), 345-369.

Bourdieu, P. (1977). Cultural reproduction and social reproduction. In J. Karabel and A.H. Halsey (eds.), *Power and ideology in education* (pp. 487-511). New York: Oxford University Press.

Bourdieu, P. (1986). The forms of capital. In L. Richardson (ed.), *Handbook of theory and research for the sociology of education* (pp. 241-258). New York: Greenwood Press.

Bourdieu, P., and Passeron, J.C. (1990). *Reproduction in education, society and culture* (2nd edition). London: Sage.

Bourdieu, P., and Wacquant, L. (1992). *An invitation to reflexive sociology*. Chicago: University of Chicago Press.

Brubaker, R. (2004). Rethinking classical theory: The sociological vision of Pierre Bourdieu. In D.L. Swartz and V.L. Zolberg (eds.), *After Bourdieu: Influence, critique, elaboration* (pp. 25-64). Dordrecht, the Netherlands: Kluwer.

Chao, R.K. (1996). Chinese and European American mother's beliefs about the role of parenting in children's school success. *Journal of Cross-Cultural Psychology, 27*(4), 403-423.

Chodorow, N. (1989). *Feminism and psychoanalytic theory*. New Haven, CT: Yale University Press.

Crozier, G. (2001). Excluded parents: The deracialisation of parental involvement. *Race, Ethnicity and Education, 4*(4), 329-341.

Dumais, S.A. (2002). Cultural capital, gender and school success: The role of habitus. *Sociology of Education, 71*(1), 44-68.

Grenfell, M., and James, D. (eds.) (1998). *Bourdieu and education: Acts of practical theory*. London: Falmer Press.

Griffith, A., and Smith, D. (2005). *Mothering for schooling*. New York: Routledge.

Hays, S. (1996). *The cultural contradictions of motherhood*. New Haven, CT: Yale University Press.

Horvat, E.M. (2003). The Interactive effects of race and class in educational research: Theoretical insights from the work of Pierre Bourdieu. *Perspectives on Urban Education, 2*(1), 1-25.

Jamal Al-deen, T., and Windle, J. (2015). The involvement of migrant mothers in their children's education: Cultural capital and transnational class processes. *International Studies in Sociology of Education, 25*(4), 278-295.

Kausar, Z. (2006*). Muslim women at the crossroads: The rights of women in Islam and general Muslim practices*. Malaysia: Laris Resources Sdn Berhad.

Lamont, M., and Lareau, A. (1988). Cultural capital: Allusions, gaps and glissandos in recent theoretical development. *Sociological Theory*, 6(2), 153-168.

Lareau, A. (2003). *Unequal childhoods: Class, race and family life.* Berkley: University of California Press

Lareau, A. (2008). Watching, waiting, and deciding when to intervene. Race, class, and the transmission of advantage. In L. Weis (ed.), *The way class works: Readings on school, family, and the economy.* New York: Routledge.

Lareau, A., and Horvat, E.M. (1999). Moments of social inclusion and exclusion: Race, class, and cultural capital in family–school relationships. *Sociology of Education*, 72(1), 37-53.

Lee, J., and Bowen, N.K. (2006). Parent involvement, cultural capital, and the achievement gap among elementary school children. *American Educational Research Journal*, 43(2), 193-218.

Liam, I.I.L. (1999). The challenge of migrant motherhood: The childrearing practices of Chinese first-time mothers in Australia. In P. Liamputtong Rice (ed.), *Asian mothers, Western birth* (pp. 135-160). Melbourne: Ausmed Publications.

Liamputtong, P. (2001). Motherhood and the challenge of immigrant mothers: A personal reflection. *Families in Society*, 82(2), 195-201.

Liamputtong, P. (2006). Motherhood and 'moral career': Discourses of good motherhood among Southeast Asian immigrant women in Australia. *Qualitative Sociology*, 29(1), 25-53.

Liamputtong, P., and Naksook, C. (2003). Life as mothers in a new land: The experience of motherhood among Thai immigrant women in Australia. *Health Care for Women International*, 24(7), 650-668.

McMahon, M. (1995). *Engendering motherhood: Identity and self-transformation in women's lives.* New York: The Guildford Press.

Mernissi, F. (1987). *Beyond the veil: Male–female dynamics in Muslim society.* Bloomington, IN: Indiana University Press.

Ochocka, J., and Janzen, R. (2008). Immigrant parenting: A new framework of understanding. *Journal of Immigrant & Refugee Studies*, 6(1), 85-111.

Reay, D. (1995). A silent majority? Mothers in parental involvement. *Women's Studies International Forum*, 18(3), 337-348.

Reay, D. (1998a). Cultural reproduction: Mothers' involvement in their children's primary schooling. In M. Grenfell and D. James (eds.), *Bourdieu and education: Acts of practical theory* (pp. 55-70). Bristol, PA: Falmer Press.

Reay, D. (1998b). Engendered social reproduction: Mothers in the educational marketplace. *British Journal of Sociology of Education*, 19(2), 195-209.

Reay, D. (1999). Linguistic capital and home-school relationship: Mothers' interactions with their children's primary teachers. *Acta Sociologica*, 42(2), 159-168.

Schleifer, A. (1996). *Motherhood in Islam.* USA: The Islamic Texts Society.

Sered, S.S. (1996). Mother love, child death, and religious innovation: A feminist perspective. *Journal of Feminist Studies in Religion*, 12(1), 5-23.

Shannon, S.M. (1996). Minority parental involvement: A Mexican mother's experience and a teacher's interpretation. *Education & Urban Society*, 29(1), 71-84.

Sohn, S., and Wang, X.C. (2006). Immigrant parents' involvement in american schools: Perspectives from Korean mothers. *Early Childhood Education Journal*, 34(2), 125-132.

Standing, K. (1999a). Lone mothers' involvement in their children's schooling: Towards a new typology. *Gender and Education*, 11(1), 57-73.

Standing, K. (1999b). Lone mothers and 'parental involvement': A contradiction in policy. *Journal of Social Policy*, 28(3), 497-495.

Tummala-Narra, P. (2004). Mothering in a foreign land. *American Journal of Psychoanalysis*, 64(2), 167-182.

Vincent, C. (2010). The sociology of mothering. In M. Apple, S. Ball and L.A. Gandin (eds.), *The Routledge international handbook of the sociology of education* (pp. 109-120). Routledge.

Wadud, A. (1999). *Qur'an and woman: Rereading the sacred text from a woman's perspective.* New York: Oxford University Press.

Windle, J.A. (2015). *Making sense of school choice: Politics, policies, and practice under conditions of cultural diversity.* New York: Palgrave-MacMillan.

CHAPTER 3

LEGISLATING ENGLISH IN NEPAL

Discourses of Social (in)Equalities

Ram Giri

Abstract

English was imported into the Himalayan nation of Nepal over a century ago. Its importation, together with the existing racial/ideological supremacy and a resultant linguistic reduction approach to education, helped establish a linguistic edge in favour of the ruling elites. This in practice created a new tier in the already prevalent caste-based divisions in Nepalese society. An example of the primacy of English is the fact that English was made a compulsory subject in education even before the official/national language, Nepali. In this way, English language education (ELE) was initially restricted to the elites, which also helped establish a form of neo-colonialism creating a further divide between the haves and the have-nots. The language became a yardstick for employment and educational and occupational opportunities which were made available exclusively to the English speaking elites. A century later, debates have erupted in ELE academia in which one school of thought sees English as neutral, democratic and, more importantly, liberating. These advocates of the autonomous approach suggest that English in 'New Nepal' is free from any ideological and cultural baggage, and, in the situation in which its need is growing, they demand the language be made 'official'. The critics of this school, on the other hand, point to the existing state of the affairs and claim that the language, indispensable though it may be, has never been and will never be neutral, and that such a move will only contribute further to the social divide that this language has already created. This chapter investigates both sides of the claim of social and linguistic injustice the language has created in the Nepalese community, and, on the basis of an analysis of the current and past discourses, elucidates to what extent the claim of the great social divide is justifiable.

Keywords: employment, English language education, social justice, neo-colonialism

Introduction

Keeping English from anyone, whether actively and indirectly, must now be seen as a social injustice.

Hall 2016

The impacts the global spread of English has exerted on different English-using contexts have been perceived and interpreted differently. While some groups of English speakers within a context have positive attitudes towards the influence of the language, others see conspiracy in the way it is practised. A large body of literature, triggered by and largely in response to the linguistic imperialism theory advocated by Robert Phillipson (Phillipson 1992), has appeared in the last three decades. The ensuing global discourses on English language education (ELE) appearing since this seminal work represent three different but sometimes overlapping theories, namely, sociocultural, politico-economic and linguistic. The sociocultural imperialism, a macro-level perspective, refers to structural dominance which society asserts by perpetuating dominant norms, values and behaviours. Ideological dominance which establishes, promotes and maintains interests and views to benefit some privileged groups of people is the politico-economic imperialism. The third theory, linguistic imperialism, on the other hand, which refers to the exercising of dominance through a dominant language, is a subset but nonetheless an integral aspect of the former two because language is the transferor of all forms of imperialisms. English linguistic imperialism, then, is the dominance that the English language exerts on its users as well as its non-users. The language, as it has been claimed, establishes and perpetuates the ideals, structures, norms and values of the Anglophiles. This claim, however, is far from settled. A counter-perspective to the claim suggests that it is an over-simplification, as it fails to take into account the micro-level complexities and local sociolinguistic realities.

The reflection of the controversies can be seen in the Nepalese ELT debates that advocate for and against the growing dominance of English in Nepal. On the one hand, a significant section of ELT academia vehemently opposes it. On the other hand, supporters of English argue that English is already working as an alternative language in administration, law, business and education domains, and that in the federal system of governance, for which different states are likely to have different official languages, English should be made an 'official' language in New Nepal. In this chapter, I examine these debates and outline different theories behind the propositions. I argue that English as a linguistic instrument employed by the elites is perceived to have created social injustice and social inequality in the impoverished Himalayan state. The chapter, thus, is a result of a critical analysis of the major discourses – either formal or informal – prevailing since the importation of English into Nepal almost a century ago. The section that follows provides an overview of the theoretical bases which the ELT discourses have drawn upon.

The Theoretical Bases

The unprecedented pace of development in the globalised world is currently experiencing may be termed a new mania, the English mania. In Nepal, one of the most impoverished nations on earth, people in great numbers flock to English language teaching institutes to learn some form of English. English institutions, parents, teachers, and above all students go to any length to be a part of a linguistic tsunami which is affecting the world over (Aryal et al. 2016; Lin 2013; Walker 2008). An investigation of the academic discourses on English language teaching and learning reveals that the tremendous drive for learning English has largely been triggered by three theories. The first of these theories is the sociocultural theory. This theory is connected to the discourses surrounding ideological dominance, with its roots in dominant social ideas and norms. Structural ideology perpetuates a social structure and the norms and values associated with its products and practices. This then serves the dominant ideological interests as the 'Centre' of the sociocultural process (Corcorum 2009). The practice of the hierarchical process makes a distinction between the dominant Centre and the dominated Periphery. The ideology of the Centre then legitimises and strengthens the sociocultural structure (Lin 2013; Tomlinson 1991). At the micro-level, ideologies, structures and practices are used to legitimise, effectuate and reproduce unequal division of power and disproportional distribution of resources (Skutnab-Kangas 1988).

The second theory for the tremendous popularity of English is the politico-economic theory. This theory follows the monolingual principle and advocates for social justice and unity among a nation's populace. It also legitimises the ideology of equal economic opportunities for all speakers of the Centre language (Canagarajah 1999). In practice, however, the theory leads to the total disregard of the peripheral norms and values, inducing a 'colonised consciousness' and neo-colonial attitudes (Pennycook 2007). On the economic front, the theory allows for monopoly over two tiers of economic opportunities – prime opportunities for the speakers of the Centre language and subordinate opportunities for all others (Auerbach 1993; Cook 2001). As a consequence of this practice, monolingualism has political and economic advantages in favour of the Centre, as it creates not only a hegemonic control over the Periphery but also a stratified and functional division of labour keeping the 'Other' at the lower level of the stratification.

Finally, the third theory is the theory of the linguistic imperialism of English. According to the theory, ELT is an act of linguistic imperialism which posits that the dominance of the Centre language serves to undermine the local languages, and therefore marginalises the speakers of the latter languages. The former language, as the principal means of communication, plays a crucial role in transmitting the norms and ideology of the Centre (the Inner Circle countries) to the Periphery (the countries of Outer and Expanding circles; see Kachru 1982, 1992). In other words, the cultural baggage (ideas, values and ways of life) associated with the language serves to develop a patronising attitude towards the speakers of other languages. English linguistic imperialism, therefore, is 'the dominance of English asserted and maintained by the establishment and continuous reconstruction of structural and cultural inequalities between the speakers of English and the speakers of other languages' (Phillipson 1992, 47). English linguistic imperialism, as a subtype of 'linguicism', drives all other types of imperialisms, namely sociocultural and politico-economic imperialisms, because it leads to marginalisation and discrimination on the basis of the language people speak (Skutnabb-Kangas 2009).

The contemporary authors in the field, however, present a different perspective to the coveted spread of English and suggest that the notions of English linguistic imperialism, and of the dominance of the Centre over the Periphery are generalisations, and therefore lack 'a view of how English is taken up, how people use English and why people choose to use English' (Pennycook 2007). Fishman (1993), for example, suggests that the growing popularity of English is the result of people's involvement in the global economy of the modern world rather than of the externally imposed English hegemony. Rejecting the linguistic restrictionism theory, he affirms that English and local languages can complement each other to satisfy different linguistic needs for different social functions (see also Fishman 1996). Davies (1996), agreeing with Fishman and rejecting the English linguistic imperialism theory, asserts that the popularity of English in a given context is because of the instrumental or egalitarian roles English plays in the context, and that any disadvantages caused in the local population are due to the faulty policies and decisions made by the individual nation-states. Similarly, Bisong (1995) examines the linguicism theory in the ESL context of Nigeria and argues that English in Nigeria is a choice which functions as a pragmatic tool and is not associated with any endangerment of indigenous languages. Any suggestion of English linguistic hegemony is, therefore, failing to understand the complexities of the local sociolinguistic situation.

Graddol (1997, 2006) also takes a positive perspective on the global spread of English and suggests that English should be regarded as a consequence of the current politico-economic order of the world rather than a consequence of any conspiracy theory. This is consistent with Pennycook (2013), Auerbach (1995) and Tollefson (1995) who argue that the global spread of English is part of a wider political, social and economic process that results in inequality, and that the current global status of English and its relationship with global inequality should be carefully examined.

Lin (2013) summarises the two sides of the argument by saying that scholars on the three theories discussed above are divided. He questions the widespread ideological view of English as an instrument of politico-economic inequality and argues that:

> The global spread of English is not a simple phenomenon of prevalence of skills or technique, but a complicated process with socio-cultural and politico-economic implications. English might not be the cause of global inequality, but has become an important factor in intensifying inequality (p. 9).

The arguments and controversies surrounding English linguistic imperialism have polarised the ELT world, and Nepalese ELT academia is not an exception to this. Since the initiation of formal English language education, the Nepalese ELT academia has been divided regarding the impact of the language on people and the status and role it should be accorded in the multilingual/multicultural nation. The following section looks into the two sides of the polarised Nepalese discourses.

The Nepalese Context

Nepal, a tiny nation-state situated in the foothills of the Himalayas, is also known as the land of contrasts. One of the many contrasts is that it is a multilingual and multiethnic country, yet multiculturalism is not part of the national policy. As a meeting point of two multilingual cultures – Tibeto-Burman and Indo-Aryan – it is a home of 123 languages and 100 ethnicities (Ethnologue 2015). However, multilingualism and multiculturalism are regarded by many as a threat to nationalism and national identity. The second contrast is English has become an integral part of Nepal's policy efforts for advancement and modernisation. The language, however, is yet to be officially included in the national language policy. English has formally been taught and learned in Nepal for about a century now but there is no clear and consistent national policy for its teaching and learning (Kansakar 1988, 2011). It was incorporated into the national curriculum as a foreign language in the first half of the 20th century, and it remains so despite its growing popularity and use among a large section of the population. Educationally, English as a language of communication and education serves practical purposes; ideologically, however, it is used to achieve what may be termed a linguistic advantage over the already dominated language groups. In the following section, I provide a historical overview of social inequality and social injustice that adoptation of the English language has created in Nepalese society.

The Historical Base

When English was first imported into Nepal in the early 1850s, Nepali was already established as the official language of the Shaha-Rana's regime. In the next 100 or so years, Nepali would become the only national language and an instrument to establish the linguistic superiority of the ruling elites. The first ever Nepal National Education Planning Commission (NNEPC), which was set up in 1954 and responsible for planning languages for education for Nepal, adopted what is known as the 'Linguistic Reduction Theory' (see also Awasthi 2004, 2011). The theory is an application of downward filtration strategies which reduce multilingualism in favour of monolingualism and controls the distribution and/or the teaching and learning of languages. The proponents of the theory believe that multilingualism and multiculturalism are a threat to national unity and cohesion, and advocates for a single language and single culture.

The de facto one nation, one language policy of the Shaha-Rana rulers was a deliberate attempt to undermine hundreds of languages and cultures, which, in practice, suppressed the development and use of other languages. In effect, however, it produced two types of linguistic attitudes, both inherently negative . First, it generated an attitude of two languages, two peoples and two cultures. The two peoples refer to the elites and the subjugated, and the two languages and cultures refer to the languages and cultures of the rulers (the elites) and those of all others. The languages of the elites, in this case English and Nepali, are the languages of the civilised, educated and enlightened people, whereas other languages are 'the speech of the illiterate' and 'the dialects of the jungle' (Malla 1979, 31). This policy, therefore, is repressive and discriminatory and promotes racial and caste prejudices and inequalities: 'Under the (Shaha)-Rana regime … the elites began to discriminate against [the speakers of] other languages' (Hutt 1986, 10).

Second, speakers of other languages, as a consequence of the situation, developed a poor attitude towards their languages, considering them insignificant and of no practical value. This, then, also gave rise to the feeling that their languages were inferior to the elite languages and therefore they too were inferior (Giri 2010, 2011).

The ELT Discourses

In the backdrop of the linguistic design outlined above, the ruling elites imported another linguistic tool, English, with a view to giving their supremacy another linguistic edge. Since its importation, English has had many faces and roles in Nepalese society. From 1851 to 1951, English education remained reserved for the ruling elites and the policy remained off limits from any public scrutiny because criticism of any policies of the autocratic regime was punishable by law. As a result of this, no discussion or debate on the government's policies, including language (education) policies, took place. The Panchayat[1] regime established by King Mahendra, nationalised all education systems of the country. These three decades of autocratic rule were extremely important so far as the language policy debate is concerned because it was during this rule, for socioeconomic reasons, that the creation of a new sociocultural order through nationalisation of language, literature and belief systems took place (Subedi 1996) which in effect suppressed the indigenous minority languages (Hangen 2007).

Nepal is currently experiencing a complex relationship between (a) globalisation from above, and (b) globalisation from below. In globalisation from above, it is the higher social and ideological structures which influence

---

1   A system of governance.

social developmental processes. In globalisation from below, however, it is the local apparatuses and practices that perpetuate and help maintain social processes. Both types of globalisation impact social ecology including language ecology. In the wake of globalisation, the value and influence of English in Nepal has risen sharply, and its current standing as a dominant language is revered, so much so that 'English is replacing Nepali, the national language, in many social, developmental and educational domains' (Rana 2008). While the local demand for English dictates its practice, the politics surrounding the language at the top level of the sociopolitical hierarchy is extremely intriguing. There is a great deal of confusion and uncertainty about its status and role in Nepalese society. The confusions and uncertainties are reflected in evolving ELT discourses. The emerging ELE discourses appear to have been guided by two distinct theoretical perspectives: the progressivist perspective and neo-colonialist perspective. These two theoretical perspectives are discussed in the following sections.

The Progressivist Perspective

The progressivist perspective is inspired by utilitarian as well as egalitarian principles. The utilitarian principle affirms that English is learned and practised to achieve certain socioeconomic goals (see also Wong 1982). As a language of educational advancement and communication, it opens avenues for educational and economic opportunities (Bhattarai 2006; CDC 1988; Khaniya 1990, 2007; Malla 1977). It serves as an instrument of modernisation. In the context that Nepal has been an important global source of particular workforces, its role in vocational education has become indispensable. Recent studies have claimed that Nepali workers who have proficiency in English are given better pay and prestige, both at home and overseas (Dahal 2000; ekantipur.com 2017).

As a means of communication, English is used for intranational as well as international communication. The ELE discourses have been tentative and inconclusive in claiming English as a language of intranational communication; however, it is widely mentioned that it is a lingua franca (CDC 1988; Giri 2007), a link language for the purpose of interstate communication (Sah 2016); a tool for better understanding between people of different language backgrounds (MO 2001; Awasthi 2004). In addition, more and more Nepalese people adopt the language to achieve equality or equal treatment across ethnicities, genders, religions, economic and social statuses and ideological beliefs (Sonntag 1995, 2003). English is regarded as the language of prestige, a means of upward mobility (Yadava 2005) and an instrument of social advancement (Sonntag 2005; Shrestha 2008). English enjoys a special privilege and prominent place in Nepal. Apart from a prestige language and a status symbol, it is increasingly becoming a household language for a vast majority of educated people.

According to the advocates of the theory, in the context in which linguistic hegemony and ethnic dominance is deeply rooted, English is regarded as an emancipator which can liberate people from linguistic and cultural prejudices. In this sense, English serves an egalitarian purpose in Nepal. English thus functions as a unifying force in the ethnically and linguistically divided Nepal. With the rise of ethnic politics, a language which is not indigenous, and therefore does not carry any cultural baggage along with it, is needed so that people of all ethnicities and backgrounds can accept it as a common language. English in this sense serves a practical purpose of inter-community communication. Furthermore, in the developing politics of federalism, English is a likely common language of inter-state communication (Sah 2016).

The Neo-colonialist Perspective

Neo-colonialist theory considers English to be a divisive instrument of creating social divisions in already ethnically divided Nepalese society. There is strong opposition to the way English is allowed to impact on the lives of average Nepalese people. The opponents believe that, despite some positive outcomes, the Nepalese people have paid a heavy price as this language has created what is known as neo-colonialism in the sense that, by not providing access to quality ELE to all of Nepal's population, it has become a power tool in the hands of the privileged few to colonise the minds of millions of people and to create a monopoly and status quo (Giri 2007, 2009). Tickoo (1993) has observed that a vast majority of Nepalese learners learn English in an 'acquisition poor environment'. English in its current form plays a divisionary role rather than an integrative one as it favours some sections of the population and contributes to furthering the social divide. As a result, this language disadvantages some people. Shrestha (2008, 200) notes that 'people living in the rural areas … have been marginalised economically, politically, educationally and culturally because of their inability to use English'.

As indicated in the previous sections, English was imported with an acculturation ideology (Giri 2009, 2015) and it still carries a sociopolitical function as it is not just a means to communicate or get understood, it is also a powerful means to elevate certain people to a superior status (Stiller 1993).

Legislating English in the Federal Republic of Nepal

The New Constitution of Federal Nepal 2015 divides the nation into seven states mainly on the basis of ethnicity and allows the states to legislate one or more local indigenous languages as the languages of the state. Nepali, the federal official language, is also the official language of all states. This means that Nepali remains the language of administration, the justice system, education and most economic activities. In the context that some ethnicities consider Nepali as a neo-colonial language, there is a call for English to be legislated as a federal official language (Giri 2015; Sah 2016). As the New Constitution is implemented, two ideologically motivated lines of thought are set to gain prominence. The first of these is the promotion and even legislating of indigenous languages as a sociolinguistic capital and a medium of elementary education at the state level (Phyak 2013, 2016). This school of thought is inspired by ethno-linguistic identity and educational principles which suggest that education in and through home languages promotes transformative, affective and cognitive development in children (Hough, Thapa-Magar and Yonjan-Tamang 2009; Phyak 2013; Taylor 2010; Yonjan-Tamang 2005, 2012). However, as discussed in the previous section, the multilingual language education (MLE) in Nepal has been disintegrated, patchwork and largely donor-driven and therefore ineffective because (a) Nepalese language planning and policy remains uncoordinated (Eagle 2000, 2010; Sonntag 2007), (b) there is an acute scarcity of adequate educational resources, both human and material (Phyak 2013, 2016; Taylor 2010), (c) the people's attitude to MLE is unconducive in that the speakers of these languages perceive their languages to be of no practical value (Giri 2009, 2011; Turin 2013), (d) the non-speakers of the languages see MLE as groupist and political in orientation which hinders the prospect of unified national identity (Awasth 2004; Caddell 2002), and (e) there is a disproportional, unregulated distribution of resources (Taylor 2010).

English has been increasingly adopted as an alternative to, and sometimes parallel to, MLE in private schools and a large number of public and community schools. These schools have already adopted a de facto English as the medium of instruction policy (Phyak 2016). Therefore, the second school of thought that is emerging strongly advocates that English be given an official status in New Nepal. As discussed earlier, despite the label of 'foreign', English has never been treated or accepted as a foreign language but as a first/primary language (Rathbone 1969; Shrestha 1983), as a second language in many public and private domains (Awasthi 2011; Giri 2015; Karn 2012), and is fast replacing Nepali itself (Rana 2008). An indication of English as a de facto official language is that the Government of Nepal has made all of its documents available in one of the two languages (Giri 2015).

The ELE discourses on legislating English of the last five years can be seen from three perspectives. The first calls for Nepal's identity in the new context to be redefined (Lal 2016) with English as an official language in it (Sah 2016). The Nepalese ELE intelligentsia led by prominent Nepal English Language Teachers' Association (NELTA) members argue that English in Nepal is no longer an elite language, nor is it tied to any caste or class (see NELTA Chautari Forum). Rather it has become everybody's language (B. Sharma 2016; S. Sharma 2009) and therefore is one of the local languages (Giri 2015; Karn 2011). The second perspective is that despite English being accepted in more and more domains by more and more people, it still carries the neo-colonial attitude and remains the basis of sociopolitical discrimination, mainly because (a) the government lacks a clear and consistent ELE policy, (b) there is a scarcity of trained and qualified teachers in rural Nepal, (c) there is a lack of access to quality ELT for all, and (d) there is a disproportionate distribution of ELT facilities and resources (Giri 2011; Phyak 2016). The third perspective, however, represents the confusions and uncertainties in ELT academia. A sizeable population of ELT practitioners are unsure whether or to what extent English has established itself as a local language, and what place it should be accorded in the Nepalese languages education policy (Daniloff-Merrill 2010; Duwadi 2010; Kamali 2010; Sharma 2014). Nonetheless, they agree that while the role and status of English in Nepalese society for development is undeniable, it must also meet the local sociolinguistic conditions and communicative needs. In other words, it must be appropriately situated in the Nepalese language situation on the principles of language ecology and linguistic co-existence (Giri 2015).

Discussion of Implications

English in today's Nepal is no longer a language of simple communication. It is a language of power, of opportunities and above all of identity. There is a consensus in the Nepalese sociopolitical and ELE discourses that English has a unique status in Nepal and its role in Nepal's policy for modernisation and economic development is instrumental. A large proportion of the available English language education discourses suggest that English in the Nepalese context is being accepted for pragmatic reasons, and, just because it is being increasingly adopted by more and more people, it is naïve to say that its culture dominates, replaces or displaces indigenous languages and cultures. The Nepalese people understand the current need and demand for English, and recognise the importance of multilingual literacy in the modern global world. They do not see this language as devaluation or marginalisation of their own language and culture and recommend a principled co-existence with English. Legislating English, therefore, eliminates the confusions, uncertainties and ambiguity that surrounds English language education today.

The other part of the discourses points to the fact that Nepalese regimes have used English as a tool to divide people between the rulers and the ruled, and as a consequence of this the sociocultural divide today is widening more than ever before. The elites, by not giving due consideration to its status and acquisition planning, use it as a tool to perpetuate the existing sociopolitical structure and maintain the status quo. The decision to include English in Nepalese education, therefore, and to 'not plan' a uniform distribution of teaching resources and pedagogic provisions at the practice level is a political one. English, in one way or another, also remains at the centre of the MLE controversy. Even the most hardline opponents of cultural hegemony have not been able to refuse to use English because of its inevitable role in one's future. These opponents, for example, despite their opposition to cultural hegemony and linguistic imperialism, do not hesitate to send their children to elite English-medium schools (Sonntag 2005).

Opponents of the proposition of legislating English present four types of arguments. First and foremost, English is collusionary in that it accompanies globalisation which endorses capitalism, and promotes homogenisation of local languages and cultures. The second argument is that the language is a false promise in the sense that English is supposedly a key to a better life for the masses and therefore an escape from grinding poverty, but in reality, it does not deliver. The gap between the rich and the poor in fact widens because of the language. Third, English is illusionary in that it gives high hopes to its learners but in practice their variety of English becomes the subject of disadvantage and disempowerment. The final but significant argument is that the language is exclusionary in the sense that the language contributes to significant sociocultural and politico-economic inequalities, and creates class divisions (Tollefson 2000).

New Nepal, therefore, faces the dilemmas of social equity, social division, and inequitable practice of English language education. Educational experts agree that ELE has to be based on the reality of the situation; it must take into account the needs of different sections of populations (Yadav 2009), and while English is the 'first' language or 'a second language for some in urban areas', it is the third or even fourth language for the rural population. It is imperative, therefore, that English be treated differently in different parts of the country. This means that there is a need of different literacy targets for different types of population which must be addressed differently. However, fair though it sounds, this approach creates a social dilemma and policy contradiction, as it may seem to deny the same level of opportunity and access to all. The ELT approach has already been accused of creating a class-based society (Giri 2007; Sharma 2016; Sonntag 2007). While we must not keep English away from anyone, as this chapter's epigraph suggests, setting different targets for different sections of the population may be seen as social injustice and is bound to polarise the issue further.

This chapter is based on an analysis of current and past ELE discourses. The relevance of its implications and recommendations may be limited. Large-scale research studies on the multiple English literacy situations, the actual needs and the resultant educational policies will be required to address the issues. But, most importantly, what is also required is a debate on the changing status and roles of English, involving ELT practitioners as well as policy makers at all levels to resolve the uncertainties and confusions that surround English language education in Nepal today.

References

Acharya, S. (2006). *Teaching management and multilingual context*. Kathmandu: Department of Education, Ministry of Education. The Government of Nepal.

Aryal, A. Short, M., Fan, S., and Kember, D. (2016). Issues in English language teaching in Nepal. In S. Fan and J. Wells (eds.). *What is next in educational research*. The Netherlands: Sense Publishers.

Auerbach, E.R. (1995). The politics of the ESL classroom: Issues of power in pedagogical choices. In J.W. Tollefson (ed.), *Power and inequality in language education*. Cambridge: Cambridge University Press.

Awasthi, L. (2004). Exploring monolingual school practices in multilingual Nepal. PhD Thesis, Danish University of Education, Copenhagen.

Awasthi, L. (2011). Importation of ideologies: From Macaulay to Wood Commission report. In L. Farrell, U.N. Singh and R.A. Giri (eds.), English language education in South Asia: From policy to pedagogy (pp. 73-88). India: Cambridge University Press.

Bhattarai, G.R. (2006). English teaching situation in Nepal: An appraisal. *Young Voices in ELT*, 5(1), 1-6.

Bisong, J. (1995). Language choice and cultural imperialism: A Nigerian perspective. *ELT Journal* 49(2): 122-132.

Caddell, M. (2002). Onward looking eyes: Visions of schooling, development and the state of Nepal. PhD Thesis, University of Edinburgh.

Canagarajah, A.S. (1999). *Resisting linguistic imperialism in English teaching*. Oxford: Oxford University Press.

Canagarajah, A.S. (2002). Globalization, methods, and practice in periphery classrooms. In D. Block and D. Cameron (eds.), *Globalization and language teaching*. London: Routledge.

CDC. (1988). *Recommendations in Second National Convention of Tribhuvan University Teachers of English*. Kathmandu: Tribhuvan University.

Corcoran, J. (2009). Linguistic imperialism and the political economy of English language teaching. Paper presented at Meeting of the Latin American Studies Association, Rio de Janeiro, 11-14 June.

Cook, V. (2001). Using the first language in the classroom. *Canadian Modern Language Review*, 57: 402-423

Davies, A. (1996). Reviewing Article: Ironising the myth of linguicism. *Journal of Multilingual and Multicultural Development* 17(6): 485-496.

Dua, H.R. (1994). *Hegemony of English*. Mysore: Yashodha Publications.

Duwadi, E.P. (2010). Nenglish: An inevitable reality or merely a mirage. *Journal of NELTA*, 15: 43-53.

Eagle, S. (2000). The language situation in Nepal. In R.B. Baldauf, Jr., and R.B. Kaplan (eds.), *Language planning in Nepal, Taiwan and Sweden*. Clevedon: Multilingual Matters.

Eagle, S. (2010). The language situation in Nepal: A 2007 update. In R.B. Baldauf and R.B. Kaplan (eds.), *Language planning in Asia. Volume 1: Japan, Nepal, Taiwan and Chinese characters*. Sydney: Multilingual Matters.

ekantipur.com. (2017). [English delivers better pay and prestige] (News). Retrieved 1 January 2017 from www.ekantipur.com

Ethnologue. (2009). *Languages of the world* (16th edition). TX: SIL International. Online version: http://.ethnologue.com/

Fishman, J.A. (1993). Book reviews: Linguistic Imperialism. *The Modern Language Journal*, 77: 399-400.

Fishman, J.A. (1996). Introduction: Some empirical and theoretical issues. In J.A. Fishman, A. Conrad and A. Rubal-Lopez (eds.), *Post-Imperial English: Status change in former British and American colonies, 1940–1990*. Berlin: Mouton de Gruyter.

Giri, R.A. (2009). English in Nepalese education: An analysis of theoretical and contextual issues for the development of its policy guidelines. PhD Thesis. Melbourne: Monash University.

Giri, R.A. (2007). The power and price of English. In L. Farrell and T. Fenwick (eds.), *Educating the global workforce* (pp. 211-224). London: Routledge.

Giri, R.A. (2010). Cultural anarchism: The consequences of privileging languages in Nepal. *Journal of Multilingual and Multicultural Development*, 31(1), 3741.

Giri, R.A. (2011). Languages and language politics: How invisible language politics produces visible results in Nepal. *Language Problems & Language Planning*, 35(3), 197-221.

Giri R.A. (2015). The many faces of English in Nepal. *Asian Englishes*, 17(2), 95-115.

Graddol, D. (1997). *The future of English?* London: The British Council.

Graddol, D. (2006). *English next: Why global English may mean the end of 'English as a Foreign Language'*. London: British Council.

Hall, C. (2016). A short Introduction to social justice and ELT. In C. Hastings and L. Jacobs (eds.), *Social justice in English language teaching* (pp. 3-10). USA: TESOL Press.

Hangen, S.I. (2007). *Creating a 'new Nepal': The ethnic dimension*. Washington, D.C.: East-West Center.

Hartford, B.S. (1996). The relationship of new Englishes and linguistic theory: A cognitive based grammar of Nepali English. In R.J. Baumgartner (ed.), *South Asian English: Structure, use and users*. Urbana: University of Illinois.

Hutt, M.J. (1988). *Nepali: A national language and its literature*. London, UK: SOAS.

Igboanusi, H, and Peter, L. (2015). The language-in-politics in Nigeria. *International Journal of Bilingual Education and Bilingualism*, 19(5): 563-578.

Kachru, B. 1988. Teaching world Englishes. ERIC/CLL News Bulletin 12: 1.

Kachru, B. (1992). Models for non-native Englishes. In B.B. Kachru (ed.), *The other tongue: English across cultures* (2nd edition). Urbana: University of Illinois Press.

Kadel, P. (2017). [Lost education of Tharu language, most schools shut down] (Feature article). *Kantipur*, 24 August.

Kansakar, T.R. (1988). The development of English in Nepal. In M.P. Mainali and G.S. Pradhan (eds.), *Education and development* (pp. 144-156). Kathmandu: CERID.

Karn, S.K. (2006). English, then and now and the days ahead. *Journal of NELTA* 11(1): 73-79.

Karn, S.K. (2011). On Nepalese English discourse: Granting citizenship to English in Nepal via corpus building. *Journal of NELTA* 16(1): 30-41.

Khaniya, T.R. (1990). Nepal: System of education. *International encyclopaedia of education* (2nd edition). London: Pergamon Press.

Khaniya, T.R. (2007). *New horizons in education in Nepal*. Kathmandu: Mandala.

Lal, C.K. (2017). Nepali nationality has not been defined even after 250 years (Interview). *The Kathmandu Post*, 23 January 2017.

Lin, H. (2013). Critical perspectives on global English: A study of their implications. *Intergrams*, 13(2), 1-24.

Malla, K.P. (1977). *English in Nepalese education*. Kathmandu, Nepal: Ratna Pustak Bhandar.

Malla, K.P. (1979). *The road to nowhere*. Kathmandu, Nepal: Sajha Prakashan.

MOE (2001). *Education for all*. Kathmandu: Ministry of Education, Government of Nepal.

Pennycook, A. (2013). Language policies, language ideologies and local language practices. In L.R. Wee, B.H. Goh and L. Lim (eds.), *The politics of English: South Asia, Southeast Asia and Asia Pacific*. Amsterdam: John Benjamin.

Pennycook, A. (2007). ELT and colonialism. In J. Cummins and C. Davidson (eds.), *Kluwer International handbook of education: English language teaching*. Norwell, MA: Kluwer.

Phillipson, R. (1992). *Linguistic imperialism*. Oxford: Oxford University Press.

Phyak, P. (2015). Reimagining education from a multilingual perspective: Policies/ practices, realities and looking forward. *NELTA Chautari Forum* – Nepal's first digital ELT magazine.

Phyak, P. (2016). Local–global tension in the ideological construction of English language education policy in Nepal. In R. Kirkpatrick (ed.), *English language education policy in Asia* (pp. 199-217). Switzerland: Springer International Publishing.

Phyak, P.B. (2013). *Language issues in educational policies and practices in Nepal: A critical review*. Kathmandu: Asian Development Bank.

Pokharel, B.R. (2003). English in broadcast and print media in Nepal. M.Ed. Thesis. Faculty of Education, Tribhuvan University, Kathmandu.

Poudel, T. (2016). English in Nepal: From colonial legacy to professionalism. *NELTA Chautari Forum* – Nepal's first digital ELT magazine.

Rana, B.K. (2008). Linguistic dynamism in South Asia: Some insights into recent change and development in different language communities in Nepal. In M.J. Warsi (ed.), *Linguistic dynamism in South Asia* (pp. 1-17). New Delhi: Gyan.

Rathbone, D. (1969). *English teaching in Nepal. Semi-annual report*. Kathmandu: Tribhuvan University.

Sah, M. (2016). [The compulsion of speaking Nepali to be Nepali]. *Kantipur*, 1 November.

Sharma, B.K. (2014). Some people should stop speaking English: Transnational Nepalese and language ideologies in YouTube discourse. *Discourse, Context and Media*, 4, 19.

Sharma, B.L., and Phyak, P. (2017), Neoliberalism, linguistic codification, and ethnolinguistic identity in multilingual Nepal. *Language in Society*, 17, 1-26.

Sharma, B.L. (2016). Economic market, elite multilingualism and language policy in Nepali schools. Retrieved from http://www.academia.edu/29784394/Economic_market_elite_multilingualism_and_language_policy_Nepali_schools

Sharma, G.N. (1990). The Impact of education during the Rana period in Nepal. *Himalayan Research Bulletin*, 10(2-3), 3-7.

Sharma, K.C. (2006). English in Nepal: From past to present. *Journal of NELTA*, 11, 24-33.

Sharma, S. (2009). ELT in New Nepal: A means for republican and global knowledge sharing. *NELTA Chautari Forum* – Nepal's first digital ELT magazine.

Shrestha, P. (2008). ELT ESP and EAP in Nepal: Whose interests are served? In M. Krzanowski (ed.), *ESP and EAP in developing countries: State of play vs. actual needs and wants* (pp. 191-110). Canterbury: IATEFL.

Shrestha, R. (1983). ESL/EFL distinction: Its pedagogy and the Nepalese context. *Contributions to Nepalese Studies*, 11(1) 45-59.

Skutnab-Kangas, T. (2009). Linguistic genocide: Tribal education in India. *Indian Folklore*, 32 (April): 4-6.

Skutnab-Kangas, T. (1988). Multilingualism and the education of minority children. In T. Skutnab-Kangas and J. Cummins (eds.), *Minority education: From shame to struggle*. Clevedon: Multilingual Matters.

Sonntag, S.K. (1995). Ethnolinguistic identity and language policy in Nepal. *Nationalism and Ethnic Politics*, 1(4), 108-120.

Sonntag, S.K. (2003). *The local politics of global English: Case studies in linguistic globalization*. Lanham: Lexington Books.

Sonntag, S.K. (2007). Change and permanence in language politics in Nepal. In A.B.M. Tsui and J.W. Tollefson (eds.), *Language policy, culture, and identity in Asian contexts* (pp. 205-218). London: Lawrence Erlbaum Associates.

Taylor, S.K. (2010). MLE policy and practice in Nepal: Identifying the glitches and making it work. In K. Heugh, and T. Skutnabb-Kangas (eds.), *Multilingual education works: From the periphery to the centre* (pp. 204-223). New Delhi: Orient BlackSwan.

Tickoo, M. (1993). When is a language worth teaching? Native languages and English in India. *Language, Culture and Curriculum*, 6(3): 225-239.

Tollefson, J.W. (1995). Introduction: Language policy, power, and inequality. In J.W. Tollefson (ed.), *Power and inequality in language education*. Cambridge: Cambridge University Press.

Tollefson, J.W. (2000). Policy and ideology in the spread of English. In K. Hall, J. and W. Eggington (eds.), *The sociopolitics of English language teaching*. Clevedon: Multilingual Matters.

Tomlinson, J. (1991). *Cultural imperialism: A critical introduction*. London: Pinter.

Turin, M. (2013). Our language in your hand. BBC radio program. Retrieved from http://www.bbc.co.uk/programmes/b01p3hnv

Wong, I.F.H. (1982). Native-speaker English for the Third World today? In J. Pride,(ed.), *World Englishes* (pp. 259-286). Rowley: Newbury.

Yadav, P.K. (2009). Rights based approach to ELT and how to adopt it in Nepal. *NELTA Chautari Forum* – Nepal's first digital ELT magazine.

Yadava, Y.P. (2007). Linguistic diversity in Nepal: Perspectives on language policy. International Seminar on Constitutionalism and Diversity in Nepal (pp. 1-18). Kathmandu, Nepal.

Yonjan-Tamang, A. (2005). Present situation of national languages of Nepal and language planning. A paper presented in Royal Nepal Academy, Kamaladi, Nepal, December.

Yonjan-Tamang, A. (2012). Bahubhashik shikhako kura [*Dialogue on multilingual education*]. Kathmandu, Nepal: Didi Bahini Offset Press.

Yonjan-Tamang, A., Hough, D., and Nurmela, I. (2009). 'All Nepalese children have the right to education in their mother tongue' – but how? The Nepal MLE program. In A.K. Mohanty, M. Panda, R. Phillipson, and T. SkutnabbKangas (eds.), *Multilingual education for social justice: Globalising the local* (pp. 241-249). New Delhi, India: Orient Black Swan.

CHAPTER 4

PERSISTENT INEQUALITY IN FEMALE EDUCATION WITHIN SOUTH ASIA

Comparing Bangladesh, India, Pakistan and Sri Lanka

Venesser Fernandes, Farzana Khan, Lavanya Raj
& Shashinie Thenabadu

Abstract

Gender inequality has been promoted through the justification of gender-based differential treatment and an inequality of resource distribution within developing nations. Through the increase in innovation in our present digital age, the existence of inequality in female education within these nations has been made profoundly transparent (UNESCO 2012). This chapter focuses on studying this issue within four countries in the South Asian region – Bangladesh, India, Pakistan and Sri Lanka – chosen due to their close geographical location and shared historical background. A long and common history of colonisation and its influence on the legal, political, economic and educational systems within these nations provide a common ground for the comparative analysis conducted in this chapter. While issues around gender inequality are highly complex in nature, the purpose of this chapter has been to highlight some of the inequalities in education faced by women in the South Asian region. In highlighting the contributing factors that influence the perpetuation of female inequality in education such as poverty, patriarchy, culture, religion, access and politics (Klugman et al. 2014; Razzaq and Forde 2014; Solotaroff and Pande 2014), this chapter focuses on developing an initial understanding of the need for a dominant praxis that addresses these issues in order to bring the transformation that is needed within the South Asian region.

Keywords: female education, gender-based education, inequality, developing nations, South Asia, colonialism

Introduction

Gender inequality can be defined as allowing people different opportunities due to perceived differences based solely on issues of gender (Parziale 2008). The 'World Atlas for Gender Equality in Education' describes the complexity of those suffering due to this inequality and considers that 'Girls and women remain deprived of full and equal opportunities for education. There has been progress towards parity at the primary level, but this tapers off at the secondary level in developing regions' (UNESCO 2012a, 1). Two out of the eight Millennium Development Goals (MDGs) (2000–2015) set by 191 United Nations member countries and relevant to the discussion on gender inequality in education include: achieving universal primary education, and promoting gender equality and empowering women (UNO 2015). The MDGs have provided the United Nations with the basis to deal with the apparent poverty and inequality prevalent across the developing world. However, in 2015, countries once again became engaged in the process of shaping and adopting a new development agenda that would build on the eight United Nations MDGs; from this agenda 17 United Nations Sustainable Development Goals (SDGs) emerged which focus on further strengthening the work done through the MDGs. From 2016 to 2030, these proposed SDGs will aim to work at ending poverty in all its forms everywhere. The special areas of concern highlighted include gender inequality and education, among others, both of which are relevant to this discussion. The emphasis at the international level provides a strong basis for a closer examination and understanding of different developing regions around the world and the contextual realities that give both agency and structure to hegemonic structures in place.

In focusing on the South Asian region of the developing world, it is found that a shared colonial history provides a major contextual reality across this region and contributes to the power structures that have been in place and continue to work within each of the four countries as well as the commonality of issues that surrounds gender inequality in this region. Interestingly enough, while available literature does not clearly highlight the state of female education during colonisation, it does indicate that 'dependency relationships based upon race, sex and class were perpetuated through social, education and economic institutions throughout the colonial era' (Lindsay 1983, 306). Education was a valuable tool 'of colonial policy in the consolidation of political power and in the acculturation of a colonial society' (Jayaweera 1990, 323). As such, during colonial rule, there was an upsurge of male education under the British raj as men were needed to correspond and transact with the British rulers (Cubero 2010). Since then and on a relatively more positive note, equality in education for women has come a long way since. One of the main positives of colonisation has been that formal education became an important aspect of the Indian subcontinent and a system of education emerged that offered education to the masses and weakened the status of education for the upper-class. This has resulted in a stronger middle class that has grown over the last 60 years with an easier access to education in urban South Asia for both males and females. Yet there is a marked inequality that continues to persist against women in this region and a number of issues become evident through this chapter as the analysis looks at the high variance found between urban and rural South Asia as well as upper classes of urban society as compared to lower classes of urban society. In fact, a deep-rooted gender inequality perpetuated by a number of factors becomes apparent.

In the next section, some of the significant contributing factors that sustain this inequality in the region are discussed at length. These include what the authors term the 'The 3Ps-based South-Asian Power Structure for Female Inequality in Education'. As seen in Figure 4.1, Poverty, Patriarchy and Politics of Caste and Culture would seem to be significantly strong factors that drive female inequality in education in South Asia. While the three factors are found to be quite deep-rooted and systemic within the South Asian region, interestingly enough, the authors found that the central factor of this power structure remains poverty. Further discussion on this is taken up in the sections below.

Poverty

Poverty continues to remain a major contributor to the issues surrounding female illiteracy in all four of these developing South Asian nations. Poverty is defined as general scarcity, dearth or the state of people lacking material and personal effects or money (Encyclopedia Britannica 2016). Poverty, which is a multidimensional concept consisting of social, economic and political fundamentals, is the root cause of issues that contribute to female inequality and perpetuates the postcolonial structures still in place that disadvantage women.

Siddiqui (2014) claims that poverty is much more complicated than just income deprivation and the nexus between poverty and education is complex (Tsujita 2012). Social Watch (n.d.) claims that the concept of poverty

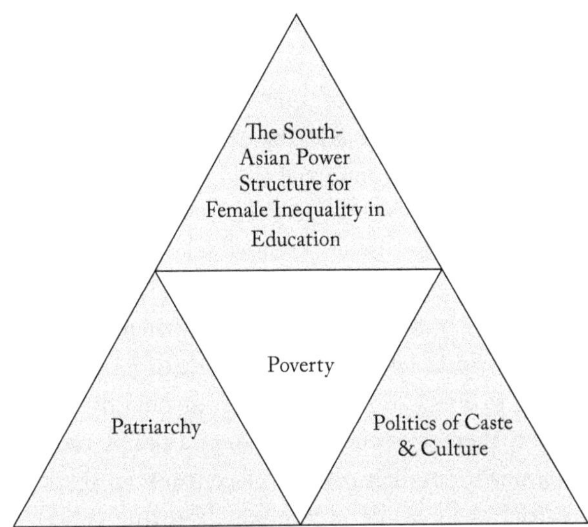

Figure 4.1: The 3Ps-based South-Asian Power Structure for Female Inequality in Education

has grown to include vulnerability, insecurity and defencelessness in the face of crisis. Factors such as malnutrition, lack of proper education, unemployment, women working abroad, alcoholism and domestic and sexual violence against women are issues that are linked to poverty, afflicting the lower social strata of these nations to a large degree. Poverty affects women disproportionately and often causes deprivation of basic education. Although basic education is freely available for all, the poorest, by virtue of being poor, are unable to access it because of direct and indirect costs attached to it. All countries in the South Asian region persistently face the problem of poverty and sociocultural factors as unrelenting obstacles to girls' education (Chitrakar 2009).

The impact of poverty on education for both boys and girls in India is such that it negatively affects initial enrolment in schools (Siddiqui 2014). Also, getting out of poverty through education is not an easy option in poorer households because of the often low educational levels of parents (Tsujita 2012). Lower income families are not in a position to afford good quality education. Government schools in India are provided with fewer resources because students are from lower socioeconomic strata (Tsujita 2012). However, it is the girl child in a poor family who is deprived of an education as it is perceived as an 'unnecessary luxury' (Chitrakar 2009, 54).

Even though it is difficult to make changes, Govinda and Bandyopadhyay (2010) suggest that the community can be empowered through decentralised decision-making such as making the school the primary unit for all interventions meant to enhance efficiency, so that more students – especially girls – are retained in schools. However, questions arise when there is an obvious gap between these findings and the actual reality of the poor masses that live in these South-Asian countries (ibid.). Will the political forces that govern educational systems be able to decentralise decision-making to the masses? And will the masses be empowered enough to take up the responsibility that comes with decision-making? In looking at traditional bureaucracies and practices that are strongly prevalent where poverty is high, how can these developed world notions of female equality be effectively implemented? According to Foucauldian thinking, at any given period of time, in a given context, there are substantial constraints placed on how people are able to think due to implicit rules in place (consciously or unconsciously active) that restrict their range of thought (Gutting 2005). This section begs consideration of the need to uncover these 'implicit rules' in the thinking of people from within these nations.

In Pakistan, almost 60 per cent of its population lives below the poverty line, with poverty higher in rural and less-developed urban areas of the nation. Pakistan has the second largest number of children out of school (6.7 million) of which 55 per cent are females (METS 2015) and has reduced its spending on education from 2.6 per cent to 2.3 per cent of GNP over the decade (UNESCO 2012b). Pakistani females carry a disproportionate burden of poverty and landlessness and comparatively have lacked equal rights with men due to male-dominated traditional patriarchal authority and pseudo-religious influences that have grown over the last few decades (Fatima 2013). 'Poverty of opportunity' has also resulted in significant disproportionate access to health and education for women compared to men (Qureshi 2004). As Mumtaz (2005) observes, 'Women living in poverty, even those desiring changes in gender relations, can frequently neither spare the time from their burdened daily existence nor risk the consequences of taking public action to advance their collective interests' (pp. 67-68). Shaukat (2009) also finds that the poor and illiterate communities prevent their daughters from acquiring education due to cultural constraints enforcing more traditional domestic roles for them. Hence, any significant improvement in their role through education has a direct impact on breaking the ongoing and vicious cycle of poverty and inadequate schooling that is in place. Fatima (2013) notes that while over the last decade there have been improvements in the ratios of female education and opportunities for female employment within Pakistan, still huge improvements are needed to implement quality education since education is the only vehicle for change. It can be noted that a political climate (see Ali - Chapter 5, this volume) that has given rise to attacks on girl students, female teachers, girl's schools and female NGO case workers has resulted from a strong patriarchal mindset. As such, these factors continue to deepen the poverty situation within Pakistan, making the task of Education for All more challenging.

As noted in the Poverty Reduction Strategy Paper II (IMF 2010), 'Pakistan must seek to employ its entire labour force, both male and female, as income generation from employment constitutes the most effective weapon in tackling poverty' (p. 8). A decade ago, Pakistan's Country Gender Assessment Report by the World Bank (2005) recommended that as low educational accomplishment has far-reaching consequences, women should be educated to benefit both inside and outside of households and society in general. A decade later, Pakistan must continue to work on the improvement of female education through improved policy and governance as well as through sound accountability systems within its educational systems to ensure poverty reduction and help Pakistani females.

Similar to the situations in India and Pakistan, poverty has plagued the lower levels of Sri Lankan society for many years. And as found in the other three countries, similar effects of poverty have had an effect on female education in Sri Lanka as well. Gender inequality in education has been of significant concern in Sri Lanka for many years despite the many efforts made in providing education to the entire nation (Fatima 2013). While education is compulsory for every child under 16 years (Kohona 2013), not all engage in higher education. Huge investments have been made to provide free education up to the secondary level along with providing technical education as an alternative path to economic stability (Fatima 2013). Fatima observes that, despite these efforts, disparity in education is seen in the rural areas of the country. Women in particular avoid engaging in higher education due to poverty and instead are married off at an early age. However, their lack of sufficient education leads them to be unemployed or underemployed. In addition to this and similar to the other South-Asian nations, violence against women, be it physical, emotional or sexual, is prevalent among the people of the lower social strata. This is mainly due to alcoholism rising from frustrations, which stem from poverty, job loss or unemployment among men. Very little evidence is present on these gender-based violent episodes as most of them go unreported (Perera 2013). Women in rural areas of the country opt either to go overseas (the Middle Eastern countries) as domestic workers or get employment in garment factories in order to become financially stable. Due to a lack of proper education or training, the options for these women are narrow and issues of violence against them are common. Research findings indicate that many of them face challenges and difficulties over continued or stable work, being underpaid, having poor accommodation, living at near starvation levels, having poor health, being victims of physical and sexual violence, and in rare cases, even death (Samath 2009).

Looking at the situation in Bangladesh, Nasreen and Tate (2007) identified poverty as the main reason for children dropping out from school. Access to tertiary education is heavily restricted and inequalities continue to widen, non-poor households being six times more likely to be enrolled in postsecondary education than children from poor households (Al-Samarrai 2008). Poverty refers to not only money or resources but also various other disadvantages related to power, status, and participation. Similar to the other three nations, poverty and patriarchy are inextricably linked in the rural areas. Girls are doubly marginalised in this social polarisation as boys are seen to have more potential for earning if parents invest more in them. Young girls who have to look after their younger siblings and share the domestic responsibilities with mothers are still a common phenomenon, especially in poor families (Blunch and Das 2014). Women in Bangladesh are continuously fighting against two odds – poverty and patriarchy – along with malnutrition, high maternal mortality rates, lack of access to resources, environmental degradation, lack of access to health, lack of paid employment and discriminatory wage rights (Nasreen and Tate 2007).

In short, although there has been progress towards gender parity at both primary and secondary levels of education globally since 2000, it still remains a challenge for world populations (UNESCO 2012c) and continues to remain a focus for the Sustainable Development Goals set by the United Nations in 2015. In all four countries, poverty has been noted as a strong barrier for access to education for boys and girls, with girls being more disadvantaged than boys due to the inherited systems of patriarchy, traditions and religious observances. It was also found consistently that inequality in enrolment widens as children move up the education system, with children in poor households being twice as unlikely to be enrolled in secondary school as their counterparts.

For poverty to be alleviated within South Asian countries, a consciousness awakening or power needs to start from the grassroots level and move upwards. Foucault (1998) considered this to be a dispersed or pervasive source of power as compared to the power wielded by people or groups as 'episodic' or 'sovereign' acts of domination or coercion. In other words, while poverty is deeply rooted and connected with patriarchy in these countries, it requires a cultural change, before reformative, sustainable improvement can be realised. Foucault suggests that 'Power is everywhere' and 'comes from everywhere', having neither an agency nor a structure (Foucault 1998, 63). In other words, the power to bring about a change in the inequality found in female education and one of its main underlying factors – poverty – requires these nations to work beyond the usual political campaigns, traditional bureaucracy and popular fear campaigns that have been evidenced during colonial and even in postcolonial times. It requires national policy and sense-making that brings about systemic reformation through a strong economic development plan but along with this it requires cultural changes that are implemented at the grassroots level through community platforms such as schools, religious institutions, health institutions, and non-government and government offices.

From a Foucauldian perspective, this would call for ongoing discourse at all levels of society as a way of critical analysis and strategic action. Foucault suggests that discourses are not necessarily always subservient to power; instead, he suggests, that in bringing about a cultural change and mindset for poverty alleviation, we must make allowances for the complex and unstable process through which these multilevel discourses can be both an instrument and an effect of dispersed or pervasive power, and a strong hindrance, stumbling point of resistance and starting point for an opposing strategy to current episodic or sovereign power structures in place. In Foucault's words, 'Discourse transmits and produces power; it reinforces it, but also undermines and exposes it, renders it fragile and makes it possible to thwart' (Foucault 1998, 100-101). This is what is needed to make explicit some of the 'implicit rules' of thinking that these nations have been subjected to for a very long time and to bring them into a vibrant 21st century discourse around female empowerment through literacy, economic standing, social and political representation and inclusion.

Patriarchy

The second common factor that impacts women's education is patriarchy which is directly related to the male-dominated power structure in these countries. Patriarchy has been identified as one of the major concerns that generates contemporary issues such as the persistence of gender discrimination, how gender roles undermine the development of healthier marriage and family relationships (and better relations among generations), the lack of full equality for women in employment, falling birth rates and rising divorce rates (Kaku 2013). Within this patriarchal power structure, girls are subject to decision making by the head of the family who determines whether or not they are allowed to go to school or how far they are allowed to go if they are sent to school. This traditional power structure curbs the rights of women to be educated since the traditional patriarchal family structure re-emphasises the common understanding of gender roles of men being superior in the power structure and the decision makers (Khan 2016). This structure is in essence performative as it is internalised through various social norms and practices where women are taught not to ask questions but to maintain the structure and to fear what will happen if they are not conforming to the structure. Butler (1990) argues that performativity of gender (how one should fit into the expected gender norms) is a stylised repetition of acts, an imitation or miming of the dominant conventions of gender, which in essence is carried out both by males and females in the family and then in society. The power intricacy lies in the defining factors of what is expected and what is accepted by the small as well as broader periphery that determines a girl's participation in education.

Much has been done to promote the agenda of gender equality in education at national and international levels in Bangladesh, India, Pakistan and Sri Lanka (Chitrakar 2009). The Millennium Development Goals have emphasised the need for concerted effort on gender equality in the education sector. In the past few years numerous gender-focused initiatives were taken that yielded remarkable changes in the status of girls' education, 'although much still needs to be done to achieve fuller equality' (Chitrakar 2009, 9). Except for Sri Lanka, patriarchy has been identified as the major reason for gender inequality in Bangladesh, India and Pakistan (Byrnes & Freeman 2012; Chitrakar 2009; Niaz 2003). Patriarchy is practised in the forms of socioeconomic advantage, child marriage, eve-teasing, religion, caste and also violence against women, which eventually stop girls from attaining education. In the previous section Foucault's theory of power was discussed in terms of ensuring education for women but, within the patriarchal social system, power works in a top-down process as it invokes the 'monolithic conception of male dominance' (Kandiyoti 1988, 275). As Kandiyoti (1988) contends, in the patriarchal social system women strategise their sense of autonomy through resistance and conformity. Within this power frame of strategising, women's autonomy remains in the domestic periphery. A question that arises is whether women can strategise or negotiate their rights to education. Another question is: does patriarchy impact boys and girls separately or in the same manner? The discussion below highlights how patriarchy curbs women's right to education.

Socioeconomic Advantage

In the earlier section, it has been argued that poverty and patriarchy are overlapping issues that put women in a disadvantageous situation, not only in terms of accessing education but also in terms of enjoying basic rights as human beings. All four countries have a strong undercurrent of patriarchal values that are materialised differently based on cultural and religious tenets. For example, in the patrilocal social system in Bangladesh, girls are seen as liabilities as when they are married they will not live with their parents and thus will not contribute to the family. In a patrilocal social system, married couples live near or with the husband's parents. When a woman gets married, she essentially ceases to be a member of her birth family and joins her husband's family - 'Under this system, parents potentially reap more of the returns to investments in a son's health and education because he will remain a part of that family' (Jayachandran 2014, 11). Similarly, Pakistan with its traditional gender roles positions women within the home and men as the breadwinners of the family.

Like Bangladesh, one of the long-term effects of patriarchy has been the preference for investment in the education of boys over girls. In their study on rural girls, Lloyd, Mete and Grant (2007) found that household economic shocks affect girls and their schooling negatively but have no such effect on boys. This would suggest that these barriers are clearly economically-driven, with parents more willing to invest in the education of their boys than their girls. Lloyd et al. (2007) further suggest that the large and persistently evident gender gap in schooling can be explained in terms of demand-side constraints which include poverty and parental concerns about the safety and mobility of their daughters and supply-side constraints which include underinvestment in girls' schooling. In India, female children are viewed as a burden and are not valued as highly as the male children (Johnson and Johnson 2001), which means parents do not provide sufficient opportunities for their education or higher education in comparison to their male counterparts; the destination of female children is often seen to be marriage, not making education a necessity. Contradictorily, in Bangladesh, with the advancement of globalisation, awareness of educating girls is on the rise as educated girls tend to attract better marriage proposals than non-educated girls (Khan 2016). If a girl is educated, she is likely to attract a more 'suitable' partner with an educated and higher-status family.

Child Marriage

As a result of the perception that girls are a burden to the family in most cases, they are married at a very young age. In Bangladesh, child marriage has been identified as one of the major reasons for girls to drop out before finishing secondary school. However, according to a UNICEF (2008) report, child marriage is slowly decreasing in Bangladesh – although the rate is still very high at 66 per cent of young girls married under 18, resulting in early pregnancy and often forcing them to leave education before completing their higher secondary education (UNICEF 2008). Moreover, in the traditional expected gender roles in Bangladeshi society, the new bride is expected to do the household chores, which automatically prevents her from attending school.

The situation in Pakistan is quite similar to Bangladesh. Early marriage of girls is a dominant practice, especially in the rural and underdeveloped urban sectors of the country. The notion of 'settling our daughters' by marrying them off not only has implications of reducing long-term expenses associated with rearing females in the family but also stems from fears for the safety of young girls. In 2014, according to United Nations Development Program (UNDP) data-sets for Pakistan, the maternal mortality ratio was 260 to every 100,000 live births, with adolescent birth rates recorded at 27.3 in every 1,000 young women aged 15–19. Compared to other South Asian countries, these statistics indicate mixed results, with the maternal mortality ratio for Pakistan being higher than Afghanistan and closer to Bangladesh and India. Better comparisons for Pakistan were found in terms of adolescent birth rates where Pakistan statistics indicated lower maternal mortality ratios than in countries such as India, Bhutan, Bangladesh, Nepal and Afghanistan, indicating gradual improvements made in the last few years. In India, child marriage has been identified as 'a substantial barrier to social and economic development and a primary concern for women's health' and education (Raj, Saggurti, Balaiah and Silverman 2009, p. 1883).

Religion

Various religious interpretations ostracise women in Bangladesh, India and Pakistan. Dreze and Sen (1995) contended that educating girls in India historically has been seen as a threat to the social order in the 'dominant Brahminical tradition' (p. 132). In this tradition, males are seen as elites and 'boys are always preferred over girls if a choice for an opportunity has to be made' (Chitrakar 2009, 54). Abortion based on sex preference, female foeticide, is shockingly prevalent in various Indian communities. Chitrakar (2009) argues, where these kinds of criminal activities are rampant, 'it is not difficult to imagine the extent to which the discriminatory general social perception against education of girls can be pervasive and deep-rooted' (p. 55). The discrimination is even worse when it comes to the lower castes in this hierarchical social system. This will be discussed in the caste section in detail.

The situation is similar if not the same in Pakistan. As Latif (2007) contends, Pakistan is an Islamic nation, and therefore should not experience gender disparity in education because in Islam equal emphasis has been given for seeking knowledge on men and women. Despite this, in some parts of Pakistan, particularly in rural and tribal areas in the north, girls are strictly forbidden from taking advantage of educational opportunities. Buzdar and Ali (2011) identified non-religious reasons in their study on parents' attitudes towards female education in tribal areas of Pakistan. The main barriers were the lack of quality public education and proper school governance; access issues for remote areas; scarcity of female teachers in public schools; preference for a religious education; and high costs of private schools in the area. Similarly, the Pakistan Education for All Review Report 2015 (METS 2015) reports similar findings including reasons such as high opportunity cost of a girl attending school as she has to undertake or help out in household chores; cultural factors, especially among tribal and conservative segments restricting female mobility; and the overall deteriorating law and order situation, discouraging parents from sending their daughters to school.

Public Harassment and Violence against Women

In Bangladesh, India and Pakistan, violence against women has become a major issue (Chitrakar 2009; Niaz 2003). According to a UNICEF (2011a) report, public harassment (popularly known as 'eve teasing') and stalking of schoolgirls have become an increasingly concerning issue for attending schools in Bangladesh. On many occasions, the outcome of stalking has increased drop-out rates as it can result in girls committing suicide as the only way out, or being murdered by their stalkers. Eve-teasing has been justified as one of the key reasons for marrying girls at an early age, to 'protect' them from predators (Unicef 2011a). This harmful practice violates the rights of children, as girls being forced to marry at a young age puts their health and educational opportunities in jeopardy. There are laws to protect girls from these kinds of sexual offences but, due to the poor implementation of law and corruption, in most cases exemplary punishments are not set. While on the one hand girls' participation in education is progressively encouraged and supported by state laws and policies with provision of attractive incentives, ironically girls walking down the street (for example, going to or returning from school) become subject to 'female infanticide, kidnapping, public assault, and acid throwing [including] rape, incest, and harassment through language, trafficking and forced prostitution' (USAID 2002, 9). The threat of caste and religion based violence as well as kidnapping, trafficking and prostitution are also major causes of hindrance for women's education in Bangladesh, India and Pakistan (Chitrakar 2009; Niaz 2003).

This section highlighted how patriarchy is practised in terms of socio-economic disadvantage, early and forced marriages of girls, religious (mis) understanding and public harassment and violence against women in Bangladesh, India and Pakistan. Patriarchy along with poverty ostracises women and hinders their equal access to education. The absence of literature in the Sri Lankan context may suggest that patriarchy is not a major concern for female inequality in Sri Lanka.

The Politics of Caste and Culture

Why are caste and other social stratification systems critical in understanding inequality in female education? Countries in the Indian subcontinent are characterised by some common histories and cultural similarities even though they are different in their political, religious and social makeup. All countries seem to share similarities in following certain social stratification systems to varying degrees. 'Certain common features like centralized government socioeconomic inequalities based on class, gender and caste and nationalistic divisive claims on ground of ethnicity has characterized the South Asian countries' (Sharma 2014). Some systems such as the Hindu caste system in India, Pakistan, Bangladesh and Sri Lanka are rigid, whereas other social stratification systems unique to specific countries or some communities in some or all countries might be more flexible. Nevertheless, it has been documented that such social stratification systems negatively impact female equality in education. UNESCO (2010) claims that due to caste-based discrimination in South Asian countries, girls, especially rural girls, have low prospects in gaining education and that legislation has not succeeded in transforming discriminatory practices in many parts of these countries.

The Indian caste system is a hierarchical segregation of people according to the birth order ordained in the Brahminical scripture *Manusmriti* through which the society was divided into Brahmin, Kshatriya, Vaishya, Shudra and Dalits. The Shudras and the present-day Dalits or Scheduled Castes are at the lowest rung of the hierarchy. This segregation extended to the labour status of an individual according to the specific caste they were born into, which meant it was not only a segregation of labour but also labourers, thus making mobility from one economic class to another almost impossible. The effects of the caste system are still prevalent: although constitutionally it has been outlawed in India, Pakistan, Bangladesh and Sri Lanka, it is culturally and socially still in practice. Within the caste system, women are considered to be inferior to men, and women belonging to the lower castes are considered to be inferior to women in higher castes, thus negatively impacting women belonging to the lower castes more so than women belonging to the upper castes. Thus, even though patriarchy negatively impacts women of all castes and classes, women belonging to the lower class and caste are *doubly* impacted because of discrimination by both men and women of all castes. Therefore, the relationship between the caste system and class is a pertinent one in understanding female inequality in education because the higher castes generally are economically forward in comparison to the lower castes and access to education is a process that is affected by economic ability and other social constraints. It can be said that the caste system then is an economic structure that not only discriminates against women but also helps maintain the status quo of the lower caste women. Although the effects of the caste system are profound in India and there is a general belief that Bangladesh, Pakistan and Sri Lanka do not suffer as much as India does, the tendency of 'caste blindness', a belief that there is no caste structure, has been observed by activists and researchers in these countries (Silva, Sivapragasam and Thanges 2009). The International Dalit Solidarity Network (IDSN 2009) strongly claims that although founded and sanctioned by Hinduism, caste discrimination cuts across religions and regions and therefore is also prevalent in Bangladesh, Sri Lanka and Pakistan.

It is to be noted here that the IDSN (2008) states that in Sri Lanka 'the state has turned a blind eye' to caste discrimination and that while Tamil-speaking communities practise caste discrimination, a caste system unique to the Sinhala community within the realm of the Buddhist culture is also practised. Ninety per cent of the population recognises it for some purpose (Thorat and Shah 2007) even though the Constitution of Sri Lanka under Article 12(2) prohibits discrimination by reason of caste. The three different communities – Sinhala, Sri Lankan Tamil and Indian Tamil – all follow practices of the caste system. Lower caste women in the Sinhala community have resorted to overseas employment as domestic help in Middle East countries to escape caste discrimination at home. Tamil nationalism and the militant form of it, known as the Liberation Tigers of Tamil Elam (LTTE), brought about the banning of caste-based discrimination among the Sri Lankan Tamils. While many underprivileged caste groups in Sinhala society have managed to uplift themselves through the welfare state, an even benefit has not been noted in all such caste groups (IDSN 2008). Women in low castes in both Tamil and Sinhala communities continue to suffer in their access to education, although they may not be excluded from accessing basic necessities, like drinking water (IDSN 2008).

In India, UNICEF (2011a) reported discrimination against students by teachers based on caste. While affirmative action policies have played a major role in extending education to the lower castes, the progress in girls' education is reported to be inadequate. A strong feudal agrarian culture with situated oppression directed towards women and Dalits, as well as the ongoing suppression of social and political institutions, has led to chaos and corruption (Dreze and Sen 1995), and resulted in a situation that mostly favours the interests of the elites. For example, there is a significant difference between Scheduled Castes (SC)/Scheduled Tribes (ST) and other castes in terms of enrolment in higher education. In 1990–1991, the share of the SCs in total enrolment in Indian higher education was only 8.7 per cent while the share of STs was only 2.1 per cent. In professional education, including engineering, the situation is bleaker with the share of SCs/STs only 6.7 per cent and 3.2 per cent respectively in 2000–2001 (Scaria 2014). These numbers are inclusive of both genders.

Dalit girls suffer multiple burdens of poverty, caste and gender (Rampal 2005). Harassment and dehumanisation by the very institutions that need to protect their educational rights have consistently been reported. For example, in Indian rural settings, it is a widely acceptable culture to force girls and boys students belonging to the Dalit communities to clean toilets in schools. Girls are also subjected to sexual abuse by upper caste teachers, thus leading their parents to remove the girls from attending school. Legal protective measures have been recommended as a key factor in reducing such discriminatory practices (Chitrakar 2009).

Although in Bangladesh some reports claim that girls' access to education is 'no longer an issue', it is made clear that research is needed in the area of determining whether girls from certain backgrounds are deprived of incentive programs and quality education and the relationship with harassment, abuse and intimidation at school (Chitrakar 2009, x). Discriminatory attitudes of teachers to children based on their caste, leading children to not attend classes, have been recorded (UNICEF 2011b). The dominant socio-cultural feature in Bangladesh is a combination of Hindu and Muslim traditions (Chowdhury 2009), both following caste and social stratifications systems that are seen to negatively impact women's education.

While 5.5 million Dalit communities are segregated based on their caste (Chowdhury 2009), the literature also indicates the many castes within Muslim communities and the graded hierarchy between them (Chowdhury 2009; Karim 1956). While Article 28(1) of the Constitution of Bangladesh proclaims that the state shall not discriminate against citizens on the grounds of caste, the Constitution does not recognise the minorities as groups distinct from the Bengalis and the existence of indigenous people in the country (Chowdhury 2009). The logical progression of such a situation leads us to an enquiry on the status of female inequality in education from this perspective, which is currently an area that requires study. Severe forms of violence such as rape and destruction of property can be seen as negatively impacting female education in Bangladesh. According to the National Sample Survey of Child Labour in 1995–96, 6.3 per cent of total 34.4 million children were involved in labour, out of which 12 per cent in the age group of 5–9, of which the male-female ratio of the children was 60:40. Further, the distinction of women into *Bhadramahila* (upper class women) and *Mahila* (lower class women) determines their social standing and when seen through a social stratification perspective, can be understood to impact girls in their access to education because they face multiple forms of discrimination both as Dalit/lower caste and as women in a patriarchal society, as young women are prohibited from making educational choices (Chowdhury 2009).

The Gender Equality Index of Pakistan, which is 0.20, indicates that girls' education is lagging behind. Although remarkable improvement has been made in the field of literacy by rural women (20.8 per cent), it is the urban women who have made a greater percentage gain (55.6 per cent). In rural Pakistan, much like in other South Asian countries, accessing education means that children will have to cross settlement or caste boundaries to reach the nearest school. In places where higher castes dominate, low-caste children, especially girls, face high barriers in attaining education (Jacoby and Mansuri 2011). In a study that calculated the distance girls needed to travel to acquire education, it was found that the low-caste girls appear to gain little from the presence of a school even in their own settlement because of the domination of high-caste households. However, low-caste children are more likely to attend school if the school is available in their settlement, but, for low-caste girls who are less mobile, the caste boundary effect is twice as large.

While Article 22 of the Constitution of Pakistan states that 'no citizen shall be denied admission to any education institution receiving aid from public revenues on the ground only of race, religion, caste or place of birth', the 2006 National Education Census showed that 21.56 per cent of villages lack educational institutions and many villages simply do not have schools for girls. Of the 12,737 schools that were included in the Census, the highest percentage were in the area of Sindh and the government report clearly mentions that the disadvantages faced by female students are multiplied if the students come from a low performing region. Lower caste women in rural areas of Sindh face some of the most severe challenges in education because people are illiterate as a result of poverty and they are poor due to illiteracy (PDSN 2013).

Having described the problems girls and women face due to caste-based discrimination, the most important reflection at this stage would be: this being the case, what next? At a time when left-wing and subaltern women's movements are strengthening in India and other South Asian countries, because of heightened discrimination, Evidence (2011) stresses that the states have obligations to prevent, investigate and punish acts of violence and that any legislation that protects Dalit women should be reviewed and strengthened. Also, law enforcements agencies must be sensitised to address caste and gender-based discrimination. All India Dalit Mahila Adhikar Manch (AIDMAM) (n.d.) provide 32 recommendations for strategic intervention on violence against women and atrocities on Dalits. Setting up of a Human Rights Commission in units within communities, districts and finally at the state level could be one of the most important steps in building a strong anti-violence system. Such recommendations are key in understanding the specific tasks that need to be undertaken so that caste-based discrimination can be minimised and the educational status of women in South Asian countries can be improved.

Since in Sri Lanka caste is not a variable in any official database, it has been reported that the National Human Rights Commission must pay great attention to understand the relationship between caste discrimination and education, especially female education (IDSN 2008). Since a resistance to investigate caste practices in Bangladesh, Sri Lanka and Pakistan has been observed in the literature, at this juncture it is safe to say that further research is very pertinent to understand the relationship between caste structures and female inequality in education.

In Foucauldian terms, the work of deep transformation and reform is required when considering the above issues around caste. This is brought about through an open and turbulent atmosphere of continuous and revolutionary criticism (Gutting 2005) directed at the status quo as well as reforms that emerge as a revolutionary response to the status quo. In short, to disable the negative agency given to caste through the religious and cultural structures in place, it will be necessary to disrupt the current status quo as well as critique the reforms that come after until a new transformation within these nations is palpably noted. But even then, all such activities require radical criticism in order to generate much needed questioning modes of thought that 'break the current mould'.

Conclusion

As discussed at length in this chapter, the whole issue of inequality in female education is deep-seated and deep-rooted within the societal framework of these nations. There are many factors that contribute to this, and some of the main factors have been discussed and critically examined in this chapter. Suggestions have also been made on how considerations around the current agency and structure in place need to be defiantly challenged to unlock the potential of overcoming previously held notions of sovereign patriarchal power and postcolonial hierarchies of power, providing new ways of thinking. In these new ways of thinking, power is dispersed and comes from everywhere, disrupting caste or cultural boundaries and combatting the ongoing condition of poverty prevalent in these nations.

In short, surface-level, narrowly defined improvements have not made a sufficient enough impact on the required gender parity needed in education. More, much more, needs to be done. This is just the beginning of the beginning. A much needed social reawakening is required that allows for South Asian females to be considered as equal, contributing, and socially active citizens of these nations. And within such a social awakening, female equality in rights to education is a central factor of the discourse around the change that is needed.

References

All India Dalit Mahila Adhikar Manch (AIDMAM) (n.d.). *Violence against Dalit women.* Retrieved from http://www.ncdhr.org.in/aidmam/key-activities-1/Submission_on_Violence_Against_Dalit_Women.pdf

Al-Samarrai, S. (2008). *Governance and education inequality in Bangladesh.* United Nations Educatonal, Scientific and Cultural Organization website. Retrieved from http://unesdoc.unesco.org/images/0018/001800/180086e.pdf.

Blunch, N.-H., and Das, M.B. (2014). Changing norms about gender inequality in education: Evidence from Bangladesh. *IZA Discussion Papers,* (8365), 1-37.

Butler, J. (1990). *Gender trouble: Feminism and the subversion of identity.* New York: Routledge.

Buzdar, M.A., and Ali, M. (2011). Parents' attitude toward daughters' education in tribal area of Dera Ghazi Khan (Pakistan). *Turkish Online Journal of Qualitative Inquiry,* 2(1), 16-23.

Byrnes, A.C. and Freeman. M. (2012). The Impact of the CEDAW Convention: Paths to Equality (February 20, 2012). UNSW Law Research Paper No. 2012-7. Available at SSRN: https://ssrn.com/abstract=2011655 or http://dx.doi.org/10.2139/ssrn.2011655.

Chitrakar, R. (2009). *Overcoming barriers to girl's education in South Asia.* Kathmandu, Nepal: Wordscape.

Chowdhury, I. U. (2009). Caste based discrimination in South Asia: A study of Bangladesh. Working Paper Series Volume III, Number 07, New Delhi: Indian Institute of Dalit Studies pp 1-58.

Cubero, A.V. (2010). Women's education in India during the colonial period. *Educación XX1,* 13(2), 185-197.

Dreze, J., and Sen, A. (1995). *India Economic development and social opportunity.* New Delhi: Oxford University Press.

Evidence. (2011). Atrocities against Dalit women and access to justice. Retrieved from http://idsn.org/wp-content/uploads/user_folder/pdf/New_files/Key_Issues/Dalit_Women/EVIDENCE_final_access_to_justice_report.pdf

Fatima, G. (2013). Gender inequality in human capital accumulation and economic growth: A comparative analysis of Pakistan and Sri Lanka. *Asia Pacific Journal of Social Work and Development,* 23(4), 242-252. doi: 10.1080/02185385.2013.778786.

Foucault, Michel (1998). *The history of sexuality: The will to knowledge.* London, UK: Penguin.

Govinda, R., and Bandyopadhyay, M. (2010). *Changing framework of local governance and community participation in elementary education in India.* Consortium for Research on Educational Access, Transitions and Equity.

Gutting, G. (2005). *Foucault: A very short introduction.* Oxford: Oxford University Press.

IMF (2010). Pakistan: Poverty reduction strategy paper II. Washington, DC: International Monetary Fund Publications. Retrieved from https://www.imf.org/external/pubs/ft/scr/2010/cr10183.pdf

International Dalit Solidarity Network (IDSN). (2008). *Dalits of Sri Lanka: Caste-blind does not mean casteless* (2nd edition). Retrieved from http://idsn.org/uploads/media/FACTSHEET_SRILANKA.pdf

Jacoby, H.G., and Mansuri, G. (2011). Crossing boundaries: How caste and gender affect schooling in rural Pakistan. Retrieved from http://www- wds.worldbank.org/external/default/WDSContentServer/WDSP/IB/2011/06/28/000158349_20110628133715/Rendered/PDF/WPS5710.pdf

Jayachandran, S. (2014). The roots of gender inequality in developing countries. *Annual Review of Economics.* Retrieved from http://faculty.wcas.northwestern.edu/~sjv340/roots_of_gender_inequality.pdf

Jayaweera, S. (1990). European women educators under the British colonial administration in Sri Lanka. *Women's Studies Inf. Forum,* 13(4), 323-331.

Johnson, P.S., and Johnson, J.A. (2001). The oppression of women in India. *Violence against Women,* 7(9), 1051-1068.

Kaku, S. (2013). *Patriarchy in East Asia: A Comparative Sociology of Gender.* Netherlands: Brill.

Kandiyoti, D. (1988). Bargaining with patriarchy. *Gender & Society,* 2(3), 274-290.

Karim, A. K. N. 1956. *Changing Society in India and Pakistan.* Dhaka: Ideal Publications.

Khan, F.Z. (2016). Negotiating the silenced 'self'. Purdah, globalization and tradition: Resistance and agency among Muslim female University graduates in Bangladesh. Unpublished PhD Thesis. Monash University.

Klugman, J., Hanmer, L., Twigg, S., Hasan, T., McCleary-Sills, J., and Santa Maria, J. (2014). *Voice and agency: Empowering women and girls for shared prosperity.* Washington, DC: World Bank.

Kohona, P. (2013). *Sri Lanka: Advancing gender equality with carefully calculated strategies.* TheHuffingtonPost.com.

Lindsay, B. (1983). *Comparative perspectives of third world women: The impact of race, sex and class.* New York: Praeger.

Lloyd, C.B., Mete, C., and Grant. M. (2007). Rural girls in Pakistan: Constraints of policy and culture. In M. Lewis and M. Lockheed (eds.), *Exclusion, gender and schooling: Case studies from the developing world* (pp. 99-118). Washington, DC: Center for Global Development.

METS (2015). *Pakistan Education for All review report 2015.* Islamabad, Pakistan: Ministry of Education, Training and Standards, Higher Education Academy of Educational Planning and Management.

Mumtaz, K. (2005). Advocacy for an end to poverty, inequality, and insecurity: Feminist social movements in Pakistan. *Gender & Development,* 13(3), 63-69. doi: 10.1080/13552070512331332298.

Nasreen, M., and Tate, S. (2007). *Social inclusion: Gender and equity in education swaps in South Asia: Bangladesh case study.* UNICEF.

Niaz, U. (2003). Violence against women in South Asian countries *Arch Womens Ment Health,* 6, 173-184.

Pakistan Dalit Solidarity Network (PDSN) (2013). Scheduled Caste Women in Pakistan - Denied a life in dignity and respect. Report prepared by the Pakistan Dalit Solidarity Network (PDSN) in association with the International Dalit Solidarity Network (IDSN) and submitted to the CEDAW Committee in January 2013. Retrieved from: https://idsn.org/wp-content/uploads/user_folder/pdf/New_files/Pakistan/SCHEDULED_CASTE_WOMEN_IN_PAKISTAN_-_Alternative_report_to_CEDAW_-_PDSN_and_IDSN_-_Jan_2013.pdf

Parziale, A. (2008). Gender inequality and discrimination. In R. Kolb (ed.), *Encyclopedia of business ethics and society* (pp. 978-982). Thousand Oaks, CA: Sage Publications. doi: http://dx.doi.org/10.4135/9781412956260.n365

Perera, A. (2013). *Women battle on after Lanka war*. Retrieved from http://www.ipsnews.net.2013/10

Qureshi, S. (2004). *Pakistan: Education and gender policy. Girl's education: A lifeline to development*. Budapest: Center for Policy Studies, Central European University. Retrieved from http://www.policy.hu/qureshi/Respaper.pdf

Raj, A. Saggurti, N., Balaiah, D., & Silverman, J. (2009). Prevalance of child marriaige and its effect on fertility and fertility-control outcomes of young women in India: A cross-sectional, observational study. *Lancet, 373* , 1883-1889. doi:10.1016/S0140-6736(09)60246-4.

Rampal, A. (2005). *Quality and equality in education: Gendered politics of institutional change*. Retrieved from http://www.ungei.org/resources/files/beyondaccess_ramphal.pdf

Razzaq, J., and Forde C. (2014). The management of large-scale change in Pakistani education. *School of Leadership and Management*, 34(3), 299-316.

Samath, F. (2009). *Sri Lanka: 25 years on, women still struggle for their rights*. Retrieved from http://www.ipsnews.net.2009/10.

Scaria, S. (2014). Do caste and class define inequality? Revisiting education in a Kerala village. *Contemporary Education Dialogue*, 11(2), 153-177.

Sharma, P. (2014). Oligarchic patriarchal political culture of women participation in South Asia: with special reference to India, Bangladesh, Pakistan. Research paper presented at the XXIII IPSA World Congress - Challenges of Contemporary Governance 19 - 24, July 2014 held at Montreal, CANADA Retrieved from: https://pdfs.semanticscholar.org/a9a6/01bafdd6c423ed528744751a6bf3d432aefe.pdf

Shaukat, A. (September, 2009). Delivering girl's education in Pakistan. Oxfam BG Discussion Document. Oxfam International. Retrieved from http://www.ungei.org/resources/files/delivering-education-pakistan-ukfiet09.pdf

Siddiqui, T. (2014). Education as poverty removal instrument: A study in India. *Global Journal of Research Analysis,* 3(6), 50-53.

Silva, K. T., Sivapragasam, P. P., and Thanges, P. (2009). *Casteless or caste-blind?: Dynamics of concealed caste discrimination, social exclusion, and protest in Sri Lanka*. Copenhagen: International Dalit Solidarity Network.

SPARC (2014). *The state of Pakistan's children – 2014*. Report prepared by Society for the Protection of the Rights of Children. Retrieved from http://www.sparcpk.org/sopc2014/Education_Chapter_2014.pdf

Solotaroff, J., and Pande, R. (2014). *Violence against women and girls: Lessons from South Asia*. South Asia Development Forum. Washington: World Bank Publications.

Thorat, S., and Shah, P.G. (2007). *Dismantling descent-based discrimination: Report on Dalits' access to rights*. Retrieved from http://www.indianet.nl/pdf/dismantling.pdf

UNDP Human Development Report (2014). *Sri Lanka HDI values and rank changes in the 2014 Human Development Report.*

UNESCO (2010). EFA Global Monitoring Report 2010: Reaching the marginalized. Paris: UNESCO. Retrieved from: http://unesdoc.unesco.org/images/0018/001866/186606E.pdf

UNESCO (2012a). *From access to equality. Empowering girls and women through literacy and secondary education* (2nd edition).

UNESCO (2012b). *Youth & skills: Putting education to work.* EFA Global Monitoring Report 2012. France: United Nations Educational, Scientific and Cultural Organization. Retrieved from: http://unesdoc.unesco.org/images/0021/002180/218003e.pdf

UNESCO (2012c). *World atlas of gender equality in education.* France.

UNICEF (2008). *Early marriage.* Retrieved from http://www.unicef.org/bangladesh/children_4866.htm

UNICEF (2011a). A Perspective on gender equality in Bangladesh: From young girl to adolescent: What is lost in transition? Dhaka: UNICEF. Retrieved from: https://www.unicef.org/bangladesh/Gender_paper_Final_2011_Low.pdf

UNICEF (2011b). Disparities in education in South Asia: A resource tool kit. Nepal: UNICEF Rosa. Retrieved from: http://www.ungei.org/files/Countering_Disparities_in_Education_Toolkit__2011.pdf

UNO (2015). *The Millennium Development Goals report 2015.* New York, NY: United Nations.

USAID (2002). *Bangladesh education sector review: Report no. 2. Status of gender equity.* Dhaka: USAID.

World Bank (2005). Pakistan – Country gender assessment : bridging the gender gap – opportunities and challenges : Pakistan – Country gender assessment – Bridging the gender gap : opportunities and challenges (English). Washington, DC: World Bank. Retrieved from: http://documents.worldbank.org/curated/en/325871468289192424/Pakistan-Country-gender-assessment-Bridging-the-gender-gap-opportunities-and-challenges

CHAPTER 5

EIL AND LEARNER IDENTITIES

Exploring Learners' Sociocultural Identities in Locally Developed English Textbooks in Pakistan

Zahra Ali

Abstract

The remarkable change in the status and role of English as an international language warrants critical focus on the notions of culture and identity in English language education. This study addresses the need to revisit the role of culture in English language teaching (ELT) by drawing on the epistemological framework of English as an international language (EIL). The epistemic position of EIL strives for breaking the dependency on Anglo-centric teaching approaches and learning materials by more fully respecting the local culture of learning and promoting the significance of contextually designed pedagogical and learning strategies. Drawing on the case of Pakistan, this chapter utilises the textual analysis approach to examine cultural representations in two locally developed secondary level English language textbooks for Grade 7, and the impact of such cultural representations on the identities of its learners. The textbooks represent the distinct teaching of English in two education systems of Pakistan: (1) the General Certificate of Education (GCE O level) and (2) the Secondary School Certificate (SSC matriculation). The analysis of the cultural and linguistic representations in the two textbooks revealed that despite inclusion of international target cultures, the cultural information was mainly presented at a knowledge-oriented level. Furthermore, the textbooks did not prepare its learners to engage in intercultural communication with English speakers from diverse cultural backgrounds. In light of these findings, some recommendations are proffered to the ELT industry reflecting the multiple perspectives inherent in the teaching of EIL.

Keywords: English language teaching (ELT), English as an international language (EIL), Pakistan, culture, identity, curriculum and pedagogy, intercultural communication, textbook analysis

Introduction

Reinforced by globalisation, recent decades have witnessed a phenomenal rise in the number of English users around the world. It is estimated that over one billion people are learning and speaking English worldwide (Beare 2010; Sharifian 2013), with the number of non-native speakers outweighing the native speakers of English. As indicated by the British Council, 375 million English users belong to the category of English as second language (ESL) speakers, while there are approximately 750 million English as a foreign language (EFL) speakers worldwide. In light of the dynamic changes in the users, role and status of English, several scholars within the field of English pedagogy (McKay 2003; Levis 2005; Matsuda and Friedrich 2011; Matsuda 2012; Alsagoff 2012; Marlina and Giri 2013; McKay and Brown 2015) have called for a change in the form of an entirely new perspective in the conceptualisation, teaching and learning of English. For instance, Kumaravadivelu (2012) calls for critically revisiting the teaching and learning of English through a 'radical reconceptualisation' (p. 14) of English language pedagogy. His approach involves moving away from the traditional dependency on Western-based approaches to learning and acknowledging the linguistic and cultural diversity of the English language.

Furthermore, in response to the epistemic shift in the way English is being conceptualised and used in the 21st century, research on language and its relation to learners' identities has recently been gaining momentum (Alsagoff 2012; Mahboob 2015). Duff and Uchida (1997) indicate how an individual's identity is 'co-constructed, negotiated and transformed on an ongoing basis by means of language' (p. 452), and likewise how the individual's language is influenced by and through their linguistic and cultural identities. Increasingly, research within many branches of linguistics views language as a system, which operates beyond the control of abstract grammatical categories – i.e., viewing language as a semogenic 'meaning-making system' (Mahboob 2015). This system recognises how language serves as a creative space for its users to construct different meanings by contextualising language to reflect certain meanings. Similarly, interest in identity in the field of ELT represents a shift from the cognitive perspectives of second language acquisition (SLA), towards the sociocultural dimensions of language learning that not only view the learner as a 'complex social being' (McKay and Wong 1996, 557), but also address the relationship between the learner and the larger social world in which they participate (Rampton 1990; Alsagoff 2012). As Norton (1997) indicates, learners' participation in the social world involves a 'mutually constitutive' (p. 419) relationship between their identity and the language they use.

This study is, therefore, an attempt to explore the formation of learners' sociocultural identities in the learning and teaching of English through examining the notion of culture in English language textbooks used in Pakistani schools. By actively drawing upon the epistemological framework of EIL, this study engages in a critical analysis of the cultural content of English language textbooks used in Pakistani schools, which have claimed to incorporate a 'global' approach to teaching and learning English. This chapter will begin by providing a brief overview of an EIL perspective of the English language, culture and identity, and the relationship between them. This will be followed by an examination of the presentation of cultures in the two ELT textbooks in Pakistan and its impact on learners' identities. Finally, in light of the findings, recommendations for future textbook writers and teachers will be provided.

EIL, Culture and Identity in English Language Teaching

The role of culture in ELT, specifically in the field of curriculum design and pedagogy, has gained significant momentum worldwide due to its long-established relationship with language. McKay (2003) discussed how cultural knowledge plays a significant role in English language pedagogy by often providing the content and topics used in language materials and classroom discussions. However, there has been ample evidence in the ELT literature of the promotion of native English speaker culture in both locally developed and internationally distributed ELT textbooks, which reproduces the linguistic and cultural dominance of Kachru's (1985) Inner Circle nations (Murayama 2000; Ilieva 2000; Shin et al. 2011). Song (2013) points out the role of powerful institutional gatekeepers such as English language proficiency tests (for instance, Cambridge examinations and the Test of English as a Foreign Language (TOEFL)) as well as Western publishing houses in reinforcing the superiority of the varieties of English spoken in Inner Circle countries. This has further led language professionals to believe that developing native-speaker-like competence also meant integrating native cultural norms (McCrum 2010). However, many scholars in the field of ELT disagree with the assumption of English learners' inclination towards the English culture. Ultimately, the role of

English as a global language means that no country can have custody over it (Widdowson 1994), and that learners of this international language do not need to mimic or internalise the cultural norms of its native speakers, since the ownership of this language has become 'denationalised' (McKay 2004; Pandian et al. 2014). Instead, the focus has now shifted towards enabling the communicative role of English as opposed to attempting to produce a native-like cultural identity (Kumaravadivelu 2012).

Garrett (2010) adds to the discussion on the changing role of English two views regarding the impact of globalisation on the culture of English users: 'cultural homogenisation' and 'cultural hybridisation'. Homogenisation of cultures is associated with 'cultural imperialism, westernisation, or Americanisation' (p. 448). Hybridisation, on the other hand, reflects the localisation of Western cultures to adapt to local tastes and contexts, so that either the associated ideologies are ignored or perceived differently in their new contexts. Recent years have observed an inclination towards the hybridisation of cultures in English texts, as Matsuda (2012) suggests that the learning of the English language is 'now intricately intertwined with a wide variety of cultures, including national and regional cultures that are not traditionally associated with English [Anglo-centric culture]' (p. 176). However, the question remains, to what extent has this been practised? Studies conducted by Matsuda (2003) and Honna (2008) in Japan, as well as numerous studies in Korea (Jung 2005; Park and Kim 2014) showed that, despite encouraging the importance of learning about diverse cultures, most of the teaching materials and courses focused entirely on Anglo-American cultures.

Furthermore, many ELT scholars have questioned the kind of cultural information presented in English language teaching materials. Adaskou, Britten and Fahsi (1989) talk about the inclusion of four cultural dimensions in textbooks: (1) the aesthetic sense (art and literature); (2) the sociological sense (customs and practices); (3) the semantic sense, the manner in which a culture's conceptual system is embodied in a language; and (4) the pragmatic sense, which pertains to linguistic and paralinguistic rules and skills that guide speakers in appropriate use of rhetorical styles for communication purposes. They further argue that the last two senses of culture, semantic and pragmatic, are necessary for the development of intercultural communicative competence. McKay (1992) adds to the discussion by suggesting that 'in order to be competent in a language, individuals need to understand the concepts that individual words embody as well as how to use the words appropriately' (p. 56). Sharifian (2009) also recognised the importance of promoting multiculturalism and development of intercultural awareness in teaching materials by pointing out that 'what is needed … is an expansion of the scope of speech communities and interlocutors engaged in intercultural communication, especially as most instances of intercultural communication in English today takes place between its non-native speakers' (p. 4).

Recognising the impact of cultural knowledge in ELT materials, many EIL scholars view the critical role of culture in English language texts as developing an 'ideological' stance (Cortazzi and Jin 1999). In other words, as Pandian et al. (2014) suggest, 'the cultural content of the textbook … reflects a worldview or cultural system, a social construction that may be imposed on teachers and students and that indirectly constructs their view of a culture' (p. 35). Therefore, it can be assumed that exposure to certain textbooks and learning materials can be understood as a manifestation of certain cultural norms. As textbooks are 'one of the first places – and one of most formal artefacts – that demonstrate what educational "norms" are intended to be transmitted in the classroom' (Khurshid et al. 2010, 427), this study views ELT textbooks as 'cultural artefacts, which serve to make English mean in particular ways' (Gray 2010, 730). Shin et al. (2011) suggest that ELT textbooks, curricula and teachers should 'provide a lens through which learners can expand their cultural awareness to include global, multicultural perspectives' (p. 265), and these insights and perspectives can facilitate learners in instances of intercultural communication that occur in international contexts. Therefore, the main research objective in this study is to examine how current ELT textbooks in Pakistan acknowledge and reflect the global diversity of cultures of English users, and the impact of inclusion of such cultural knowledge on the identities of its learners. In order to achieve this objective, the study identified and examined the cultural content presented in two locally developed ELT textbooks, followed by an analysis of the impact of these on learners' sociocultural identities.

In terms of the context of the research, Pakistan is categorised as a peripheral colonial country, where English was imposed and 'successfully transplanted' (Hall and Eggington 2000) during the British colonial rule. Much of the language research in postcolonial countries shows how the practice of colonisation continues to permeate ELT practices and that its effects are still evident today. Many scholars in the field of ELT including Phillipson (1992), Ramanathan (1999) and Kumaravadivelu (2012) agree that core countries like Britain and the USA exercise major control over the political and economic domains of the periphery countries, including the educational arena through giving importance and preference to native-speaker accents, native-like competency, teaching methods developing and emerging from Western universities, and textbooks published by Western publishing houses. Therefore, one of the aims of this research study is to critically evaluate the English learning materials used in Pakistani classrooms to see whether they present an Anglo-centred or a globally-oriented/hybridised cultural view of the world. Since culture and identity are inextricably linked, this study further investigates how the diversity of the uses, users and cultures of English presented in the ELT textbooks influence learners' identities.

In regard to the notion of identity, this study has adopted the postmodern view that no longer treats individuals' identity as singular, static or stable, but rather as a plural, multiple and mutable entity (Dumitrescu 2001). Identity is seen beyond the rigidity of fixed social categories and as something that 'is constantly and endlessly invented and reinvented' (Kumaravadivelu 2012, 11), and negotiated throughout the contexts of local and international discourses and interaction. As discussed earlier, the hybridisation of cultures in English, therefore, involves learners and users of this language negotiating their identities as a balance between their global and local use of English. In terms of the localised status of English, this language serves the diverse local needs of its multilingual users through reflection of their cultural norms and values. On the other hand, English's position as a global language enables its users as intercultural speakers to understand, acknowledge and respect other English users as individuals with complex multiple identities, regardless of their national and ethnic origins (Alsagoff 2012).

To summarise, the analytical framework for this study was designed to answer the following research questions:

1. What, whose and how are cultures depicted in ELT textbooks in Pakistan?

2. How do the cultural representations in the English language texts project, shape and manage learners' sociocultural identities?

Samples and Context of Research

For the purpose of examination and analysis, two secondary level English textbooks for Grade 7, representing two different education systems in Pakistan, were taken as samples. The first textbook was Oxford Progressive

English 7, published by the Oxford University Press Pakistan for students studying English for the General Certificate of Education (GCE O level). The second ELT textbook was *English for Grade VII*, published by the Punjab Textbook Board and taught as part of the secondary school certificate (SSC matriculation), which is equivalent to GCE in the local education system of Pakistan.

The teaching of these textbooks is consigned to two types of schools in Pakistan, namely the 'government-funded' and the 'private' schools. For instance, *English for Grade VII* is taught as part of the secondary school certificate (SSC) in all government schools in Punjab. The content for this textbook is developed based on the guidelines included in the National Curriculum (2006) of the country, which is decided by the Ministry of Education Curriculum Wing of Pakistan. On the other hand, the General Certificate of Education (GCE) is administered by the examination boards in the United Kingdom, and Oxford University Press generally provides the textbooks. Akhtar and Saeed (2014) noted that there were 432 institutions in Pakistan approved by the British Council to offer GCE to its students, and most of these belong to the elite private sector of the country. Mahboob (2015) further comments on the difference in the medium of instruction between the government and private schools by indicating that in government schools 'English is only taught as a subject for a few hours a week, whereas students in elite private schools study all their subjects in English' (p. 155).

Data Collection and the Analytical Framework

This study selected and adapted the textbook analysis approach developed by Murayama (2000), which deals with a detailed cultural content analysis of learning materials by beginning to look at whose culture is depicted (aspect of culture) and places them in one of the following three categories of presentation of cultural information (Cortazzi and Jin 1999):

- *source culture*, which depicts the learners' own culture as content;

- *target culture*, information representing the culture of the country where English is spoken as the mother tongue or first language; and

- *international target culture*, representation of the diversity of cultures belonging to Kachru's (1985) Outer Circle and Expanding Circle countries.

Following this, the framework then situates the cultural information presented within the categories of 'level of culture' and 'how the culture is represented' (Dinh 2014; Murayama 2000; Shin et al. 2011). The 'level of culture' helps identify the presentation of cultural information at the level of *general culture* and/or *specific culture*. Dinh (2014) differentiates between the two categories by indicating 'culture in texts can be categorised into culture-general (addressing general issues, non-identifiable country's culture) or culture-specific (capturing a specific country's culture through cultural hints)' (p. 148). The final category of 'how the culture is represented' looks at the presentation of the cultural information at either the *knowledge-oriented* or *communication-oriented* level. The knowledge-oriented cultural presentation, according to Shin et al. (2011), looks at the 'traditional way of presenting cultural information through the presentation of facts' (p. 263). On the contrary, the communication-oriented level presents culture in the form of dialogue and interaction amongst people. In other words, the learning material in a communication-oriented format aims to promote cultural sensitivity in instances of international interaction through activities like discussion and comparison of diverse and distinct cultural information and ideas.

Finally, in light of the results, the study looks at how learners' identities are managed through the types of cultural information presented in the texts.

Findings

English for Grade VII – the Punjab Textbook Board

Published by the Punjab Textbook Board for Year seven, this English textbook was designed to address the basic skills of reading, writing, listening and speaking in all of its units, along with developing the identities of its learners as globally-oriented individuals through introduction of cultural knowledge from across the globe. For instance, the textbook claims:

> Students are exposed to a variety of extracts to gain knowledge of the world. The literary texts also offer a range of genres (poem, stories) written by the authors from different cultures ... This activity centralises [English] language as a vehicle for communication, prompting students to share their opinions with others and leading them to accept and understand different points of view. (Baig et al. 2014, vi)

Table 5.1: Table of contents of *English for Grade VII* published by the Punjab Textbook Board

English for Grade VII – Table of Contents
Unit Title
1. The Last Sermon of the Holy Prophet Hazrat Muhammad (صلى الله عليه وسلم)
2. Our Villages
3. Eid-ul-Azha
4. Rain in Summer (Poem)
5. Traffic Sense
6. Pollution
7. A Dengue Patient Visits a Doctor
8. A Nation's Strength (Poem)
9. Kaghan Valley
10. Quaid-i-Azam
11. The Rooster and the Fox
12. I Dream a World (Poem)
13. Inventions and Discoveries
14. A Terrible Earthquake

Upon detailed textual analysis of the textbook, it was found that the majority of the units represented the students' source culture (Pakistan). There were a total of six literary texts, out of which two represented the Pakistani culture through display of local practices: the creation of the system of 'panchayat' (p. 17), a local council that comprises five members, organised as a governing body of a village in Pakistan; and the social issue of dengue outbreaks in Pakistan. On the other hand, out of the eight non-literary texts, six represented the Pakistani culture at a knowledge-oriented level in the form of religious events (Eid-ul-Adha and Khutbat-ul-Hajja-tul-Wida, also known as the last sermon of Hazrat Muhammad PBUH); local places (Kaghan Valley in northern Pakistan); social issues (the 2005 Kashmir earthquake); and local heroes (Quaid-i-Azam, the founder of Pakistan and its first Governor General). The remaining six literary and non-literary texts were written by authors mostly from the US, but did not represent the culture of their authors at either the knowledge or communication-oriented level. The three non-literary texts merely provided discrete facts and general information on issues such as pollution, scientific inventions and medical discoveries, without addressing any specific culture or country.

So was the case with the literary texts, comprising three poems, which lacked the identifying culture of their authors and addressed general topics such as the rain and the qualities required to build a strong nation. To summarise, the focus of the textbook relied predominantly on the students' source culture in a knowledge-oriented format, and did not correspond to any of the cultures across the world. Dinh (2014), in her study of local Vietnamese ELT textbooks, had similar findings: 'there has been an overrepresentation of the Vietnamese society across the textbooks, leaving minimal chance for students to get immersed in the reality of diversity' (p. 145).

The second aim of the textbook addressed the skills of oral communication, as the authors suggest that each unit builds students' 'communication skills using selected linguistics exponents to communicate appropriately for various functions and co-functions of opinions, feelings, emotions, instructions in real-life situations' (Baig et al. 2014, vii). This aim was supposed to follow the communication-oriented format of cultural presentation by introducing students to instances of intercultural communication and various negotiation strategies required as part of real-life international exchanges. However, teaching of the oral communication skills in the textbook relied on teachers prompting the students to read an excerpt of a dialogue exchanged between two characters and to reproduce the same dialogue by 'practise this conversation in pairs' (p. 12) (Figure 5.1).

In addition to the format of the presentation of cultural knowledge, the language of the content is also crucial to managing, shaping and maintaining learners' identities. In the case of the textbooks approved by the government/provincial textbook boards of Pakistan, certain linguistic cues from the onset indicate the promotion and maintenance of the learners' Islamic identities. There are two major examples of how the textbook analysed in this study encouraged the importance of Islamic principles and credo. Firstly, the textbook began its introduction with the phrase بسم الله الرحمن الرحيم (I begin in the name of Allah, most gracious, most merciful). Mahboob's (2015) research on the language of the Grade 1 English textbook endorsed by the Sindh Textbook Board also indicated similar results, with the textbook initiating with the same Arabic phrase, thus evidencing the promotion of Islamic ideology as a shared feature of all the Pakistani Government authorised textbooks. Another instance of the use of Arabic phrases was observed in the first unit of the textbook:

Our Villages

Group Activity:

Practise this conversation in pairs.

Fatima:	Where are you going?
Rani:	I am going to fetch water from the well.
Fatima:	Do you need water badly?
Rani:	Yes, all the pots and pitchers are empty. Yesterday I could not go to the well, because I was ill.
Fatima:	Are you fine now?
Rani:	Yes, I am fine now. I can bring out and take water home.
Fatima:	May I help you?
Rani:	No, thanks.

Guidelines for the Teacher:

- Help the students to conduct all the activities in the classroom situation.
- Involve the students in teaching-learning process using no cost / low cost teaching material.

26

Figure 5.1: *English for Grade VII* (p. 26).

Table 5.2: Culture representation in *English for Grade VII*

Unit	Whose culture			Level of culture		How culture is represented	
	Source culture	Target culture	International target culture	General culture	Specific culture	Knowledge-oriented	Communication-oriented
1	✓			✓		✓	
2	✓				✓	✓	
3	✓			✓		✓	
4	-	-	-	✓		✓	
5	-	-	-	✓		✓	
6	✓			✓		✓	
7	✓			✓			✓
8	-	-	-	✓			
9	✓				✓	✓	
10	✓			✓		✓	
11	-	-	-	✓		✓	
12	-	-	-	✓		✓	
13	-	-	-	✓		✓	
14	✓			✓		✓	

'The last sermon of the Holy Prophet Hazrat Muhammad' 'صلى الله عليه و سلم' (p. 1), where the authors used the Arabic phrase instead of its English counterpart ('Peace be upon him – PBUH'). Further reference to Islam was projected in the promotion of its ideological beliefs and practices. For instance, the first unit of the textbook began with the statement, 'Islam covers all the aspects of human life. It is not only a religion but a complete code of life' (p. 1). Mahboob (2015) reflects on the dominance of Islamic ideology in ELT textbooks in Pakistan and indicates how it is 'used to construct an Islamic identity in and through English' (p. 165).

To review briefly, some of the major findings from the textual analysis of the *English for Grade VII* textbook include:

- The culture(s) represented in the texts mainly captured the students' source culture, that is, the Pakistani culture. The majority of the textual units focused on Pakistani culture (8 out of 14 units), emphasising local places, events, personalities and practices. The rest of the units, however, depicted general issues without addressing the norms or values of either the target or international target cultures.

- The cultural information was presented at both the level of general and specific culture; however, the propensity was more towards the presentation of general cultural information.

- Cultures were represented in the knowledge-oriented format through display of cultural facts, rather than manifestation of intercultural communication as part of the communication-oriented format.

Oxford Progressive English 7 – Oxford University Press Pakistan

This textbook is part of the Oxford Progressive English series, which prepares learners for the General Certificate of Education (GCE). It has been written according to the guidelines provided by the UK and the Pakistan National Curriculum that aims to enhance learners' reading, writing, speaking and listening skills through the teaching of a wide range of texts from prominent Pakistani and foreign authors. There are 10 units in the textbook comprising a range of texts from fictional and non-fictional prose and poetry.

The textual analysis revealed the dominance of target culture content in the textbook (8 out of 10 units), specifically the culture of the UK. There were instances of certain texts that addressed the content of the students' source culture (two non-fictional Pakistani readings) and the international target culture (for example, Burma, Japan and West Africa). The presentation of the cultural information in these texts was mainly at a culture-specific level, including local names such as Simasiku Pumulo (Zambia), Pahom (Russian); local titles and practices, for example the Burmese title of 'thakin' addressing a man of respect, and Origami, the Japanese art of paper folding; local heroes (Sadako Sasaki from Japan); historical places and events, such as the Sri Dalada Maligawa Temple in Sri Lanka and the Battle of Paniput 1526; and lastly metaphors, for instance reference towards elephants in Sri Lanka as symbolising abundance and fertility. Moreover, despite the themes of certain fictional and non-fictional texts focusing on inter-cultural contact between characters, the texts were still displayed in

Table 5.3: Table of Contents of *Oxford Progressive English 7* published by Oxford University Press Pakistan

Oxford Progressive English 7 – Table of Contents
Unit Title
1. Elephants
2. War and Peace
3. London
4. Sugar and Spice
5. Danger!
6. Lesson
7. Water
8. Family Feelings
9. Other Worlds
10. Achievement

a knowledge-oriented format with none of the characters being involved in instances of intercultural communication.

Textbooks bear a direct influence on the teaching of culture and it is through this medium that the values and norms of a particular culture are enforced on its teachers and learners. As Khodadady and Shayesteh (2016) reveal, 'textbooks are not only the sole conveyers of subject knowledge, but also the tools of ideological reproduction' (pp. 604-605). Upon detailed analysis of the textual content of *Oxford Progressive English 7*, it was confirmed that, through the use of certain linguistic items, learners' identities were positioned along a conformist orientation. Mahboob (2015) describes how learners' conforming sociocultural identities are 'shaped in relation to the dominant and powerful sociocultural beliefs and practices' (pp. 156-157). In the case of postcolonial contexts, the authority of the native-speaker's English has shaped and influenced the teaching of the language, thus influencing the identities of its learners to acknowledge, legitimise and conform to native-speaker English and Western cultural beliefs. This linguistic and cultural hegemony has been described as a form of epistemic orientation of marginalisation and self-marginalisation (Kumaravadivelu 2012) that continues to dominate the mainstream English education, a form of dependency on Anglo-centred teaching methods.

The research context of this study still found itself dominated by the native-speaker episteme that continues to regulate the coloniality of English language teaching and learning. For instance, this textbook, although published by the Pakistani branch of Oxford University Press, still seems to be loaded by the native-speaker culture. This dominance also carries with it the stance of the native-English speakers' speech as the 'gold standard of grammatical correctness and perfect pronunciation' (Walkinshaw and Oanh 2014, 1). This was observed through the inclusion of a pronunciation key by the author in the units specifically focused on the target culture of the UK (Figure 5.2).

There were a number of readings in the textbook, which focused on the students' source culture and represented the international target cultures of Burma, West Africa and Japan, through inclusion of local names and items.

London

Vocabulary

gaolers (Paragraph 7)

jail / gaol (both pronounced [jale]) and *jailer* **/** *gaoler* **are**

spelling variations which are both correct. A *gaoler* **or** *jailer* **is**

the person guarding the prisoner in prison.

Note the spellings and pronunciation of:

gaol [jale] = prison

goal [gole] = and objective or an aim

To score a goal is to get the ball through or into the net in netball or football.

Definitions

a rack = an instrument of torture used to extract information from prisoners at this time. As a wheel was turned, the prisoner tied to the rack was stretched out further and further.

disembowel = to cut out the entrails or bowels.

Spelling

parliament – pronounced [parl-a-ment], but remember the 'ia' in the middle!

Figure 5.2: *Oxford Progressive English 7 (p. 73)*.

For instance, the first unit in the textbook 'Elephants' (p. 2) introduced its learners to a wide range of Burmese vocabulary like 'thakin' (a term of respect), 'oo-si' (an elephant handler or rider) and 'cheerot' (a kind of cigar). However, unlike the pronunciation key provided for the units focusing on the target culture of the UK, the textbook lacked a pronunciation key for the local terms used in international target culture texts. In view of these findings, there is no doubt that the identities of the learners were managed to integrate within the native-English community by acquiring their exact language use and consequently, their cultures.

Table 5.4: Culture representation in *Oxford Progressive English 7*

Unit	Whose culture			Level of culture		How culture is represented	
	Source culture	Target culture	International target culture	General culture	Specific culture	Knowledge-oriented	Communication-oriented
1			✓		✓	✓	
2		✓	✓		✓	✓	
3		✓			✓	✓	
4	✓	✓			✓	✓	
5		✓		✓		✓	
6			✓		✓	✓	
7		✓			✓	✓	
8		✓		✓		✓	
9		✓			✓	✓	
10	✓	✓			✓	✓	

As displayed in Table 5.4, the textbook attempted to promote teaching and learning of diverse cultures through the incorporation of texts displaying students' source culture, the target culture of the UK and various international target cultures. However, with the dominance of the knowledge-oriented pattern of cultural presentation, the textbook did not prepare its learners to meet the reality of global communication in which not only do people exchange information but simultaneously negotiate cultural differences during intercultural communication.

Pedagogical Implications

A critical analysis of the two English language textbooks used in Pakistani schools revealed that despite inclusion of students' source culture and international target cultures, the cultural information was predominantly presented at a knowledge-oriented level. Also, the textbooks lacked preparation of students for communicating across cultural borders, thus limiting students' views and awareness of the real-life communicative aspect of English as an international language. In light of the dominance of knowledge-oriented cultural information in the textbooks, it seems as if the identities of the learners are being managed as passive receptors; according to McManus (2001), they are assumed to have 'minds like empty vessels or sponges to be filled with knowledge' (p. 424). Sturman (1997) identifies this passive role of learners as a form of 'social injustice' in education. By classifying students as 'disadvantaged', he encourages application of three aspects of social justice in order to ensure equity in education: 'social justice should include components of distribution, principles of curriculum justice, and should also draw attention to non-material components of equity, such as empowerment' (p. 116). Sturman emphasises the importance of empowering students by equipping them with the opportunity of 'decision-making' (p. 118).

This is also consistent with research in the fields of curriculum design and teaching (Eisner 2002; Milner 2010; Doecke and Parr 2009) that views learners' language and experience(s) as an indispensable resource for effective learning. Barnes (1976) talks about the power that learners often exercise – the power 'of opting out; they conform, and even play the system, but many do not allow the knowledge presented to them to make any deep impact upon their view of reality' (p. 17). In fact, learners have a personal history outside their classrooms and curriculum, which they tend to utilise when making sense of new knowledge. Kim (2006) encourages that, in order to motivate and engage students in making sense of the knowledge presented to them, teachers should incorporate their 'voices', while involving them in activities such as intercultural encounters and conflicts. Doecke and Parr (2009) also agree on enacting a curriculum that 'treats the language and experiences students bring to school as an indispensable resource for meaningful engagement in schooling' (p. 67).

This research study therefore makes a strong case for radically changing the way English is being taught in Pakistan by leading towards an EIL pedagogy which aims to promote: (1) an acknowledgement and understanding of the plurality in the present-day use, users and cultures of English; (2) preparing learners to collaborate in a global society by interacting appropriately with speakers of English from different cultures; and (3) a sense of ownership of the local varieties of English. Due to Pakistan's background as a peripheral colonial country, this study acknowledges Mignolo's (2010) advice of 'delinking from the concepts of coloniality and the extension of coloniality of power and knowledge' (p. 451), which would eventually lead to a 'de-colonial epistemic shift and bring to the foreground other epistemologies, other principles of knowledge and understandings' (p. 453). The notion of EIL stands as the other epistemological orientation, which strives to separate itself from an epistemic position that exercises native-English hegemony in education.

What is needed is for the debate to revolve around the trend of promoting discourses of multiculturalism, multilingualism and internationalisation, which translates into 'the promotion of a pedagogy that is highly sensitive to diverse uses, users, functions, and contexts of English' (Selvi 2014, 575). For this purpose, a balance is necessitated between the local and global teaching of English, where the learners' identity is recognised as a multicompetent user (Cook 1992, 1999) of English, in which 'instead of being cast as imperfect native speakers … learners are now re-imagined as multilingual agents in control of complex linguistic repertoires that serve their identity needs' (Alsagoff 2012, 114-115).

In conclusion, the outcomes of this study argue for an urgent need to critically examine and revisit the current ELT textbooks in Pakistan in light of the ongoing internationalisation of the English language. Owing to time constraints, this study only investigated two textbooks and therefore a richer and more in-depth perspective is required in the form of a large-scale research project, exploring students' and teachers' views regarding the learning content, classroom observation and analyses of other teaching materials.

References

Adaskou, K., Britten, D., and Fahsi, B. (1990). Design decisions on the cultural content of a secondary english course for Morocco. *ELT Journal,* 44(1), 3-10.

Akhtar, M., and Saeed, A. (2014). A comparative analysis of the effectiveness of mathematics curriculum taught at GCE (O-level) and SSC systems of schools in Karachi. *Academic Research International,* 5(4), 318-329.

Alsagoff, L. (2012). Identity and the EIL learner. In L. Alsagoff, S.L. McKay, H. Guangwei and W.A. Renandya (eds.), *Principles and practices for teaching English as an international language* (pp. 104-122). New York: Routledge.

Baig, M.G., Ahmad, M., Tajammal M., and Sadaf, T. (eds.). (2014). *English for Grade VII* (p. 26). Urdu Bazar, Lahore: Ch. Ghulam Rasul & Sons.

Barnes, D.R. (1976). *From communication to curriculum*. Harmondsworth: Penguin.

Beare, K. (2010). *How many people learn English globally?* Retrieved 1 August 2015 from http://esl.about.com/od/englishlearningresources/f/f_eslmarket.htm.

Cook, V. (1992). Evidence for multicompetence. *Language Learning*, 42(4), 557-591.

Cook, V. (1999). Going beyond the native speaker in language teaching. *TESOL Quarterly*, 33(2), 185-209.

Cortazzi, M., and Jin, L. (1999). Cultural mirrors: Materials and methods in the EFL classroom. In E. Hinkel (ed.), *Culture in second language teaching* (pp. 196-219). Cambridge: Cambridge University Press.

Dinh, N.T. (2014). Culture representations in locally developed English textbooks. In R. Chowdhury and R. Marlina (eds.), *Enacting English across borders: Critical studies in the Asia Pacific* (pp. 143-167). Newcastle upon Tyne: Cambridge Scholars Publishing.

Doecke, B., and Parr, G. (2009). 'Crude thinking' or reclaiming our 'storytelling rights'. Harold Rosen's essays on narrative. *Changing English*, 16(1), 63-76.

Duff, P.A., and Uchida, Y. (1997). The negotiation of teachers' sociocultural identities and practices in postsecondary EFL classrooms. *TESOL Quarterly*, 31(3), 451-486.

Dumitrescu, M. (2001). Modernism, postmodernism, and the question of identity. *Dialogos*. Retrieved 25 July 2015 from http://www.romanice.ase.ro/dialogos/03/7-Dumitrescu.pdf.

Eisner, E. (2002). *The educational imaginations: On the design and evaluation of school programs* (3rd edition). NY: Macmillan.

Garrett, P. (2010). Meanings of 'globalisation': East and West. In N. Coupland (ed.), *The handbook of language and globalisation* (pp. 447-474). Oxford, West Sussex: Wiley-Blackwell.

Gray, J. (2010). The branding of English and the culture of the new capitalism: Representations of the world of work in English language textbooks. *Applied Linguistics*, 31(5), 714-733.

Hall, K.J., and Eggington, G.W. (eds.) (2000). *The sociopolitics of English language teaching*. Clevedon: Multilingual Matters Ltd.

Honna, N. (2008). *English as a multicultural language in Asian contexts: Issues and ideas*. Tokyo: Kuroshio Publishers.

Ilieva, R. (2000). Exploring culture in texts designed for use in adult ESL classrooms. *TESL Canada Journal*, 17(2), 50-63.

Kachru, B.B. (1985). Standards, codification and sociolinguistic realism: The English language in the outer circle. In R. Quirk and H.G. Widdowson (eds.), *English in the world: Teaching and learning the language and literatures* (pp. 11-30). Cambridge: Cambridge University Press.

Khodadady, E., and Shayesteh, S. (2016). Cultural and linguistic imperialism and the EIL movement. Evidence from a textbook analysis. *Issues in Educational Research*, 26(4), 604-622.

Khurshid, K., Gillian, I.G., and Hashmi, A.M. (2010). A study of the representation of female image in the textbooks of English and Urdu at secondary school level. *Pakistan Journal of Social Sciences*, 30(2), 425-437.

Kim, Y. (2006). Secondary Korean ESL students' perception on culture learning and cross-cultural adjustments. *English Teaching*, 61(4), 109-131.

Kumaravadivelu, B. (2012). Individual identity, cultural globalisation and teaching English as an international language. In L. Alsagoff, S.L. McKay, H. Guangwei and W.A. Renandya (eds.), *Principles and practices for teaching English as an international language* (pp. 9-27). New York: Routledge.

Levis, J. (2005). Changing contexts and shifting paradigms in pronunciation teaching. *TESOL Quarterly, 39*(3), 369-377.

Mahboob, A. (2015). Identity management, language variation and English language textbooks: Focus on Pakistan. In D.N. Djenar, A. Mahboob and K. Cruickshank (eds.), *Language and identity across modes of communication* (pp. 153-177). Berlin: Mouton de Gruyter.

Marlina, R., and Giri, R. (2013). We provide the best international education and use international-oriented learning materials: Questioning the international from the perspective of English as an international language. In N. Zacharias and C. Manara (eds.), *Contextualising the pedagogy of English as an international language: Issues and tensions* (pp. 75-98). Newcastle upon Tyne: Cambridge Publishing Scholars.

Matsuda, A. (2003). The ownership of English in Japanese secondary schools. *World Englishes, 22,* 483-496.

Matsuda, A., and Friedrich, P. (2011). English as an international language: A curriculum blueprint. *World Englishes, 30*(3), 332-244.

Matsuda, A. (2012). Teaching materials in EIL. In L. Alsagoff, S.L. McKay, H. Guangwei and W.A. Renandya (eds.), *Principles and practices for teaching English as an international language* (pp. 168-185). New York: Routledge.

McCrum, R. (2010). *Globish: How the English language became the world's language.* London: W.W Norton and Company.

McKay, S.L. (1992). *Teaching English overseas: An introduction.* New York: Oxford University Press.

McKay, S.L., and Wong, C.S. (1996). Multiple discourses, multiple identities: Investment and agency in second-language learning among Chinese adolescent immigrant students. *Harvard Educational Review, 66*(3). 577-608.

McKay, S.L. (2003). EIL curriculum development. *RELC Journal,* 34(1), 31-47.

McKay, S.L. (2004). Teaching English as an international language: The role of culture in Asian contexts. *The Journal of Asian TEFL,* 1(1), 1-22.

McKay, S.L., and Brown, J. D. (2015). *Teaching and assessing EIL in local contexts around the world.* New York: Routledge.

McManus, D. (2001). The two paradigms of education and the peer review of teaching. *Journal of Geoscience Education,* 49, 423-434.

Mignolo, W.D. (2010). Delinking: The rhetoric of modernity, the logic of coloniality and the grammar of de-coloniality. In W.D. Mignolo and A. Escobar (eds.), *Globalisation and the decolonial option* (pp. 303-368). London: Routledge.

Milner, R.H. (ed.) (2010). *Culture, curriculum, and identity in education.* NY: Palgrave Macmillan.

Murayama, Y. (2000). *The promotion of intercultural understanding in English language teaching: An Analysis of textbooks and teacher training courses for upper secondary schools in Japan* (unpublished Master's Thesis). The University of York, UK.

Norton, B. (1997). Language, identity, and the ownership of English. *TESOL Quarterly,* 31(3), 409-429.

Pandian, A., Ling, C., Lin, D., Muniandy, J., Choo, L., and Hiang, T. (eds.) (2014). *Language teaching and learning: New dimensions and interventions.* Newcastle upon Tyne: Cambridge Scholars Pubishing.

Park, K.J., and Kim, K.M. (2014). Teaching and learning of EIL in Korean culture and context. In R. Marlina and R.A. Giri (eds.), *The pedagogy of English as an international language: Perspectives from scholars, teachers, and students* (pp. 47-61). Switzerland: Springer International Publishing.

Phillipson, R. (1992). *Linguistic imperialism*. Oxford: Oxford University Press.

Rampton, B. (1990). Displacing the native speaker: Expertise, affiliation, and inheritance. *ELT Journal*, 44, 97-101.

Redford, R. (2015). *Oxford progressive English 7* (p. 73). Karachi: Oxford University Press Pakistan.

Selvi, A.F. (2014). Myths and misconceptions about non-native English speakers in the TESOL (NNEST) movement. *TESOL Journal*, 5(3), 573-611.

Sharifian, F. (2009). *English as an international language*. Bristol: Multilingual Matters.

Sharifian, F. (2013). Globalisation and developing metacultural competence in learning English as an international language. *Multilingual Education*, 3(1), 1-11.

Shin, J., Eslami, Z.R., and Chen, W.C. (2011). Presentation of local and international culture in current international English language teaching textbooks. *Language, Culture and Curriculum*, 24(3), 253-268.

Song, H. (2013). How international is EIL?: A critical discourse analysis of cultural representations in a Korean EFL education television program. *Critical Intersections in Education: An OISE/UT Students' Journal*, 1(2), 97-110.

Sturman, A. (1997). *Social justice in education*. Melbourne, Australia: The Australian Council of Educational Research.

Walkinshaw, I., and Oanh, D.H. (2014). Native and non-native English language teachers: Student perceptions in Vietnam and Japan. *SAGE Open*, 1(9), 1-9.

Widdowson, H.G. (1994). The ownership of English. *TESOL Quarterly*, 28(2), 377-389.

CHAPTER 6

POWER AND IDENTITY EMBEDDED IN THE PERSIAN FIRST PERSON PRONOUN /MÆN/

A Sociolinguistic Perspective

Hossein Shokouhi & Alireza Fard-Kashani

Abstract

This study reports on the use of the first person singular pronoun /mæn/,[1] 'I', in Persian, and its different social functions in terms of power and identity. The motivation for this investigation originates from the frequent use of this pronoun by Persian speakers, particularly males, which is often linguistically expressed as 'mæn-æm zædæn', meaning 'to boast about one's power – physical or mental – and knowledge'. We hypothesise that the use of /mæn/ reflects an exaggerated expression of one's ability; hence an identity marker. Based on the assumption that an individual's perception of the world is linked to the language they speak, this study uses Bakhtin's dialogism (Bakhtin 1981; Bourdieu 1991; Hall, Vitanova and Marchenkova 2004) to analyse five pairs of conversations by Persian speakers, who have lived in Australia for a range of 5 to 10 years, with a focus on this distinct identity marker – /mæn/. Six types of /mæn/ have been identified as marking power. Two of these directly indicate power imposition, and the rest either implicitly convey the same message or intend to expose the supremacy of the speaker's knowledge over his interlocutor(s). The results contribute to our understanding of the power dynamics in social interactions, which may affect the perception of the recipient in conversations in terms of the speaker's control of power.

Keywords: power, masculinity, femininity, gender, identity

---

1 /mæn/ is the phonetic transcription of first singular pronoun 'I' in Persian. The vowel sound in this word is similar to the English word 'can'.

Introduction

The role of language, among other markers, is the most captivating and controversial since it is a means of both communicating one's emotions and affirming or rejecting one's 'identity' from others (Jaspal 2009). Not only do individuals identify themselves with their language at a personal level, but also perceive language as a symbolic marker of social or ethnic identity. Therefore, people of one language find themselves belonging to one united whole, making language the overriding means for sifting others as *'us'* from *'others'* as strangers (Tajfel 1978). Ivanic (1995 cited in Tang and John 1999, 30-31) points out that '[w]hen someone uses a particular discourse type, they identify themselves with the interests, values, beliefs and power relations which are associated with it'; that is, language is an inseparable component of identity (see also Djité 2006; Pavlenko and Blackledge 2004). We also need to realise that identity is fluid and dynamic. For instance, Wenger (1998) defines identity as 'something that we constantly renegotiate during the course of our lives' (p. 154). To Pavlenko and Blackledge (2004), identity negotiation is 'a transactional interaction process in which individuals attempt to evoke, assert, define, modify, challenge and/or support their own and others' desired self-images' (p. 4). More precisely, identity is 'multiple' (Norton 2000; Pavlenko and Blackledge 2004), 'dynamic', 'fluid' (Hall 1997), and 'context-dependent' (Derrida 1978). Our identities are always in a state of flux and actively involved in an ongoing process of *becoming* as opposed to *being* and *fixed* (Jackson 2004). For instance, '[o]ne can be Muslim in the mosque, Asian in the street, Asian British at political hustings and British when travelling abroad, all in a single day' (Cohen 2000, cited in Jaspal 2009, 17). Therefore, it would be appropriate to study this timely transition of change or *becoming* among speakers of a language who reside in a country that is different from their country of origin.

According to Bramley (2001, v) pronouns have a major role in the construction of 'self' and 'other'. They are not solely a means for expressing grammatical categories, such as person, number and gender or even pragmatic categories, such as referential and deictic purposes. Pronouns must be seen in the 'context of interaction and in terms of the "identity work" that they accomplish'. So, although grammatically speaking Persian allows the dropping of pronouns (a characteristic of pro-drop languages), the first person pronoun in Persian persists in conversations; hence its frequency raises curiosity in terms of social use and identity marker. We argue in this study that the choice of a specific pronoun can have direct connection with

the ways in which speakers present themselves, their identity to other interlocutors, their power relations, and the ways they approach their goals in a
given context (Benveniste 1971; Watson 1987; Wilson 1990).

As such, this study intends to explore whether Persian speakers, living in
Australia, still use the first person pronoun as frequently to indicate 'mæn-
æm zædæn' as a unique identity marker. Along the same lines, this study
investigates the possible identity roles and power relations that Iranian
Australians experience in their everyday talks through the use of the first
person pronoun /mæn/ and presents a classification of different types of
this frequently used pronoun in the Persian language.

In the following, we present a brief background on the grammatical roles
of the first person singular pronoun /mæn/, 'I', in Persian. We then discuss
the theoretical framework upon which the grammatical roles of /mæn/ are
based to mark its socially significant roles, namely identity and power.

Persian /mæn/–
Its Grammatical Roles and Its Role of Identity Marker

In Persian grammar, particularly in conversation, pronouns are often elided.
Regardless of the presence or absence of pronouns in a sentence, the verb is
always marked for tense and person. The grammatical roles that /mæn/ can
take in a given sentence are: the role of the subject (or nominative role), the
role of the object (direct object, indirect object, and dative), and the possessive role (or genitive role). Table 6.1 summarises the different grammatical
forms and roles of /mæn/.

Table 6.1. Grammatical forms and roles of Persian /mæn/

Persian example	Transliteration	English translation	Role of /mæn/
.من رفتم	**mæn** ræftæm.	<u>I</u> went.	Subject/nominative role
.رز من را دید	Rose **mæn** rɑ: did.	Rose saw <u>me</u>.	Direct Object role
.او به من گفت	u: be **mæn** goft.	S/he said to <u>me</u>.	Indirect Object role
.این برای من جای سوال دارد	in bæra:ye **mæn** ja:ye soa:l da:ræd.	For <u>me</u>, this is a question.	Indirect Object (Dative) role
.این ماشین من است	in ma:shin-e **mæn** æst.	This is <u>my</u> car.	Possessive/genitive role

Among the set of pronouns, the first person singular 'I', Persian 'mæn', is mostly associated with identity. This pronoun can take various roles in addressing the social status of interlocutors, their perceived identity and knowledge, and a means of empowering speakers to enact their ideologies on their listeners. For instance, it provides its speaker with the power to claim a right over a topic and win interlocutors' support and approval. Also, as Watson (1987) shows, 'I' can be used to separate self from others, and, as Wilson (1990) further explains, 'I' is used as a tool for establishing rapport with the audience and for displaying personal involvement. Moreover, Bramley (2001) finds this pronoun acting politically, differentiating between self and other.

Theoretical Framework: Language, Identity and Power

In recent years, there have been a few studies on the use of first person singular 'I' and plural 'we' among Persian speakers (e.g., Rezvani and Mansouri 2013; Tayyebi 2012; Yazdi-Amirkhiz, Abu Bakar and Hajhashemi 2014). While Tayyebi (2012) and Rezvani and Mansouri (2013) have investigated 'I' and 'we' in written texts and have shown how authors claim authority and construct their own writer identity in academic disciplines, Yazdi-Amirkhiz et al. (2014) have compared the typology and frequency of the pronouns used in the oral interactions of four Iranian females and four Malaysian females. They showed that Iranian participants use 'I' and 'you' more often than their Malaysian counterparts, who, in turn, use more 'we'. Also, they tested the participants' verbal data set against the 'Power Distance Index' (PDI) scale (Hofstede 1986) and have found that Iranians rank 29, which means a stronger individualistic tendency (i.e., using more 'I' than 'we') whereas their Malaysian counterparts rank 1.

In this study, the aim is to explore the different types of the first person singular /mæn/ in Iranian-Australians' casual conversations and analyse the occurrences in which they mark identity and signal power. The premise is that the participants in this study, who have settled for a period of five or more years in Australia, would have integrated into the Australian culture in a way that they now avoid frequent use of the first person pronoun in their conversations for marking power as a feature of identity. This was considered reasonable given that the participants were either postgraduate students at an Australian university for at least four years or had a job for at least two years at the time of partaking in the conversation for this study. The rationale for this premise is that Australia is an egalitarian society, and equity is be the basis of arguments and negotiations, whereas in the Iranian culture and society, predominately patriarchal in nature, social power is exercised linguistically in interactions (Bourdieu 1991). The current study approaches the notions of language and identity in terms of poststructuralism. As such, the analyses are built around two theoretical frames: Bakhtin's 'dialogism' (1981) - demonstrating the significance of power relations in dialogic interactions and Bourdieu's notions of language, power and equity (Bourdieu 1985).

According to Bakhtin (1981), language is never neutral and can be categorised as 'authoritative' and 'internally persuasive', hence a site of struggle, which evolves through dialogue and dialogic interactions. Bakhtin considers 'utterance' as the unit of dialogue and assigns two defining features to each utterance: 'addressivity' and 'responsivity', by which he means that each utterance is always constructed to be addressed to someone and be also replied to with a response. Therefore, an utterance is always shared between and owned by both addressor(s) and addressee(s), and its specific meaning emerges only through dialogic interactions when multiple voices (heteroglossia) come into contact. As for identity, Bakhtin recognises it as a dynamic and fluid notion which is constantly constructed and reconstructed through language socialisation and interpersonal dialogicality within various contexts, and this becomes the basis for meaning, in a given culture (Bakhtin 1981).

As mentioned above, to obtain a better depiction of the role of /mæn/, this study also relies on Bourdieu's notions of language, power and equity. Bourdieu views society in terms of domination and imposition which is the consequence of unequal distribution of assets and resources, known as 'capitals', among individuals in the society (Weiss 2006). As influential sources of power are transformable to each other, capitals are divided by Bourdieu (1985) into: Economic (i.e., money, property, and inheritance), Cultural (i.e., knowledge, skills, educational credentials, cultural inheritance), Social (i.e., social connections to people of high positions), 'Symbolic' (i.e., prestige, reputation, distinction), and Linguistic (i.e., as a particular form of cultural capital which concerns the knowledge of a particular language or dialect). Any type of capital, when recognised as 'legitimate' in a particular context, is considered as valuable and respectable in others' view and gives its possessor higher power and status in a given field or community. This, in turn, enables the individual to project their desired identities as well as impose identities on others. For Bourdieu, communication is 'an act of power' (Bourdieu and Wacquant 1992, 145), which means linguistic capital is a mechanism for implementing power to pursue one's own interests rather than a tool merely for communication; that is, a 'symbolic power' for its user/speaker. Enjoying the hidden symbolic power, language speakers can be successful at convincing others or imposing their particular point of views on them. This means, speakers can also negotiate their desired identity position in an interaction and place themselves as the unquestioning power (Bourdieu 1985).

In this study we have incorporated Bakhtin's and Bourdieu's views to explore how the participants' existing/emergent capitals, especially their linguistic capital, would enable them to devise some strategies to be seen and acknowledged as a 'legitimate speaker' in different contexts in their verbal interactions.

The Study

As was mentioned above, the original idea for this study comes from the old Persian saying 'mæn-æm zædæn' which means 'to boast about one's power physically or knowledge-wise'. Further, many of the works on enclaving and cultural integration are theoretical explanations about immigrant behavior and settlement (Portes and Mozo 1985; Zolin, Chang and Steffens 2014, among others). This study, however, uses live conversational data to look at immigrants' enclaving or integration into a new society. To this end, this study looks at a number of dialogues occurring among Persian migrants who have been living in Australia for a considerable length of time. The aim is to investigate the identity roles and power relations that Iranian Australians experience in their everyday talk through the use of the first person pronoun /mæn/.

The participants were 10 Iranian adult immigrants (seven males and three females) with an age range of 30–55 years who had lived in Australia for 5 to 10 years at the time of the study. Their educational qualifications ranged from undergraduate to postgraduate including PhDs in a range of disciplines (e.g., Science, Humanities, Social Sciences, and Engineering). The data used in this study is taken from a wider study about referent tracking, which consisted of 5,000 utterances. The data was collected through informal meetings and talks on various issues including social, cultural and educational matters. Each pair of interlocutors were fairly familiar with each other and the researcher. The contexts wherein the conversations took place were predominately informal. The data were audio-recorded and transcribed shortly after the meetings. All occurrences of the first person singular pronoun outlined in Table 1 above were identified. An attempt was then made to identify whether the occurrence containing that particular grammatical role had any social function in terms of power as a marker of identity.

Results and Discussion

This section presents the findings about /mæn/ in the collected conversational data. An attempt is made to divide the types of /mæn/ broadly into subject role, different object roles, and possessive role. As was mentioned above, those in the subject role are further classified into three subtypes in terms of social functions: establishing power, invitation to the acceptance of power, and evidential. The evidential refers to those in which the speaker presents some kind of evidence for his statement, which could be evidence from personal experience or otherwise. The evidential was itself classified further into two reportative types: reportative type I and reportative type II (Shokouhi, Norwood, and Soltani 2015). The former is used when the role is the subject of the sentence, such as the English 'I' as in 'I have witnessed this myself', and the latter when the role is the object of the sentence, as the English 'for me', as in 'As for me, the experience is different'. Finally, it is /mæn/ in the possessive role which marks power, especially power in signifying the speaker's claim of supremacy in knowledge over his conversant(s). The following figure sketches the different social roles and functions that are attributed to their respective grammatical roles.

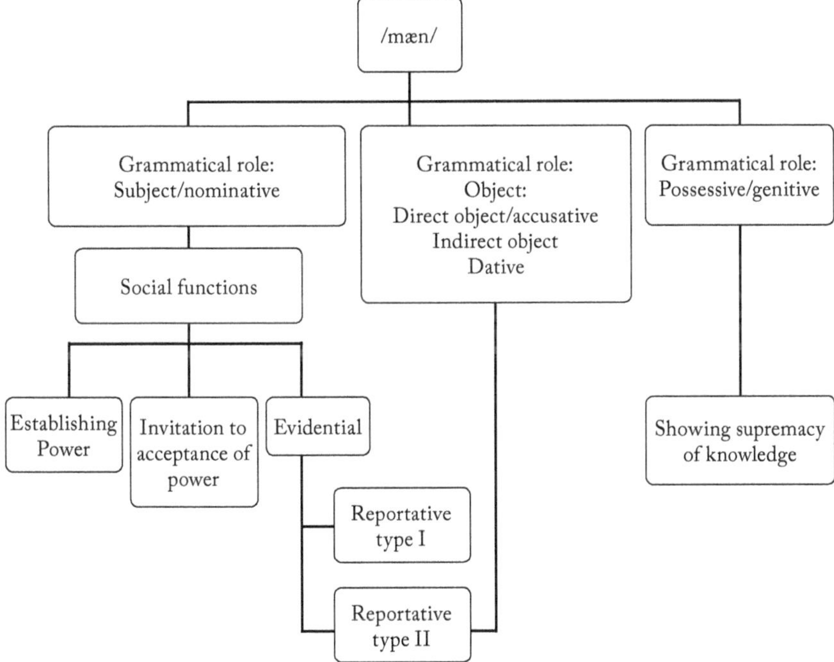

Figure 6.1: Classification of Persian /mæn/ in conversation in terms of social functions

Subject/Nominative Role – Establishing Power

As seen in example (1), the speaker attempts to establish and exert his power by using /mæn/ in its subject role evidenced by the rise of the pitch on the expression 'særih hærf mizænæm'/ 'I speak bluntly'. 'Særih', 'bluntly', indicates an openness in conversation without any consideration for redressing or Persian 'ta:rof', politeness. Persian speakers often appeal to 'ta:rof' to avoid bluntness. As the speaker reaches the word /mæn/, he gives the utterance a rising intonation and the rise even intensifies over the next word 'Særih'.

(1)

næ	næ	<u>æslæn</u>	bebin-id	<u>mæn</u>	<u>særih</u>/ (rising pitch)	hærf	mizæn-æm/
no	no	never	see	I	bluntly	speak	IMPF-hit-1SG

'No, no, never ever. Look! I talk bluntly'.

In example (2) there are numerous explicit and implicit indications to power. Although this is a casual conversation, it sounds as if the utterance is articulated in a formal speech before a crowd. The words that indicate evidence to power in this example are: a) /mæn/ emphasised by the following expressions 'be onva:ne næma:yændeye', 'as the students' representative', as well as 'ta: æla:n chændin ba:r', 'so far so many times', and b) the second /<u>mæn</u>/, clustered with the word 'ræsmæn', 'officially', followed by rising intonation shown by symbol /, signals contrast, hence forcefully exerting power. Then it is emphasised by the clause 'az harf**æm'**/ ku:ta:h nemia:m', 'will not retreat from my word', which is a further evidence to show his authority. All of these expressions before and after /mæn/ strengthen the power embedded in this pronoun.

(2)

bæle	<u>mæn</u>	be	onva:ne	<u>næma:yændeye</u>	da:neshju:ha:ye	Ira:ni	ta:	æla:n
yes	I	as	title	representative	students	Iranian	to	now

chændin	ba:r	næzær-æm	ro	**mæn**	ræsmæn/	ela:m	kærd-**æm**
several	time	my idea	RA	I	formally	announce	did

æz	<u>hærfæm</u>	hæm/	<u>ku:ta:h</u>	<u>ne-mi-a:m</u>
from	my word	also	short	NEG-come

'Yes, I, as the Iranian students' representative, have officially stated my idea; I won't retreat from my word'.

These two examples lend themselves to 'authoritative discourse' (Bakhtin 1981) whereby both speakers, as we have explicated above, take a strict stance towards the matter. They both demand their interlocutors to accept and acknowledge their viewpoints, hence indicating a higher-status identity of themselves. In the first example the speaker is trying to 'legitimise' (Bourdieu 1976) his strong disagreement by distancing himself from the rest of the interlocutors by invoking the idea that he is the only trustworthy person through his emphasis on power (e.g., 'særih', 'blunt and clear', indicating that there is no chance that he is being flexible on this, as flexibility is often seen as a positive characteristic among Persians).

In the second sentence, the speaker is placing himself as one of the dedicated members of the group he is leading. Here, the speaker's use of 'I' signifies his identity as a loyal and determined representative who cannot be compromised to give up his group's interests at any cost (i.e., 'ku:ta:h nemia:m', a typical Persian masculine expression meaning 'there is no way I lay low on this', which exerts the power of the articulator with utmost force). Both speakers in the two examples above take the best advantage of their linguistic capital (Bourdieu 1976) and metalinguistic features such as appropriate wording, inspiring speech, intonation, and use of direct disagreement clues, to claim their dominance over group members.

Subject/Nominative Role – Invitation to the Acceptance of Power

The next subtype involves the 'invitation-to-action' type which is brought to attention through the following examples:

(3)

bebin-id	mæn	mig-æm	bi-a:-yd	bitæræfa:ne	gheza:væt	kon-im
look	I	say	come	neutrally	judge	do

'Look, I say let's judge objectively'.

Normally, when an utterance is inclusive, as in this example, the speaker suffices with 'let's' and does not want to use 'I', as 'I' has the potential to carry force. Despite the inclusive 'let's', uttered as 'bi-a:-yd', this utterance carries a further tone of force because of the explicit 'I'. However, the force is being reduced by the offer of inviting the listeners to accept the speaker's power. The use of 'I' expects an action on the part of the listeners (i.e., Bakhtin's dialogicality). Here the speaker as a member of the group chooses self-exclusion and isolation from the group and tries to lead them to his desire for authority that Bourdieu and Passeron (1977) refer to as *representations of legitimacy*, which indicates that the speaker tries to gain legitimacy by fabricating a linguistic structure with the inclusive expression 'let's'. In fact, it can be argued that he demotes 'let's' by asserting it in the middle of the sentence.

Subject/Nominative Role – Evidential

In a study on evidential, Shokouhi et al. (2015) divide the Persian evidential into two major types of 'inferential' and 'reportative' and the latter into four sub-types based on the source of the evidence. In example (4) below the speaker attempts to state his authority as a source of knowledge, thus he recommends to his fellows that he believes they should study history books in order to understand the issue. Here /mæn/ is used assertively and it occurs initially as a departure point without any redressing. In other words, the speaker seems to imply that he has sufficient critical understanding of historical documents, and negotiates his identity as a person with more knowledge than his interlocutors, hence implying a cultural and social capital (Bourdieu 1991) to claim his rights and appropriate position in the power hierarchy among his interlocutors. This is generally how individuals utilise language as a tool of discrimination (Bourdieu 1991) in order to empower themselves by acknowledging the knowledge and education they possess.

Evidential – Reportative Type I

(4)

Bebin-id	inju:r	ghezavat	kærd-an	kheili	<u>sæthinegæri</u>	mishe,
look	this	judge	do	very	superficiality	become

<u>mæn</u>	mig-æm	ægær	be	keta:ba:ye	<u>ta:rikhi</u>	nega:h	kon-im
I	say	if	to	books	history	see	do

'Look, this way of judging is so superficial, I say if we have a look at history books …'

However, reportative evidential does not always occur in subject role. It is sometimes in a preposition phrase with 'for', as in the following example. In this instance, the speaker sees himself as a source of authoritative knowledge but is not exerting his power directly. He implies to his group members that 'I' am the source of knowledge because I have experienced this situation several times. It seems there is an exaggeration in the speaker's utterance by quantifying the number of occurrences of experience, which is not unusual or unheard of in Persian speakers' speech. Furthermore, as Chafe (1976) states, such dislocated construction (e.g., promoting 'for me' to the beginning of the utterance) is often used for the sake of contrast, thus bringing the promoted or dislocated element to the foreground of the hearer to give it a special emphasis. Having been promoted to the focal attention of the interlocutors, this exaggerated prepositional phrase operates as valuable experience.

Evidential – Reportative Type II

In example (5) the speaker establishes himself as an authority by producing evidence. Whether or not the evidence can be substantiated is a different matter altogether, hence we attribute it to the reportative type.

(5)

bærɑ:	<u>mæn</u>	<u>hæm</u>	chændin	bɑ:r	in	ghæziɛh	pish	umæd-eh
for	me	too	several	times	this	issue	forward	came

'This issue has also occurred to me several times'

Example (6) is interesting as the speaker is expressing his gratitude to a successful and highly-academic person whose source of authority in knowledge is valued. It implies his personal sense of appreciation and sincerity to that person. That said, he is also building on his social capital through making connections to a high-achiever to expand his social network of friends, colleagues, etc. (Bourdieu 1985). The university degree he is aiming to achieve (i.e., *cultural capital*) and acquiring two foreign languages (i.e., *linguistic capital*) are bringing him symbolic power which could lead to *recognition* that he is internalising all of the high-achiever's values as true and unquestionable (Bourdieu 1991).

(6)

ishu:n	<u>bærɑ:ye</u>	<u>mæn</u>	kheili	ærzesh	dɑ:r-e	chon	gereftæne	mædræke	doktorɑ:
he	for	I	very	value	have	since	getting	degree	PhD

væ	yɑ:dgiriye	do	tɑ:	zæbɑ:ne	khɑ:reji	kɑ:re	<u>hærkasi</u>	<u>nist</u>
and	learning	two	quantifier	language	foreign	work	anybody	not

'He is very valuable for me, because not everyone can get a PhD degree and learn two foreign languages.'

Object/Dative Role

Although in the object/dative role, /mæn/ cannot directly and explicitly show dominance, as in the subject role the contrastive state (Chafe 1976) that it creates is significant enough to account for it as an authoritative relation. Such is the case in example (7) where the speaker considers himself an authority of knowledge and believes that among so many existing reasons, what he believes stands out.

(7)

be	næzære	mæn	dælil	asli	ke	sene	ezdevɑːj	balɑː	ræfte	hæmin-e
to	opinion	I	reason	from	that	age	marriage	up	went	this

'To me, this is the chief reason why marriage age has gone up'.

Possessive/Genitive Role

The speakers utilise this type of /mæn/ to claim their ownership of something or someone, such as 'my idea', 'my class, 'my team', 'my wife', etc. Excessive use of the possessive/genitive role could imply an individual's abundant access to various capitals which others cannot or are not allowed to have, so leading to inequality and power hierarchy. The following is one example.

(8)

næ/	injori	nist\ (falling pitch)	mæn/ (rising pitch)	khodæm	ghodræte	fekriye
no	this way	not	I	myself	strength	thinking

mæn	va	tævanaiːhaye	tæhliːliːye	mæn	hæmishe	komæk	bood-æn	bæraye	inke
I	and	abilities	analytical	I	always	help	be	for	that

joze	behtærinha	bɑːsh-æm	che	tu	kɑːr-æm	che	tu	dærs-æm
among	the best	be	what	in	work	what	in	lesson

'No, it is not like this. Personally, my thinking ability and my analytical mind have always been a great help to me to become among the best, whether in my work or in my studies.'

Statements like this could induce a negative feeling in the interlocutor because they seem egotistic (e.g., the use of 'my thinking ability' and 'best … in my work or in my duties'). Although linguistically not as salient as in the subject/nominative role, possessive /mæn/ is almost as strong as the subject/nominative in terms of the conveyance of power.

Conclusion

This study has taken the first person Persian /mæn/ as its point of reference to focus on power and identity roles that this word plays. Following Bakhtin's dialogic discourse (1981) and Bourdieu's notion of power and equity (1991), the analysis of /mæn/ has identified six distinct social functions related to power and identity. This study confirms, although in making a different classification, the findings of the classic work of Tang and John (1999) who found various identity roles emerging through the use of the first person pronoun in academic writing. The authority represented by /mæn/ is chiefly either the kind of authority that directly imposes an ideology on others, or the authority that demonstrates supremacy of knowledge over others in the group. This could be explained by the competing power between males and females in a conversation.

However, it may not be a surprise that Persian speakers use /mæn/ often to mark power, as this would be expected of a male-dominated society. It is worth pointing out that females demonstrated little use of /mæn/ to mark power. This also agrees with our intuition because our prediction was that it would be males who predominately employ this pronoun as a marker of power. However, it should also be mentioned that this could be due to the lower number of female participants in our study.

Nevertheless, the more surprising finding of this study is that despite relatively long residency periods in Australia, the 10 Persian speakers whose data were used in this study *still* used /mæn/ as a marker of power to expose their identity. It seems that immigrants would want to maintain their identity markers embedded in linguistic forms and may even accentuate them in the new language and culture environment. As Portes and Rumbaut (2006) maintain, immigrants, as well as their descendants, do not completely dissolve into the mainstream culture. Many of them seem unwilling to do so, and instead prefer to preserve and enclave their unique ethnic identity rather than seek complete cultural integration. Needless to say, further studies on Persian speakers living in Iran can present a better picture for comparison.

This research, as one of the few studies dealing with the Persian pronoun /mæn/ in marking power and identity, is a step in raising consciousness of the Persian speakers living abroad to become cognisant of the term /mæn/, the power imbalance, and the wide-range of identities that the term could be associated with, in different contexts. This kind of awareness could enable interlocutors to project their desired self during conversations. We conclude by stating that the less people make reference to themselves (i.e., less use of first person pronoun), the healthier they are (Chung and Pennebaker 2007).

References

Bakhtin, M. (1981). *The dialogic imagination: Four essays by M.M. Bakhtin*. Austin, TX: University of Texas Press.

Benveniste, E. (1971). *Problems in general linguistics*. Coral Gables, Florida: University of Miami Press.

Bourdieu, P. (1976). The economics of linguistic exchanges. *Social Science Information,* 16(6), 645-668.

Bourdieu, P. (1985). The social space and the genesis of groups. *Theory and Society*, 14(6), 723-744.

Bourdieu, P. (1991). *Language and symbolic power*. Cambridge, UK: Polity Press.

Bourdieu, P., and Passeron, J.C. (1977). *Reproduction in education, society and culture*. London: Sage.

Bourdieu, P., and Wacquant, L.J.D. (1992). *An Invitation to reflexive sociology*. Chicago: The University of Chicago Press.

Bramley, N.R. (2001). *Pronouns of politics: The use of pronouns in the construction of 'self' and 'other' in political interviews*. Unpublished PhD thesis, Australian National University, Canberra, Australia.

Chafe, W.L. (1976). Givenness, contrastiveness, definiteness, subjects, topics and point of view. In C.N. Li (ed.), *Subject and topic* (pp. 27-55). New York: Academic Press.

Chung, C., and Pennebaker, J. (2007). The psychological functions of function words. In K. Fiedler (ed.), *Social communication* (pp. 343-359). New York: Psychology Press.

Derrida, J. (1978). *Writing and difference*. Chicago: The University of Chicago Press.

Djité, P.G. (2006). Shifts in linguistic identities in a global world. *Language Problems and Language Planning*, 30(1), 1-20.

Hall, S. (1997). The work of representation. In S. Hall (ed.), *Representation: Cultural representations and signifying practices* (pp. 13-64). London: Sage.

Hall, J.K., Vitanova, G., and Marchenkova, L. (2004). *Dialogue with Bakhtin on second and foreign language learning: New perspectives*. Mahwah, New Jeresy: Lawrence Erlbaum Publishers.

Jackson, F. (2004). Representation and experience. In H. Clapin, P. Slezack and P. Staines (eds.), Representation in mind: New approaches to mental representation (pp. 18-39). New York: Elsevier.

Jaspal, R. (2009). Language and social identity: A psychosocial approach. *Psych-Talk* 64, 17-20.

Norton, B. (2000). *Identity and language learning: Gender, ethnicity, and educational change*. Harlow, England: Pearson Education.

Pavlenko, A., and Blackledge, A. (2004). *Negotiation of identities in multilingual settings*. Clevedon: Multilingual Matters.

Portes, A., and Mozo, R. (1985). The political adaptation process of Cubans and other ethnic minorities in the United States: A preliminary analysis. *International Migration Review* 19, 35-63.

Portes, A., and Rumbaut, R. (2006). *Immigrant America: A portrait* (3rd edition). Berkeley: University of California Press.

Rezvani, R., and Mansouri, T. (2013). Stripped of authorship or projected identity? Iranian scholars' presence in research articles. *The Journal of Teaching Language Skills*, 5(1), 91-110.

Shokouhi, H., Norwood, C., and Soltani, S. (2015). Evidential in Persian editorials. *Discourse Studies,* 17, 449-466.

Tang, R., and John, S. (1999). The 'I' in identity: Exploring writer identity in student academic writing through the first person pronoun. *English for Specific Purposes*, 18, 23-39.

Tajfel, H. (1978). *Differentiation between social groups: Studies in the social psychology of intergroup relations*. London: Academic Press.

Tayyebi, M. (2012). Personal pronouns in English and Persian medical research articles. *English for Specific Purposes World*, 36(12), 1-12.

Watson, D.R. (1987). Interdisciplinary considerations in the analysis of proterms. In G., Button and J.R.E. Lee (eds.), *Talk and social organisation* (pp. 261-289). Clevedon, Philadelphia: Multilingual Matters.

Weiss, A. (2006). Comparative research on highly skilled migrants. Can qualitative interviews be used in order to reconstruct a class position? Forum: *Qualitative Social Research*, 7(3), Art. 2.

Wenger, E. (1998). *Communities of practice: Learning, meaning, and identity*. Cambridge: Cambridge University Press.

Wilson, J. (1990). *Politically speaking: The pragmatic analysis of political language*. Oxford: Blackwell.

Yazdi-Amirkhiz, S.Y., Abu Bakar, K., and Hajhashemi, K. (2014). The use of personal pronouns: A comparison between Iranian and Malaysian dyads. *International Journal of Applied Linguistics & English Literature*, 3(1), 245-248.

Zolin, R., Chang, A., and Steffens, P.R. (2014). The role of the ethnic enclave in facilitating immigrant business performance and social integration. In P. Davidsson (ed.), *Australian Centre for Entrepreneurship Research Exchange Conference 2014 Proceedings* (pp. 1212-1224), Queensland University of Technology, Sydney.

CHAPTER 7

'I CANNOT IMAGINE GOING TO A PUB'

Expectations, Lived Experiences and Identity Construction of Asian Students in Australia

Melinda Kong

Abstract

In response to globalisation and the internationalisation of education, many international students are pursuing their postgraduate Teaching English to Speakers of Other Languages (TESOL) degrees in English-speaking countries. Studies have shown that most TESOL programs focus on providing academic qualifications to these students. However, little attention is given to the students' academic and out-of-class non-academic expectations, as well as their experiences and identity construction (particularly outside class). Understanding these dimensions can help assist universities and educators in enriching the students' overall educational experiences. This chapter aims to explore these underexplored aspects through the notion of identity and its construction in relation to perceptions of culture and difference in the experiences of individuals. In-depth semi-structured interviews, email correspondence and informal conversations over six months were collected from five international students from Taiwan, Indonesia and China, who were furthering their studies in Australia. Findings suggest that the participants constructed their identities grounded in their expectations, their perceived differences in 'cultures', and their moral beliefs. Their reactions and choices of activities were closely linked to aspects of their identities, as well as their beliefs regarding what would benefit them and their communities. These findings contribute to new knowledge in terms of how international students adjust to studying and living in an English-speaking setting, by considering their identity construction in light of their expectations and lived experiences.

Keywords: identity, international education, international students, cultural adjustment

Introduction

International students offer significant financial contributions to English-speaking countries (see Citizenship and Immigration Canada 2013; NAFSA: Association of International Educators 2013; Department of Education and Training 2016). As an illustration, these students supplied $19.5 billion to Australia's export income in 2015 (Department of Education and Training 2016). In light of the importance of international students' economic value, various studies have explored these students' academic, cultural and social experiences in English-speaking settings (e.g., Novera 2004). Research in this area is mainly connected to language use, in particular, English, as well as how the students react and adapt to their environment, by, for example, learning about their new surroundings from students with the same backgrounds (e.g., Myles and Cheng 2003). In recent years, some researchers have also begun to include investigation on the identities of international students (e.g., Lutersz 2011). Understanding these students' lived experiences and identity construction can assist prospective international students in adapting to studying and living in English-speaking countries. Such knowledge can also help international education providers, for instance, to think of ways to enrich the overall experiences of international students (Kong 2016) and to attract prospective international students, in order to maintain and strengthen the international education industry.

A further review of literature in Teaching English to Speakers of Other Languages (TESOL) suggests that most TESOL programs seem to concentrate on providing academic knowledge (see, among others, Park 2012) to international students who are pursuing their postgraduate studies in TESOL, while overlooking how they construct and negotiate their identities in relation to not only their lived experiences, especially outside class (Kong 2014), but also what they expect to gain from studying in English-speaking contexts (Kamhi-Stein 2009). Attending to these aspects is important, especially when some of these students may expect what they learn in class to be merely part of their experiences abroad and value their experiences outside class as well (Kong 2016). This chapter aims to contribute to an understanding of the perceived gaps by firstly reviewing literature on identity, particularly in connection to culture, expectations in studying overseas, and differences. It subsequently briefly describes the methodology for the current research, and finally presents, discusses and interprets the findings of the study.

Identity: A Complex Notion

Identity is a complicated construct with various attributes. Although the notion of identity has many complex features, due to space constraints this chapter will focus on how Asian international students' multifaceted identities (e.g., as students and as users of English) are linked to culture and language (Frosh 1999), and negotiated in terms of difference (Phan 2008) in relation to their expectations (Kong 2014) and experiences (Frosh 1999), while pursuing their studies in Australia. This is because when these international students relocate from Asia to Australia to pursue their postgraduate degrees, they will most likely encounter what they perceive as cultural and linguistic differences. Characteristics of identity that are related to these students' relocation will be elaborated in the following sections.

Identity, Culture and Expectations

As suggested earlier, Frosh (1999) associates identity with individuals' experiences, language and culture. He provides a comprehensive view of identity, by stating that:

> … a person's 'identity' is in fact something multiple … constructed through experience and linguistically coded. In developing their identities, people draw on culturally available resources in their immediate social networks and in society as a whole. (p. 413)

Although Frosh's definition of identity is extensive and is linked to culture, he does not clarify the notion of culture, a term which is contested and ambiguous. In understanding the concept, for the purposes of this chapter, it is useful to consider Holliday's (1999, 241) idea of 'small' culture, which is non-essentialist and relates to the 'cohesive behaviour in activities within … social grouping[s]'. Holliday's notion is employed not to interpret prescriptive and normative perceptions of ethnic, national and/or international differences, but to seek explanations for the emergent behaviour for a particular group of individuals. A 'small' culture can be constructed for a short or long period of time by individuals from various groups. The term includes processes, activities and perceptions that are linked to group cohesion. It is fluid and involves an ongoing process that assists members of a group to make sense of and function meaningfully within changing circumstances. What group members say about 'their culture' is viewed as ways in which they socially construct their representation of 'their culture', instead of being a *direct* portrayal of their culture.

While Holliday (1999) gives clear arguments on the concept of culture and connects the notion to group membership and cohesion, Duff and Uchida (1997) provide further insights into how identity is related to culture, language and group membership. They point out that individuals' membership in a wider cultural or linguistic group assist them in shaping their identities. That is, individuals' identities are co-constructed, negotiated and expressed through language (Duff and Uchida 1997; Baker 2009), as well as their language use and attitudes (Winchester 2009). Pellegrino (2005) elaborates on this idea by stating that identities are associated with interactions, interpersonal relationships and culture. Individuals' interactions with the cultural setting, into which they are socialised, shape their perceptions of what is viewed as appropriate and/or inappropriate in their daily practices and values.

In a previous study that involved identity, culture and individuals' expectations, I attempted to fill the perceived gaps previously mentioned in the introduction. In Kong (2014), I illustrate how a postgraduate TESOL international student, Thinh, re/constructed her multifaceted identity as an international student, a learner and a user of English, based on her expectations of studying and living in Australia. In order to fulfill her expectations of improving her spoken English and learning about the Australian culture, she worked part-time at a local restaurant. Although she became familiar with the English used academically as a Master's student, she faced difficulties in understanding the English spoken outside class. However, she positioned herself as a learner in all her interactions with others. Such positioning of herself as a learner assisted her in learning new lexical items related to non-academic contexts and in exploring the local culture. Thinh's ongoing identity re/construction helped her to adapt to studying and living in Australia, and achieve her expectations.

Identity and Difference

As mentioned earlier, besides being linked to culture and individuals' expectations, identity can be connected to difference. Winkler and Olivier (2016) state that identity is 'a product of differential relations' (p. 95). Bourdieu (1986) elaborates that what governs our behaviour as groups and individuals is to differentiate ourselves socially. He believes that persons may choose to be individuals within a particular context by being different. They may gain their individuality and become distinguishable through differences in their thoughts, actions and mannerisms. Nord (2005) adds that individuals can manifest their identities and reveal their differences to others when they choose a specific position. Nevertheless, like identity itself, the concept of difference is fluid and constantly constructed and reconstructed (Dolby 2000).

In differentiating individuals from one another, Reed (2005) uses the term 'identity filters' (p. 187) to separate persons based on various 'categories'. For instance, individuals can be 'filtered' simplistically as locals or non-locals based on their place of birth and/or physical appearances. Nevertheless, Reed problematises categories as being potentially reductionist and essentialist (if not used with caution), and warns against being pulled towards fixed and narrowly defined categories. Instead, various categories can be created in new and unfamiliar ways. The concept of 'filtering' is, therefore, dynamic, with individuals using diverse sets of categories and 'identity filters'. When individuals and groups attempt to differentiate and 'filter' others, it can be inferred that they are simultaneously connecting themselves to individuals who share commonalities with them. Reed explains that individuals can connect themselves through different characteristics such as being from the same place of origin and/or using the same language. In elaborating on the concept of 'filtering', Illésfalvi (2011) points out that individuals construct their identities through their own interpretations and experiences of culture. Like Holliday (1999), as discussed in the previous section, Illésfalvi contends that individuals do not express their culture directly. Instead, similar to Reed (2005), Illésfalvi suggests that different individuals possess 'identity filters', and represent their culture in varied ways. Earley, Ang and Tan (2006) add that individuals' 'identity filters' affect how they interpret and react to diverse circumstances.

In relation to findings that involved identity being different and 'identity filters', Phan (2008) carried out research with a cohort of postgraduate Vietnamese students when they were obtaining their Master of Education in Australia and when they returned home, as well as with a batch of Vietnamese teachers who went back to Vietnam after studying in other English-speaking settings. In her work, Phan (2008) explains that morality is the focus of teacher development in Vietnam because of the influence of religious traditions in the country. She clarifies that '[t]he aim of education in Vietnam is to help people to become good citizens in terms of both knowledge and morality. ... [T]eachers tend to develop themselves both in knowledge and morality to meet the social, cultural and educational expectations of themselves as ... moral guides' (p. 6). From her findings on Western-trained Vietnamese teachers, Phan explores how these teachers negotiated their identities as teachers and as moral guides. Some of these teachers grouped themselves by using morality as an 'identity filter' and excluded teachers for whom morality was not a decisive factor in constructing their identities as students or teachers. She also proposes that these teachers constructed their identities through difference when they differentiated themselves from non-Western-trained teachers of English. Their exposure to new practices and values in an English-speaking context had made them different from what they used to be and from other teachers who were trained locally.

Contextualising this Study

Hailey, Suharto, Mei, Faye and Xhing were five participants of a larger study (with some preliminary findings discussed in Kong 2014), who were pursuing their Master in TESOL at a world-ranking university in Australia. Their background information is given in the following table.

Table 7.1: Summary of participants' background information.

Participant (Pseudonyms)	Country	Gender	Age	Languages (Written and Spoken)
Hailey	Indonesia	F	27	Bahasa Indonesia and English
Suharto	Indonesia	M	33	Bahasa Indonesia and English
Mei	Taiwan	F	32	Mandarin and English
Xhing	China	F	24	Mandarin and English
Faye	China	F	32	Mandarin and English

The objectives of the study were to examine the expectations, lived experiences and identity construction of Asian international students from non-English-speaking contexts, who were pursuing their postgraduate studies in Australia. Two questions that guide the aims of this chapter are:

1. What are the academic and out-of-class non-academic expectations of Asian international students while they are pursuing further studies in Australia?

2. How are these students' expectations linked to their lived experiences and identity construction, particularly outside class?

Three in-depth semi-structured interviews and four email correspondences were carried out with the participants during the final semester of their Master's course. Throughout the six months of data collection, I also had informal dialogues and further email correspondence for verification and clarification with the participants.

The Participants' Expectations and Identity Construction

Similar to the participant in Kong (2014), the findings of the study suggest that all five participants expected to improve their English, besides having various other expectations. Hailey expected to 'learn the language that is [used in an] Australian context' other than having the main goal of obtaining new knowledge in theories on teaching and learning. Suharto hoped to improve his English and increase his knowledge in teaching the language. Mei wished 'to study English, … speak to other international students and native speakers', and to assimilate 'into the local culture'. She also anticipated making 'more friends from different cultures'. In terms of teaching, she expected to find ways to solve her students' learning problems. Besides enhancing her English proficiency, Xhing wanted to experience life abroad, while Faye wanted to 'learn the [Australian] culture, … speak English more fluently, … [and] learn the way they write and study'. Her personal wish was to get married and settle down in Australia. However, she remarked, 'If [I] can't stay here, I have to go back. Maybe, I can have the opportunity to teach in a university in China'.

With the participants' expectations in mind, the following sections discuss and interpret how the participants constructed their identities based on their expectations in studying abroad (Kong 2014) and in relation to difference (Phan 2008). The participants had diverse reactions towards what they perceived as differences in various issues, especially outside class. Their responses seemed to help them in adapting to living in Australia. These responses can be seen as different from the ways other international students adapted in English-speaking countries (see, among others, Myles and Cheng 2003). In the current study, the participants adjusted to their surroundings by generalising 'cultural differences', and 'filter[ing]' (Reed 2005, 187) aspects that they perceived as in/appropriate based on their expectations, views of 'culture' and perceptions of morality.

'Cultural Differences'

Firstly, access to different worlds allowed the students to compare and make generalised observations regarding 'cultural differences' in their home countries and in Australia. Mei, from Taiwan, who expected to experience 'different cultures', was able to try out diverse 'cultural experiences'. She tasted South American food and enjoyed a football match with her Chilean, Japanese and Vietnamese friends. She also befriended an Australian student through a 'Buddy Program' in order to improve her English and understand the 'local culture'. She spent a night at her Australian friend's house and 'saw how local people talk to their parents and their ordinary life'. Mei made generalised comparisons between 'Western and Asian lifestyles' after the one-night stay. She claimed that Australians are more open in discussing personal problems with their parents, while as an 'Asian' she would not talk about such issues with her father due to reverence and fear.

Suharto also generalised concerning differences in Australian and Indonesian 'cultures'. He noticed that in general Australians line up to buy drinks, make appointments before meeting up with anyone and respect individuals' privacy, in contrast to many Indonesians who do not practise such habits. Faye, who was seeking personal relationships in Australia, made an identical assertion as Suharto with regard to most Australians respecting others' privacy. She compared the Australians that she observed to some 'busybodies' from China who were exerting pressure on her to get married because she was already in her thirties. Similar to Mei, she claimed that Australians are 'open-minded'. She explained that many of her Australian classmates continued learning despite being 'old'.

By making such generalised assertions and comparisons, the participants seemed to signal their membership in a larger cultural group (Duff and Uchida 1997) that was non-Australian. It can be suggested that their sense of identity was affected by what they viewed as their own 'cultures' (Holliday 1999) after their interactions with others (Pellegrino 2005) in Australia. Moreover, the participants appeared to differentiate Australians from Asians by making sweeping claims regarding the behaviour of these individuals (Bourdieu 1986). It seems that they were keen on socially constructing their identities as 'Asian', 'Indonesian' and/or 'Chinese', and establishing their differences by choosing their positions (Nord 2005) in comparing themselves to Australians.

Although some of the participants seemed to adopt particular positions by making these generalised observations regarding perceived 'cultural differences' from their Australian experiences, some of them tried to reconcile the two sets of 'cultural values' by accepting their diversity (Chowdhury 2008). For instance, Faye accepted her experiences in Australia as distinct from her previous experiences in China. She thought that 'Australians think very differently from Chinese people'. She expected her Australian coursemate to invite her out on a date again after declining his first invitation, as she claimed that Chinese men would do so repeatedly. However, her Australian friend did not ask her again and her personal hope of getting married to an Australian was not fulfilled. From her experiences, however, Faye learnt both the 'Australian' and 'Chinese' ways of doing things. She did not however sense any confrontations or feel that her interactions with Australian men affected her Chinese identity. Faye's responses suggest that, although she was exposed to Western viewpoints, she did not necessarily embrace the new ways of thinking.

Differentiating by 'Filtering'

Secondly, the international students seemed to define and differentiate themselves from others by using 'filters' (Reed 2005, 187). They allowed only some degree of 'cultural interpenetration' (Rizvi 2005, 82) by choosing what they perceived as 'good aspects' from the Australian 'culture' that would benefit their communities and/or themselves. They were resistant towards other aspects that they perceived to be inappropriate and/or against their own 'culture' (e.g., using 'four-letter' words). Nevertheless, the participants were different in terms of the extent of their 'filter[ing]'. Their 'filters' (Reed 2005, 187) can be connected to their expectations, perceptions of 'culture' and views of morality, as elaborated in paragraphs that follow.

Examples of these international students' 'filters' being linked to their expectations and perceptions of 'culture' are suggested in the participants' responses and experiences (or lack thereof) outside class in Australia. Since Xhing went to Australia expecting to experience life overseas, she explored pubs, drank beer for the first time and developed a romantic relationship with her local Australian coursemate. It can be interpreted that she did not seem to 'filter' activities that she associated with local Australians and opportunities to use English.

Unlike Xhing, Suharto and Hailey seemed to 'filter' activities based on their views of 'culture'. Their filters can be inferred when they resisted going to pubs to socialise and speak English, although they expected to improve their English. They claimed that going to pubs was not a part of their 'culture'. Hailey stressed, 'I cannot imagine going to a pub, … [it is] different from my culture'. In addition, unlike Xhing, Suharto and Hailey did not have the expectation of exploring life abroad. Instead, Suharto expected to increase his knowledge in his academic pursuits, particularly in learning English in formal contexts. He emphasised that his focus was only on 'formal' spoken English 'in a good setting, a good environment'. In fact, his desire to improve his formal spoken English was one of the reasons that motivated him to participate in the current project. He reported learning new vocabulary from me during the interview sessions. Hailey's main expectation was to advance her knowledge on theories pertaining to how to teach English. The complex intersection of the expectations and views of culture for Suharto and Hailey could have contributed to them not participating in social activities in which they might have more opportunities to speak English. It can also be interpreted that when they talked about not going to pubs, they seemed to be socially constructing their own understanding (Illésfalvi 2011) and image of their culture (Holliday 1999) as justification for their behaviour. They appeared to be simultaneously implying their perceptions that they belonged to a community, with members who also did not join such social activities.

Furthermore, Suharto and Xhing gave the impression that they possessed morality as 'identity filters'. Like the participants in Phan's (2008) research, they appeared to link their identities as teachers to moral values. In this study, the participants also associated morality to their identities as users of English and to features of the language. For example, although Suharto loved English, he resisted using words such as 'bloody' because he believed that it was not suitable for him to use such words since he is a teacher of the language.

He thought that teachers are role models to students and communities in speaking appropriate language. Consequently, his identity as a speaker of English was also closely connected to his identity as a teacher of English. A possible interpretation is that he was expressing a multifaceted identity through his attitude and language use (Winchester 2009) and/or non-use.

For these international students from Asian countries, teachers who did not pay attention to their own behaviour and/or speech were perceived negatively and were viewed as 'bad role models' to students and their communities. In particular, although Xhing did not reject going to pubs and drinking beer, she still possessed a 'filter' according to her own beliefs on how 'good' teachers should behave. For instance, she disapproved of her American teacher in China who used 'four-letter' words in class.

It is implied from the above discussion that these international students constructed their identities through difference with 'filter[s]' (Reed 2005, 187) that were affected by their expectations of studying and living abroad, perceptions of 'culture' and sense of morality (that included aspects of language). Hall (1991) states that an individual's identity is constructed 'through the eye of the needle of the other' (p. 21). Chowdhury (2008) adds that '[w]e can see ourselves through the eyes of others' (p. 144). Consequently, when the international students differentiated themselves from others, they were also constructing their own identities through their views (Phan 2008), expressions of their 'culture' (Holliday 1999), and descriptions of other individuals and their values.

Conclusion and Implications

As a case study, the purpose of this research is not to represent and generalise findings to other settings or individuals. The research is a small-scale study, involving participants from a specific cohort of international students, with their unique circumstances, at a particular time and context. Additionally, while identity is complex with many dissimilar features, the focus of this chapter is on how identity is constructed in connection to perceptions of culture and difference based on the expectations and experiences of a particular group of postgraduate TESOL international students in Australia.

To summarise, like the international students in the study by Myles and Cheng (2003), some of the participants' experiences are indeed related to using English. However, unlike the students in their research, who learned about the new context from students from similar backgrounds, the participants in this study appeared to adjust to their new environment in different and unique ways. The participants seemed to generalise concerning differences in 'cultures' by contrasting themselves to Australians after interacting with them. With their generalised observations, they also differentiated themselves from Australians and accepted their distinct characteristics. Moreover, the participants could be seen as 'filtering' their activities and what they believed as in/appropriate. The complicated intersection of filters that were related to their expectations of studying overseas, perceptions of culture and moral values could have caused them not to participate in certain social activities and/or using certain words. Their complex use of various sets of filters helped them to justify their actions and concurrently signal their membership in their communities that may share similar views with them. This study contributes to further knowledge about the identity construction of international students from Asian countries by looking at how they responded to their expectations and lived experiences (especially outside class) in a new English-speaking context with which they were not familiar.

The findings of this study, suggest that universities and educators need to be aware of factors pertaining to identity that may influence the lived experiences of international students from Asian countries. One practical implication is for universities and educators to develop practices that respond to the perceived needs (Carroll and Appleton 2007) and identity construction of international students. For example, international students can be given opportunities to voice their opinions and feelings concerning their expectations and lived experiences (particularly outside class), as well as how they can be supported. Since all the international students in this study sought to improve their levels of English proficiency, they can be provided assistance to develop their standard of English (Matsuda 2003) and have ongoing improvement in the language (Lee 2004). These international students can be requested to identify their personal linguistic needs, set their own objectives (Kamhi-Stein 2000) and examine various kinds of strategies that can help them improve their English language proficiency.

In light of the findings of this study, it is hoped that universities and educators can better enrich international students' overall study abroad experiences in English-speaking settings, instead of merely focusing on the content and activities of programs.

References

Baker, W. (2009). Language, culture and identity through English as a Lingua Franca in Asia: Notes from the field. *The Linguistics Journal, Special Edition*, 8-35.

Bourdieu, P. (1986). The forms of capital. In J.C. Richards (ed.), *Handbook of theory and research for the sociology of education* (pp. 241-258). New York: Greenwood.

Carroll, J., and Appleton, J. (2007). Support and guidance for learning from an international perspective. In E. Jones and S. Brown (eds.), *Internationalising higher education* (pp. 73-84). London: Routledge.

Chowdhury, R. (2008). *Globalisation, international education and the marketing of TESOL: Student identity as a site of conflicting forces*. Unpublished PhD Thesis, Monash University, Melbourne.

Citizenship and Immigration Canada (2013). *First time in Canadian history over 100,000 international students welcomed*. Retrieved from http://www.cic.gc.ca

Department of Education and Training (2016). Australia's international education sector worth more than previously estimated [Media release]. Retrieved from https://ministers.education.gov.au/colbeck/australias-international-education-sector-worth-more-previously-estimated

Dolby, N. (2000). Changing selves: Multicultural education and the challenge of new identities. *Teachers College Record, 102*(5), 898-912.

Duff, P.A., and Uchida, Y. (1997). The negotiation of teachers' sociocultural identities and practices in postsecondary EFL classrooms. *TESOL Quarterly, 31*, 451-486.

Earley, P.C., Ang, S., and Tan, J.S. (2006). *CQ: Developing cultural intelligence at work.* Stanford: Stanford University Press.

Frosh, S. (1999). Identity. In A. Bullock and S. Trombley (eds.), *The New Fontana dictionary of modern thought.* London: Harper Collins Publishers.

Hall, S. (1991). The local and the global: Globalization and ethnicity. In A.D. King (ed.), *Culture, globalization and the world-system: Contemporary conditions for the representation of identity* (pp. 19-39). London: Macmillan.

Holliday, A. (1999). Small cultures. *Applied Linguistics, 20*(2), 237-264.

Illésfalvi, I. (2011). *Towards a theory of cultural identity filters.* PhD Thesis, Eötvös Lóránd University, Hungary.

Kamhi-Stein, L. (2000). Adapting U.S.-based TESOL education to meet the needs of non-native English speakers. *TESOL Journal, 9*(3), 10-14.

Kamhi-Stein, L.D. (2009). Teacher preparation and nonnative English-speaking educators. In A. Burns and J.C. Richards (eds.), *The Cambridge guide to second language teacher education* (pp. 91-101). Cambridge: Cambridge University Press.

Kong, M. (2014). Shifting sands: A resilient Asian teacher's identity work in Australia. *Asia Pacific Journal of Education*, 34(1), 80-92.

Kong, M. (2016). On teaching methods: The personal experiences of teachers of English. *RELC Journal: A Journal of Language Teaching and Research*, 1-13. doi: 10.1177/0033688216661251.

Lee, I. (2004). Preparing nonnative English speakers for EFL teaching in Hong Kong. In L.D. Kamhi-Stein (ed.), *Learning and teaching from experience: Perspectives on nonnative English-speaking professionals* (pp. 230-249). Ann Arbor, MI: University of Michigan Press.

Lutersz, N. (2011). *Teacher identity: International students and their professional practice experience.* Unpublished PhD Thesis, University of Melbourne, Melbourne.

Matsuda, A. (2003). Incorporating World Englishes in teaching English as an international language. *TESOL Quarterly, 37*(4), 719-729.

Myles, J., and Cheng, L.Y. (2003). The social and cultural life of non-native English-speaking international graduate students at a Canadian University. *Journal of English for Academic Purposes, 2*, 247-263.

NAFSA: Association of International Educators (2013). *The economic benefits of international students to the U.S. economy: Academic year 2011–2012.* Washington, DC.

Nord, H. (2005). *Writing against oneself: German lecturers in South Korea.* Unpublished PhD Thesis, University of Melbourne, Melbourne.

Novera, I.A. (2004). Indonesian postgraduate students studying in Australia: An examination of their academic, social and cultural experiences. *International Education Journal, 5*(4), 475-487.

Park, G. (2012). 'I am never afraid of being recognized as an NNES': One teacher's journey in claiming and embracing her non-native-speaker identity. *TESOL Quarterly, 46*(1), 127-151.

Pellegrino, V. (2005). *Study abroad and second language use.* Cambridge: Cambridge University Press.

Phan, L.H. (2008). *Teaching English as an international language: Identity, resistance and negotiation.* Clevedon: Multilingual Matters.

Reed, G.G. (2005). Fastening and unfastening identities: Negotiating identities in Hawai'i'. In Y. Nozaki, R. Openshaw and A. Luke (eds.), *Struggles over difference: Curriculum, texts, and pedagogy in the Asia-Pacific* (pp. 183-198). Albany: State University of New York Press.

Rizvi, F. (2005). International education and the production of cosmopolitan identities. In A. Arimoto, F. Huang and K. Yokoyama (eds.), *Globalization and higher education* (pp. 77-92). Higashi-Hiroshima: Research Institute of Higher Education, Hiroshima University.

Winchester, J. (2009). The self concept, culture and cultural identity: An examination of the verbal expression of the self concept in an intercultural context. *The Linguistics Journal, Special Edition*, 63-81.

Winkler, R., and Olivier, A. (2016). Identity and difference. *Journal of the British Society for Phenomenology*, 47(2), 95-97.

CHAPTER 8

REPRESENTATION OF EFL INSTRUCTORS' IDENTITIES THROUGH CLASSROOM DISCOURSE

A Case Study in a Japanese University

Kaoru Matsunaga

Abstract

Teacher identities are multiple, ongoing, and influence the ways teachers practice, and share meanings and personal values with students in a classroom. This article reports on intricate relationships of four English as a foreign language (EFL) instructors' identities constructed across different times and spaces, and their representation of identities through teacher-talk in their classrooms in a Japanese university. It examines how instructors' identities have impacted the ways they transform their knowledge and negotiate meanings with students. The findings demonstrate that the instructors explore their sense of self through experiences with power, resistance and changing emotions, and through the narrativisation of self. In their classroom discourses, the instructors with long-term transnational experiences demonstrated multiple cultural lenses and familiarity with global contexts of English as well as students' native culture and language, which allowed them to acknowledge students' translinguistic identities and competences.

Keywords: teacher identity, EFL, teacher talk, narrativisation, classroom discourse

Introduction

Construction of teacher identities plays an important role in how they position and represent themselves in classrooms, what they deliver in classrooms pedagogically and socially, and how they transfer their knowledge, skills, values and understandings in relation to course content (Duff and Uchida 1997; Tsui 2007; Warwick 2008; Kiely and Askham 2012; Nagatomo 2012;

Trent 2012; Cojocnean 2013). Their identities are often shaped by biographical factors including past learning and cross-cultural experiences (Morita 2004), their imagination of their students (Natgatomo 2012), and more immediate contexts, such as the institutional culture, local classroom culture, as well as curriculum and textbooks (Duff and Uchida 1997), all of which influence the ways teachers enact their lessons. Overall, teachers' identities develop within 'a network involving macrolevel sociocultural circumstances and ongoing microlevel private and public interactions inside and outside of the classroom' (Simon-Maeda 2004, 409). While there is a large amount of existing literature on teacher identity construction processes, its focus has been mostly confined to single or few aspects of what constitute a person's identity which include biographical or institutional factors, learning and teaching experiences, or transnational life experiences. Typically, they have been sought without specific references to talk-in-interaction between a teacher and students. This chapter attempts to investigate how multidimensional factors under sociocultural circumstances and past and ongoing interactions across multi-communities shape and reshape EFL instructors' identities which, as a result, induce the instructors to share meanings associated with their personal positions and values with students through teacher-talk in their classrooms.

The central purpose of this study is to better understand how instructors' representation of identities are reflected upon in classroom discourse or 'language in use' (Pennycook 1994, 117) in conversations, and how they are implicated by the identity construction processes in the past or in the present within and outside classrooms. I adopted the notion of discourse as a way of organising and understanding meaning, and constituting the social world through 'talk-in-interaction' (Jones and Mejia 2008). It is about 'creation and limitation of possibilities' (Penyccook 1994, 128) which determine our social and individual actions; it is a 'system of power/knowledge within which we take up subject positions' (Pennycook 1994, 128). In order to investigate the instructors' identities that arise from meaning of language in use in discourse, relationships between meaning of words and meanings supplied by the context play a crucial role. This is done by looking at 'the intentions or purposes of the language use, the adherence to or flouting of conversational rules, and general forms of inferencing from the context or background knowledge' (Pennycook 1994, 119).

In doing so, this study looks into three specific issues. Firstly, it explores instructors' understandings of their own personal and professional identities. It then investigates how they perceive their representations of identities that are reflected in their classroom discourses and what contributes to such an approach. Thirdly, it further identifies how instructors represent their identities in classroom discourse and what constitutes them in terms of their past and present experiences and emotional changes. Through such methods, we are able to uncover complex and multiple factors associated with the instructors' identity construction and how such phenomena are intertwined with what instructors deliver in classroom conversation.

The next section problematises some of the most important notions of this chapter including identity, discourses, relations of power and subjectivity, and relations of subjectivity and practices in the light of existing literature. It is then followed by an outline of research design. In the later section, data from interviews, observations, and reflective journals are analysed which then leads to a conclusion and further research suggestions and recommendations.

Construction of Identities

The concept of professional teacher identities has increasingly been paid attention to and critically analysed by Teaching English to Speakers of Other Languages (TESOL) and English as a Foreign Language (EFL) professionals themselves, researchers and theorists in the last two decades. Identity is multifaceted and needs to be looked at from a variety of angles. For instance, Zembylas (2003) regards identity as 'what we know best about our relations to self, others, and the world, yet grounded in multiple ways of knowing with affective and direct experiential knowledge often being paramount' (p. 112). Lave and Wenger (1991) and Wenger (1998) see identity as associated with learning which is situated and transformative. In their terms, it is 'a way of talking about how learning changes who we are and creates personal histories of becoming in the context of our communities' (Wenger 1998, 5) through participation, non-participation and reification. Hence in the classroom context, we could say that it is through learning that we constitute and transform our identities.

As well as being an internal and psychological phenomenon emerging from within ourselves, or as a social category, identity is also a social and cultural phenomenon (Clark 2013). According to Miller (2009), it is a 'way of doing things but is inflected by what is legitimated by others in any social context' (p. 173). In other words, we can accept, deny or contest the power of interlocutors which others either impose on us or we impose on ourselves, which then determines and confines our actions. As we engage in multi-communities, one's subjectivity is produced in various social sites, and 'structured by relations of power in which the person takes up different subject positions' (Norton 1997, 411). Thus there is a dichotomy of the 'Self' or 'I', and the 'Other' or 'You' in the identity itself. Hall (1996) argues that 'identities are positions which the subject is obliged to take up while always "knowing" that they are representations, that representation is always constructed across a "lack", across a division, and from the place of the Other' (p. 6) and such positions can only be recognised and legitimatised by reference to the 'Other'. Our identities emanate from resistance and negotiation of power through difference, and what is considered the 'Other', peripheral, legitimatised, marginalised, or being in or out in a particular social and cultural setting. Hence, it is important to understand how instructors in this research see themselves and define their own identities in multi-communities.

Furthermore, our identities are constructed within discourse, a set of 'statement which gives expression to the meanings and values of an institution' (Kress 1989, 7). Discourses 'define, describe and delimit what it is possible to say and not possible to say with respect to the area of concern of that institution, whether marginally or centrally' (Kress 1989, 7). The examination of instructors' classroom discourses in this research will help us understand what constitutes them in terms of their past and present experiences and emotional changes in their multi-communities of practice and what contributes to their pedagogical approaches. Their discourse will display a full participant or a legitimate participant in a community as they negotiate their identities through participation and non-participation, and by learning what can be said and cannot be said (Lave and Wenger 1991; Kress 1989).

Pennycook (2001) refers to identity as 'not so much as fixed social or cultural categories but as a constant ongoing negotiation of how we relate to the social world' (p. 149). Similarly, Hall (1996) contends that our identities are 'points of temporary attachment to the subject positions which discursive practices construct for us' (p. 7). More precisely, teachers belong in diverse communities across different times and spaces. Their past and present negotiation of meaning and legitimacy of membership in a particular community construct their identities.

The nature of identity, therefore, involves individuals' sense of self in several different communities and practices in which they belong at any given time, and the meaning making processes through experiences, changing emotions (Zembylas 2003), and with connections to the communities and to the wider world. In such 'communities of practice' as Wenger (1998) calls them, our identities are never fixed or singular, but multiple and constantly negotiated over and changed across time and space.

While identities are constructed through such ongoing interactions and experiences, they also arise from narrativisation of the self (Hall 1996). Connelly (1999) addresses identity as 'stories to live by' (p. 4), by which knowledge, context and identity can be interlinked and understood narratively. Many studies adopted narrative analysis in investigating the relationships between teachers' identities and their modes of culture transmission in their classes (Duff and Uchida 1997; Warwick 2008), their teaching experiences and practices in a particular institution (Tsui 2007; Le Ha 2008; Kanno and Stuart 2011; Park 2012; Cojocnean 2013) and transitions in teachers' career trajectories (Simon-Maeda 2004). They indicate that teacher identity is intertwined with everything that a teacher did in the past or does in the present, which consequently influences what they do in classrooms. Teachers with transnational life experiences and tranlinguistic identities (such as the participants of this study), for instance, refer to their own cross-cultural and cross-lingual experiences and understandings of global context of languages and culture in developing students' translingual and cross-cultural awareness and competence (Warwick 2008; Jain 2014).

Teachers' perceptions of their identities may also potentially influence their pedagogical practices, values and attitudes toward students and professional practices, and vice versa. Nias's (1989) research on primary school teachers' identities draws attention to how teachers make personal and professional connections between themselves and students, and shows intricate ties between their identity and their levels of commitment and investments in their work. Nagano's (2012) study reveals how teachers' perceptions of themselves permeated through their experiences as students and how they aligned their teaching practices with their current students shape their teaching practices.

Day, Kington, Stobart and Sammons (2006) note that teachers will define themselves not only by personal and social histories and current roles but through 'their beliefs and values about the kind of teacher they hope to be in the inevitably changing political, social, institutional and personal circumstances' (p. 610). Similarly Ha (2008) argues that certain built-in qualities teachers regard necessary for their profession are united and integrated with personalities which enable them to 'fasten their identities to claim their insider status' (p. 109). Such teachers' roles perceived as part of identities are determined by themselves and by reference to the 'Other'.

Nias (1984) points out that teachers 'selves' are dependent upon internalised and externally supported values emphasised through socialisation with fellow teachers. Her research reveals that when teachers define their roles and what they do based on their own personalities and values, allowing for self-expression, the identification between self and work becomes closer which consequently affects not just the role but also the identity of the individual. On the other hand, when teachers find themselves not measuring up to their own standards as an 'ideal teacher', it makes their identification of themselves difficult both as a self and as a teacher in comparison to those who perceive themselves as a 'person-in-teaching' with teaching allowing for self-expression.

The current study examines relationships between teachers' identities and their teaching practices through discourses enacted in classrooms. In such contexts, discourses are the agent of 'how certain things come to be said at certain times and in certain places' (Pennycook 1994, 123). According to Norton (1997), identity constructs and is constructed by language. Pedagogical choices involving teacher talk and classroom discourse are closely intertwined with a sense of self, and these identities are constructed, enacted and transformed through discourse (Man 2008). More precisely, teachers' identities determine how they deliver or negotiate meanings in classroom discourse and in turn, what they deliver in classroom discourse constructs their identities. Such perspectives will be further examined and expanded upon as we will be able to see how classroom discourses are impacted upon and are intertwined with teachers' past and present negotiation of meanings in various communities of practice.

The next step then is to unveil the implications of this on learning. The in-depth understanding of teachers' identities will, for instance, provide more convincing arguments for Effion's (2015) research, as he claims instructors' presentation and social factors can trigger higher levels of foreign language anxiety (FLA). It may also reveal the types of compelling agents, conflicts and resistances experienced by students when 'plurality of identities, differences and alternatives are celebrated' (Man 2008, 130) in discourse between a teacher and students. However, this paper does not seek to understand how instructors' representation of identities implicates the process of students' identity construction or learning; rather, it focuses on how instructors' identities impact the ways they transform their knowledge and negotiate meanings with students.

Study Design

This study employed a qualitative case study to gain understandings of participants' in-depth and intricate 'socially constructed nature of reality' (Denzin and Lincoln 2010, 8) and it is limited to viewing certain EFL instructors' representation of identities in a Japanese university.

The study involved four different EFL instructors who held Master's degrees in different areas of expertise from Japanese or overseas universities. They all worked at the same university in Japan and belonged to three different faculties: Literature, Foreign Language Education, and Global Culture and Communication. Two were Japanese, one was from the Philippines, and the other was from the UK. They all previously had long-term or short-term intercultural and interlingual experiences abroad other than their countries of origin. Their classes and course contents varied, and they taught different age groups from 1st year to 4th year undergraduate students. Their teaching experiences ranged between two years and 30 years.

In collecting data, triangulation of multiple methods, including a survey, a pre-classroom observation interview, a classroom observation, five-day journal entries, and brief post-observation questions and feedback were carried out. Throughout the data collection, both verbal and non-verbal meta-linguistic elements were recorded and such elements were accounted for to enrich interpretation of data.

Data analysis began during the data collection itself and later they were divided into emerging themes using thematic analysis. Five stages of thematic analysis as suggested by Braun and Clarke (2006) were adopted including generating initial codes, followed by searching for themes, reviewing themes, defining and naming these, and producing the report.

The Instructors' Identification of the Self

At the beginning of individual interviews, instructor participants were asked to define their own identities and professional identities through the questions 'What makes you the person you are?', 'How do you describe yourself?', 'How do you understand what kind of EFL instructor you are?', and 'How do you want to be seen by students?'.

Daniel, a 55-year-old male British instructor, identifies himself as British with Jamaican background. He had lived in Japan for more than 20 years since 1990, went back to England in 2010 and came back to Japan again four months prior to this research. He had been teaching English in various universities for more than 30 years. Prior to his teaching career, he worked as a qualified youth community worker. He was born and raised in the UK with his Jamaican parents. For him, growing up learning both British and Jamaican culture in his household, there was never a conflict of identity between two cultures due to being surrounded by a multicultural and multiracial environment. He can understand and speak English spoken in Jamaica which had colonial influences with borrowed words from African, Spanish, Dutch and so forth. However, he only uses it when he is with people from Jamaica or family members. According to Daniel, his identities are shaped and transformed through intercultural experiences in Japan by adopting certain cultural behaviours, values and mannerisms about time, politeness and respecting people.

He considers his teacher role to be a way of delivering himself as an example of culture, to 'widen students' perspectives', to make students 'incorporate ideas' and 'think outside the box'. His roles and perceptions of himself as a teacher are scaffolded and developed along past educational and professional experiences (Duff and Uchida 1997). His appreciation for and strict expectation of both his and his students' organisational skills and discipline come from his schooling experiences of attending a strict all-boys grammar school. Such a position is reflected in his account as he indicates 'I'm not here to do a song and dance … I'm not here to entertain'. Furthermore, he believes that his professional roles as a teacher are established on the job through voluntary work at special schools as a youth community worker, together with the theoretical knowledge gained in graduate school, in which readiness to work, or 'furnished imagination' in Kiely and Askham's (2012) terms, emerged. Such 'insider trajectory' (Wenger 1998, 154) contributed to the formation of his personal and professional identities.

Bianca, a 31-year-old Filipino who has Chinese ancestry on her mother's side and Spanish on her father's, has constantly been establishing, re-establishing and re-negotiating her own identities across different times and communities. She has been living in Japan for more than nine years, out of which two years and five months have been spent on teaching English at several different universities. Prior to her teaching career, she did undergraduate and postgraduate degrees and worked as an English program coordinator in Japan. She attributes her identity to 'everything that has ever been in and out of' her life including her 'genetic dispositions' and 'environment and experiences'. In her account, she explains that she thinks about her identities all the time in Japan due to constantly having people asking her about her nationalities, the reasons behind her lack of Filipino accent and her non-Filipino looks.

Bianca describes her identity as 'culturally flexible'. Although she prefers not to be asked why she is the way she is, different from other Filipinos culturally, socially and linguistically, racial ambiguity is what she believes 'makes you interesting', 'is a strength', and 'fun to play with'. Her identities are confirmed, disconfirmed, shaped and reshaped by negotiating her own self and relating to others (Ha 2008). Linguistically and socially, she believes English, which she first started acquiring since she was four, dominates her identities and feels more comfortable being around people of an 'eclectic mix of nationalities'. Furthermore, the reasons behind her lack of Filipino accent in her English comes from the belief that 'if you are going to speak English, you should sound right'. In the Philippines, there is an emphasis on clear English as it is 'indicative of social background, it gets you more jobs and the cleaner your English is, the more intelligent you sound', thus English yields symbolic power and is used as a powerful tool for providing global economic access (Park 2012).

Drawing on her teachers' roles as part of her identities, she presents herself as a 'person', as teaching is a 'very personal profession'. She believes it is associated with students' 'confidence'. Notably she makes sure that she 'sees them', shows that she 'cares', 'remembers', 'listens', 'knows what students' part-time jobs are', and does her best to 'make it [English lesson] interesting' through presentations. It appears that her professional engagement as a teacher reflects an affective nature (Ha 2008). Pedagogically, while she believes a lesson is a 'show' or 'performance', it should also be instructive and conducive to learning. Her institutional identities are evoked through peripheral participation (Wenger 1998) as she expresses herself as being a 'part-timer' and not being part of 'the bigger mothership', and feeling detached from it, yet she appreciates the 'freedom' in which she can be creative.

Mai, a 33-year-old Japanese EFL instructor, had previously lived in the US for eight years and six months in total. She spent four years in the US from the age of two, and the rest of her time was spent on completing her Master's degree and working as a Japan outreach initiative coordinator, introducing Japanese culture in the US. She completed her undergraduate degree at the current workplace and she has been in the teaching field for more than eight years. She describes herself as Japanese, female, in her 30s, and single. She also considers herself a person who values harmony and the collective nature of a community in a variety of social settings. She believes that the underlying reasons behind such values come from her childhood memories of being a person on the periphery in Japan. When she came back to Japan after four years in the US with her family when she was six, due to her unique background and the accent in her Japanese, she felt she was being teased by her peers and that other parents gave her 'strange looks'. She expresses that she felt the need to speak Japanese and English like other Japanese people by 'faking the accent' in order to be assimilated, to be the same, and to not be marked as a conspicuous figure. The power relationship 'generated in interpersonal and intergroup relations' (Norton 2000, 9) coercively made her feel the need to accept the status quo as normal which consequently affected negotiation of her identity. Her feeling of being an outsider and marginalised appears to be strong even now as she spoke about her experiences and changing emotions with tears in her eyes. Her emotions created and still create 'sites of social and political resistances' and 'self-formation' (Zembylas 2003, 110). In communities of practice, learning and 'marginalities of competence' (Wenger 1998, 216), experiences and emotions as well as negotiation of power through difference seemed to have transformed her identities.

Drawing on her identities as a teacher, she categorises herself as a 'mother-like' or 'sister-like' figure, who stands as a 'role model' for her students as she herself is a graduate of the same institution. She expresses her job as a way to 'nurture students' and 'open another door' to allow an opportunity to come in by letting students experience the enjoyment of using English. She appears to construct her identities through 'mutuality of engagement' (Wenger 1998, 152) and alignment as she strives to relate to her students. She indicates her institutional identities as 'individual' and 'insignificant'. Such views reflect the struggle and negotiation of membership in a bigger community.

Just like Mai, Risako a 32-year-old Japanese female EFL instructor, previously completed her Bachelor's degree from the same institution she works at, with her Master's degree from a different university in Japan. She has also been teaching for more than eight years. Her intercultural experiences include travelling in the US, Australia, England and Greece, all of where her duration of stay had been less than a month. She first considered her own identities as a 'difficult question to answer'. Despite having ambiguous views about 'identities' as such, her narratives represent a transition of her dispositions as they shifted from being 'shy' and 'passive' to 'active', 'optimistic', and 'vigorous' since she started learning English. Linguistically she feels 'at ease' to give her opinions in English. While she values Japanese cultural rules, she identifies herself as a mixture of both cultures and recognises a 'hybridity' in her values (Bhabha 1994). This hybridity of cultural values or 'Third Space' in Bhabha's (1994) term represents the 'articulation of cultural difference' (p.28) which is 'neither One nor the Other but something else besides, in-between' (p. 219). Professionally, she describes her pedagogical identities and roles as 'fun', 'with a smile', 'open', and 'practical' by introducing various English phrases, music and movies to let students experience the 'real English'. Using her own past learning and teaching experiences she feels that she is able to give students advice on 'how to study English'. Learning and teaching English not only helped her change performances but also converted, constructed and reconstructed her identities and pedagogical values (Ha 2008).

The instructors perceive themselves and their identities based on socio-cultural and family backgrounds (Simon-Maeda 2004), dispositions (Kiely and Askham 2012), linguistic identities (Park 2012), intercultural and interlingual identities (Duff and Uchida 1997; Warwick 2008; Jain 2014), and interpersonalities (Ha 2008). Their professional identities were expressed in relation to four themes including past educational and professional experiences (Duff and Uchida 1997; Kanno and Stuart 2011; Canagarajah 2012; Nagano 2012), interpersonal and affective nature (Nagano 2012), pedagogical identities (Warwick 2008), and institutional identities (Zembylas 2003; Tsui 2007; Cojocnean 2013). Such identifications of the selves are vital in understanding how they are implicated and reflected in teacher-talk as they construct, reconstruct and negotiate their identities through discourse.

The nature of the instructors' narrative accounts suggests that the construction of their identities is a dual process. The first process involves the multiple opportunities through which instructors learn and negotiate meanings through participation, experiencing emotional changes in communities of practice over different times and spaces in accordance with the existence of power and their subject positions. The second process involves their own narratives. Narratives allow them to organise their ideas where they make sense of themselves, which consequently evoke, construct and reconstructs their identities. The instructors' identities appear to be constructed within the narrativisation of the self, including perceptions of teacher values and what constitutes a good teacher which are partly 'imaginary' and 'constructed in fantasy' (Hall 1996, 4). This 'imagination' creates and determines who they are and what they are about to become as it plays with 'participation and non-participation, inside and outside, the actual and possible, the doable and the unreachable, the meaningful and the meaningless' (Wenger 1998, 178) through social interactions. Furthermore, their professional roles and identifications reflect their personal selves as they share their own personal values, learning experiences and trajectories, present themselves as examples of culture, and use skills they gained from their past educational and professional experiences. By doing so, they strive to relate and align themselves to students, contribute their knowledge and understanding of the world which they consider to be conducive to students' learning, and establish one-to-one relationships with each student.

Representation of Identities in Classroom Discourse

In drawing together the instructors' own understandings of their identities, in this section I would like to highlight their representations of identities in classroom discourse. As indicated by Duff and Uchida (1997), instructors' sociocultural identifications and displays are rooted in and developed along a biographical and professional basis and a more immediate contextual basis. The findings suggest that the instructors represented their identities based on their personal histories, cross-cultural/cross-lingual experiences, evaluation and feedback, perceptions of learning materials, their expectations of students, and pedagogical advice.

Personal Histories

Daniel, Bianca and Mai used personal narrative accounts to represent themselves by interlinking their experiences in wider communities outside the classrooms; in other words, their identities as 'negotiated experience' (Wenger 1998, 149). Their identities were invoked as they shared their cultural and family backgrounds, and current and past stories of self with their changing emotions and thoughts, with their students. For instance, Daniel presented a lesson on 'Japanese quality food' in which he first introduced the topic by letting students guess how he eats or prepares food every day without a refrigerator in his apartment. After students correctly guessed, he then went on sharing about the habitual practice of going to restaurants every night, where and what he ate last night, who he saw at the restaurant, his tendency to order the same meal at a restaurant, the waiting staff's reactions, and his feelings and thoughts throughout. After briefly explaining his eating habits and lifestyle, he asked students to share what they ate last night and who prepared the meal for them. In response to these questions, one of his students answered that the student cooked carbonara for himself and his father the night before. The student's narrative indicated that the student and Daniel's son, who was 16 at the time of the observation, liked to prepare food themselves. After hearing the student's answer, Daniel contributed his son's story to connect it with the student's account:

> My son is 16. He likes to prepare food himself. Often when I go home, he prepares food for me. Yeah, so my son cooks for my daughter, my mother sometimes, and for me. I don't know if it's a little odd or strange but it's very natural in my family. So you do the same and your father appreciates that. Good, I hope he does.

This indicates that his identity consists of what he knows best about his relations to self, others, in this case students, and the world (Zembylas 2003). On other occasions, he differentiated himself from students as he talked about his dislike of mayonnaise; connections to his multicultural background and preference for multicultural cuisine; growing up in a Jamaican household and preference for slow cooked food; an unusual but exquisite experience of eating *odoriebi*, an 'alive jumping prawn'; and eating out at a Jamaican restaurant in Japan, all of which were described with marked emotions. It is plausible that the 'processes of emotion formation are fundamentally interrelated with the formation of identity' (Zembylas 2003, 112). It appears that he was participating in and renegotiating the meanings, and sharing the ownership of meanings with the students through his own stories (Tsui 2007).

In addition, such construction of identities by marking differences and similarities, and highlighting familiarities and unfamiliarities, known and unknown, acted as a pedagogical factor as Daniel provided a modelled answer through his own anecdotes and asked students to share their own knowledge and experiences. A similar pattern was seen in Mai's class as she demonstrated in her own introduction at the first seminar at the time of the observation. The display and representation of their identities could both be pedagogical and personal.

Bianca's case was slightly different as her identities did not induce an explicit provision of modelled example but rather they highlighted her sense of self outside the classroom and in another lesson more implicitly. The classroom focus was on 'US culture and society'. At the beginning of the course she gained permission from the students to take pictures in a class and make an album to show them to other students to inspire and motivate them. As one of the students prepared jambalaya for the whole class, she mentioned 'I'm going to take pictures to add to my collection'.

Her representation of identities became an implicit pedagogy. Above all, the lived experiences of the instructors' selves which they had negotiated through discourse constitute their identities as a member of the classroom, institution, and wider community. Meanings are shared through exploration of identity that is a 'work in progress, shaped by efforts, incorporating the past and the future in the experience of the present, negotiated with respect to paradigmatic trajectories' (Wenger 1998, 158). By sharing meanings with students, the instructors demonstrated that the individual teacher and each student in the classroom were connected by what Wenger (1998) calls a 'nexus of multi-membership', as we are all required to take part in the work of reconciliation to maintain our identities across boundaries.

Expectation and Advice

During the recorded practice, only Mai explicitly presented her expectations and advice through her 'transnational' identities. The recording took place on the first lesson of the course, programmed for students who were planning to participate in an internship in the US and to equip themselves before leaving for the US through a range of discussions, presentations and projects. The first lesson involved a brief summary of the program followed by an introduction of the instructor and the students, and instructions on rewriting an application form which students had already written prior to the class. In Mai's account, she expressed her expectations as the following:

> Let's do a brief introduction of ourselves because we don't know who is here in this class. Please include your name and faculty. I prefer not to care too much on everyone's ages and grades. You will understand eventually, but let's try not to call senior members *senpai* (senior) and junior members *kouhai* (junior) … because people in the US won't care about that … Anyway, I would like all of you to stand together as a group without a hierarchical relationship …

In other instances, she also mentioned to 'get to know each other well' and 'build a strong bond' amongst themselves because 'if something happens they are the people who are to be relied on'. Such messages came from her own experiences of joining the exact same internship program she had completed at the same institution more than 10 years ago. This indicates the likelihood of her transnational, transcultural and translingual experiences being paramount in inducing her to represent her identities through discourse. Her transnational and intercultural identities involved 'negotiated investment in seeing the world through multiple cultural lenses' (Warwick 2008, 622). It appears that such multiple cultural lenses, together with a deep understanding of students' dominant culture and their needs, became resources for addressing what is likely to happen in students' lives abroad and for understanding the investments they need to make in the near future.

Risako's journal entries displayed a similar pattern throughout; however, they were more strategic and methodology based. She drew on her own learning experiences of English in Japan and advised students about the methods of learning, and how to study English in Japan. These included utilising university facilities and learning materials, managing time wisely, and pursuing life-long learning skills. Her journal entries indicated only these methods of approach. Consequently, it is plausible to consider that the instructors' long-term transnational experiences in countries other than their home countries helped them constitute their transnational identities as they negotiated their sense of self in communities of practice in which the emergence of legitimacy, periphery and power came into play, which consequently became resources in developing students' transnational competences (Jaon 2014).

These two models also indicate that through 'imagination' (Wenger 1989) of students' current situation and their future, these instructors saw their own practices as 'continuing histories that reach far into the past' (p. 178) and that they let themselves and students 'conceive of new developments, explore alternatives, and envision possible futures' (p. 178).

Cross-cultural and Cross-lingual References

While some instructors represented their identities of multimembership by sharing personal histories and commenting on students' possible future directions, they also presented their transnational, traslingual and transcultural identities by making cross-cultural and cross-lingual references.

Mai and Daniel referred to their cross-cultural and cross-lingual experiences abroad and in Japan in order to help students develop their intercultural competence and awareness. Their narratives indicate that their transnational life experiences helped them construct and define their own intercultural identities and determine the means to approach intercultural (Warwick 2008) and interlingual issues with their students. Mai, for instance, explained about the ways the Americans treat everyone the same regardless of age differences, as she advised students to dispense with the fixed concept of 'seniority rules' that exist in Japanese society. This happened straight after she presented her expectations to the whole class as discussed above.

In other instances, she made interlingual references. On several occasions, she attempted to raise awareness of the linguistic differences in nuance between Japanese and English based on what students wrote on application forms about their objectives for joining a volunteering program abroad. For instance, she indicated that the phrase 'to feel culture' from direct translation of Japanese, *bunka-wo-kanjiru*, would not be understood in the West. What it really should be was 'to experience another culture'. Another example was given as a student wrote 'I want to break the wall', *kabe-wo-norikoetai*, meaning 'I want to overcome an obstacle or difficulty'. In addition, she raised a point about Japanese people's tendency to write in a vague manner to avoid being impolite, while in English we were required to be straightforward and to the point in order for us to be understood. Instructors with 'translinguistic identities' (Jain 2014) who are familiar with global contexts of English, including the students' native culture and language such as Mai herself, can better acknowledge students' translinguistic identities and competence.

While Daniel did not make such linguistic comparisons, he emphasised more on sociocultural factors. Through his narratives, he recounted the transformation of his position between two nations:

> If I was in the UK, I would never do that. I would never go to a restaurant and sit down by myself because people would think 'Why is he by himself?' [laughs]. That kind of feeling. I feel uncomfortable. But here, not a problem at all.

Such agency indicates identity as 'temporary points of belonging and identification, or orientation and installation, creating sites of strategic historical possibilities and activities, and as such they are always contextually defined' (Grossberg 1996, 102). Through verbalising his agency that shifts depending on cultural contexts, he constructs and shares the meanings associated with social powers and legitimacy involved in different cultures and community settings with the students. His discourse demonstrated the 'dual nature of power', and 'interplay between identification and negotiability' (Wenger 1998, 207) as he claimed legitimacy of membership, while implicitly showing its vulnerability and keeping the meaning of ownership open to negotiation.

Pennycook, A. (1994). Incommensurable discourses? *Applied Linguistics*, 15(2), 115-138.

Pennycook, A. (2001). *Critical applied linguistics: A critical introduction*. New Jersey: Lawrence Erlbaum Associates.

Rymes, B., and Pash, D. (2001). Questioning identity: The case of one second-language learner. *Anthropology and Education Quarterly*, 32(3), 276-300.

Simon-Maeda, A. (2004). The complex construction of professional identities: Female EFL educators in Japan speak out. *TESOL Quarterly*, 38(3), 405-436.

Tsui, A. (2007). Complexities of identity formation: A narrative inquiry of an EFL teacher. *TESOL Quarterly*, 41(4), 657-680.

Trent, J. (2012). The discursive positioning of teachers: Native-speaking English teachers and educational discourse in Hong Kong. *TESOL Quarterly*, 46(1), 104-126.

Warwick, J. (2008). The cultural and intercultural identities of transnational English teachers: Two case studies from the Americas. *TESOL Quarterly*, 42(4), 617-640.

Wenger, E. (1998). *Communities of practice: Learning, meaning, and identity*. Cambridge: Cambridge University Press.

Zembylas, M. (2003). Interrogating 'teacher identity': Emotion, resistance, and self-formation. *Educational Theory*, 53(1), 107-127.

CHAPTER 9

HIERARCHY IN HIGH SCHOOL ENGLISH CLASSROOMS IN VIETNAM

Power Relationships and Learning Opportunities

Hoang Thi Hanh & Pham Thi Ngoc Thanh

Abstract

This study seeks to investigate how power relationships, especially unequal ones, are (re)produced through teacher–student and student–student interactions in high school English language classrooms in Vietnam, and how such practices affect students' equal chance of learning participation. The study used video recordings of six teachers' lessons, audio recordings of six hours of retrospective interviews with nine individual students, and focus group interviews with six students. Content analysis of the triangulated data reveals that the teachers' practices not only reflect a hierarchical relationship, or power distance, between teacher and students, but also help create a hierarchical academic 'order' among peers of high school students of English language classes. As a result, these practices not only contribute to the unequal participation of students in class activities but also impact the way students position themselves and are positioned in relation to others in a hierarchy. The study problematises such taken-for-granted hierarchy as an unquestioned cultural value and argues that, in order to ensure more equitable academic participation and culturally appropriate pedagogy in the Vietnam context, we need to listen to students' voices and take equity and power relations into consideration.

Keywords: classroom interaction, hierarchy, power relations, learning opportunity, Vietnam

Introduction

The import of Western methods of teaching English to 'Eastern' contexts has often been criticised as culturally inappropriate. The effort to find a more culturally appropriate teaching methodology and to adapt the teaching theories and methods from the West to the East involves investigating and understanding the cultural teaching and learning styles of the East and contextualising teaching methods accordingly.

In the context of Vietnam, a high power distance culture, where people expect and accept unequal distribution of power (Hofstede 1986), the power to distribute learning opportunities in class almost exclusively belongs to teachers, who have higher power. Hadley (2001) further proposes that power differences in classrooms of high power distance cultures are shown through the differential treatment of students by both teachers and students depending on their hierarchical positioning. With such descriptions by Hofstede (1986) and Hadley (2001), we can hypothesise that the unequal power distribution realised in teacher–student and student–student classroom interactions may reinforce social injustice and inequity. Nonetheless, both Hofstede and Hadley conclude that such unequal distribution of power is cultural learning and teaching style, and suggest that the responsibility to adapt to the cultural learning style should belong to the teachers.

We recognise the necessity to seek a more culturally appropriate pedagogy. However, we argue that finding such pedagogy does not mean simplistically adopting the Western methods or reproducing the observed patterns of classroom interaction of the East without considering factors like power relations realised therein. If the power relations are not facilitating equity, it is necessary to challenge such relations rather than reproduce them. We assume that a culturally appropriate pedagogy should not only take into consideration cultural features of the academic context but also facilitate learning by promoting equity.

We are interested in understanding whether teachers consciously or unconsciously teach hierarchy and thereby reinforce or perpetuate inequality among students through classroom interaction. The study seeks to investigate how power relationships, especially unequal ones, are (re)produced through classroom practices in the less studied context of Vietnam. By listening to students' voices about such practices, we hope to better inform understanding and practices of both local and international teachers in their process of seeking teaching methods which not only are culturally sensitive but also help address equity and social justice.

In this chapter, we first introduce central theoretical concepts that inform the study, including hierarchy or power distance, social positioning, learning opportunities, and how these relate to equity and social justice. Afterwards, we contextualise the study by describing the high school

English classrooms and the participants. We then analyse the data, mostly from students' voices, to see how the classroom practices position students in a hierarchy and limit chances of participation in the learning of certain students, and how students fail to negotiate more desirable positions. We conclude by considering ways in which unequal distribution of power and learning opportunities might be interrupted in order to facilitate more equitable academic participation among learners.

Power Relations

The power relations in some Asian cultures are described as higher power distance ones in which people expect and accept unequal power distribution (Hofstede 1986). Teachers therein are respected and have higher social position compared to students. Students expect teachers to initiate and control classroom interactions. On the other hand, students are expected to accept such unequal power distribution and follow the teacher's directions when participating in activities, and are expected to neither contradict nor publicly criticise their teachers.

Hadley (2001) further expands the patterns of interaction in high power distance cultures to include student–student interaction. She specifies that in the Asian context, especially in Japan, there are different positions for students in class, and those in differing positions are treated differentially both by teachers and other students, and that each student knows their own position. Both Hofstede and Hadley's descriptions come from their own observation and inference without consideration of in-depth emic views from the students.

Vietnam is found to be one of the higher power distance cultures (Hofstede, Hofstede and Minkov 2010). Thus, Vietnamese classroom interaction is expected to follow the patterns described by Hofstede and Hadley. However, Hoang (2013) finds that Vietnamese students in group work may expect unequal power distribution, but they do not necessarily accept it. Such distribution, which is an unquestioned assumption, creates a competition among students trying to achieve higher power positions. In such competition, those who could not win would not be able to achieve positions of power in making their ideas or decisions accepted and followed by the group, and they would feel dissatisfied. The classroom interaction, if realised as described above, would allow little opportunity for students, especially 'weaker' ones, to negotiate more powerful positions (Holliday, Hyde and Kullman 2010), and thus possibly create dissatisfaction and demotivation among those students. Therefore, we need to explore how such power relations are played out in the classroom interaction and seek the emic views of the students towards such social relations.

Social Positioning and Learning Opportunities

The dynamic construction of who we are in relation to others in social interaction is defined as social positioning (Parrot 2003). In a discursive process, according to Kayi-Aydar (2013), one can be assigned a position by others or can assign a position to ourselves. Classroom interactions play an instrumental role in determining students' position in relation to others, and this has been found to have different effects on students' access to the learning process (e.g., Black 2004; Kayi-Aydar 2013, 2014). Positioning is dynamic, fluid and situatedly constructed; thus, it can change through the process of interaction and allow students' agency, 'the socioculturally mediated capacity to act' (Ahearn 2001, 112), to play a part in either accepting or rejecting the position assigned by others (see Duff 2002; Talmy 2009). Such positioning and the negotiation process of students can either facilitate or hinder learning processes. For example, in Duff's (2002) study, Chinese immigrant students chose to remain silent and not to answer their teacher's question in a Canadian social studies class to resist the teacher's positioning them as knowledgeable about Asian cultures. In another study by Lee (2008), also in a Canadian classroom, teachers repeatedly viewed China from white perspectives which were not shared by students from China. By reasserting his own perspectives on China and positioning the students' different views as uncritical, the teacher unconsciously silenced the students, and he, consequently, contradicted his own attempt to promote critical thinking. Lee further argues that we need to look deeper at the structure of the activity and social relations that might prevent students' participation rather than just simplistically and superficially encouraging participation of a particular 'silent' student.

Studies have also been conducted in L2 classrooms to investigate how the social positioning process plays out and how positioning impacts learners' learning opportunities. In more student-centred language classrooms, as in Talmy's (2009) study, for example, students were found to use their own agency, their capacity to navigate interactions and negotiate positions, to resist their teachers' and their peers' positioning of them as newly arrived immigrants. In Kayi-Aydar's (2013) study, a more dominant student was found to use frequent assertive commands, control others' actions to assign a stronger position to himself, create his own learning opportunities, and deny access to learning for others. The teacher responded to this student by providing learning opportunities to him but not to others because the conversation merely developed between this student and the teacher. In another study also by Kayi-Aydar (2014), two different dominant students positioned themselves as more competent and active members of the class. However, only one was gradually accepted and included in conversations with their peers. The other was assigned the position of an arrogant and inconsiderate student. Their classmates chose silence and avoidance to position the second student as an 'outsider' and denied him access to learning opportunities by refusing to talk to him. Kayi-Aydar also notes that, in this class, the teacher's attitudes and reaction towards these two students might have contributed to their peers' different positioning of the two students. While the teacher was more supportive of the first student, she was less supportive of the second as she stopped the second from participating several times to allow more opportunities for other students.

It can be seen that positioning is socially constructed as students, their peers and teachers can actively participate in negotiating positions for themselves and for others. Teachers have not only been found to contribute to the process of peer positioning but have also been found to actively participate in the positioning process, which impacts students' learning participation. Menard-Warwick (2008) finds that when the teacher in a language classroom in California assumed a particular role for her Latina immigrant woman student as a homemaker, the student's attempt to position herself as a businesswoman failed to obtain the teacher's recognition, which undermined her chance to participate in the language practice task. Martin-Beltrán (2010) indicates that students who were publicly declared and authorised as more proficient speakers by teachers were those who could gain more access to the classroom discussion. Overall, the above studies indicate that micro-analysis of the classroom interaction can help us have insight into the dynamics of positioning, participation and learning opportunities in the classroom.

This study investigates the process of positioning in English as a foreign language (EFL) classrooms in Vietnam and takes into consideration the students' 'resistance', and their capacity to navigate interaction and negotiate positions. Differing identity positions held in the learning context may limit and constrain certain students' learning opportunities while enhancing opportunities for interaction and learning for others (cf. Norton and Toohey 2001, 2011). Such learning opportunities here are a chance for learners to practice language use, or receive access and encouragement, which are essential to the second language acquisition process (van Lier 2001). Within this study, it is assumed that all opportunities to participate or to be invited to participate are considered as learning opportunities. We do not take into consideration the complexity of the effects of different types of learning activities, but only look at the (in)equality of distribution of access and encouragement related to chances to practice.

The Study

The study aims to investigate how classroom practices manifest hierarchical relations, how such practices influence students' chance of learning participation and their constructed positions in relation to hierarchy, and how such practices promote or hinder equity and social justice.

The study was conducted in a general mainstream public high school in Hai Phong city, Vietnam. Its curriculum and English textbooks are designed to meet the requirements and goals set by the Ministry of Education and Training (MOET). The public school provides education for Grades 10 to 12 students who are 15 to 18 years old. The research participants are all Vietnamese including three high school English teachers (teachers A, B, C) having 10–20 years of teaching experience, and their students in three mixed-ability classes. The students had been studying English as a compulsory subject since primary school. However, their English proficiency levels vary, from beginning to around intermediate levels. These students have five English lessons per week in which they use the English textbooks for most of their activities in class. Each English lesson lasts 45 minutes. In classroom interaction, the teachers and the students used both Vietnamese and English.

Observation, retrospective interviews and focus group interviews were employed to generate data. First, each class was observed and video recorded twice in order to familiarise students and teachers with the process. There was a camera positioned at the back of the class to capture the whole classroom dynamics. Two lessons from each class were then observed and video recorded to collect data for analysis. The purpose of the video recording was to capture how power distance was played out in the teacher–student and student–student interactions as described by Hofstede (1986) and Hadley (2001). While observing classroom dynamics, the researcher wrote down some patterns of interaction in relation to power distance. After each lesson, the researcher watched the videos again to take more detailed notes and to develop the interview protocol for the retrospective interviews. Nine students (three from each class) voluntarily participated in retrospective interviews on the day immediately following their recorded English lessons. While watching the video again with the researcher, those students were asked to reflect on their thinking, interaction and contribution to class activities. In addition, six more students participated in a focus group interview discussing the general practices of their classroom relating to power distribution such as classroom management and turn-taking during teacher–student interaction.

The data analysis of this study focused on the retrospective interviews with nine students in triangulation with the other data sources. At first, the video recordings were viewed to observe the pattern of interaction between teachers and students, to see who had the power to distribute participation opportunities and how students negotiated such distribution. Instances of positioning were noted and grouped into themes and patterns. The interview data was coded based on such instances to identify how power is played out through teachers' practices in classroom interaction, and how such practices influence the distribution of learning opportunities, as well as the way students position themselves in relation to their peers in groups. According to Gee (2011), students' and teachers' different access, different power status and different opportunities enacted through classroom practices represent 'the root source of inequality'. As a result, we see the analysis of classroom practices as a means to connect 'to matters of equity and justice' (p. 30).

Findings and Analysis

Teacher-led Classroom Interaction

It was observed that teachers initiated almost all classroom interaction and activities. These activities mostly followed the order of textbook exercises. The most frequent activity was calling on specific individual students to answer questions or read aloud certain texts. Retrospective interviews with students revealed their reaction to the way teachers organised activities.

When the teacher asked the whole class to do something, the students were seen to follow the instructions. For example, when the teacher asked students to read after him/her, the students followed suit, 'we just read after her' (Duong). However, some students expressed their disapproval:

> [We are] so grown-up like this! And he [the teacher] still asked us to read after him. At that time I thought 'Why do we have to read after him like that?' (Phuong)

The tone of Phuong's voice showed her dissatisfaction, which was hardly observed through the classroom interaction itself since, during the lesson, she still read after the teacher as required. She mentioned their age, as 'grown-up like this', to claim a more powerful position of negotiation. The student here positioned herself on *equal* footing with the teacher in the negotiation of the choice of task by demanding explanation from the teacher, and by expressing her wish to be treated as an adult. However, such strong reactions were only expressed to the researcher, not directly to the teacher. The obedience observed seemed to hide the strong resistance simmering underneath.

In such situations when students did not like the activities and were not given the chance to initiate activities or negotiate choices of activities, they chose to exert power in certain ways. The video showed a quiet class with one or two students being called on repeatedly to answer questions. For example, in class A, Hue and Lan and in class C Thang and Luyen were repeatedly called on because they seemed to speak more fluently and seemed to have more correct answers (see more analysis in the next section). In contrast, there were many other students who were sitting quietly and some students were even putting their heads down on the table. The class activities seemed to be the place for the participation of only a few learners and the teacher while the other learners did not directly show any response or reaction. However, in the retrospective interviews, a variety of feelings and reactions were expressed. When finding teacher-initiated activities not interesting or difficult to understand, students chose to 'sit still', 'not raise their hands', 'not care' (Thuy) or 'just sleep' and 'not want to hear' (Duong).

> Especially during the listening task, we can't hear English and we don't want to hear. Some can hear and they do. I can't hear English and *I just sleep*, I don't understand anything. She often speaks English and *I am fed up and don't want to hear. Frustrated.* I don't ask my classmates around me because they don't know anything about English either, and *I am afraid to ask the teacher* … Only when there are games or interesting topics that they care about will they speak. Asking [out-of-context] questions like this is *boring; they don't care.* (Duong)

During the lesson, although the students could not hear, could not understand anything and felt 'frustrated' or 'bored', they did not seem to actively show any reactions to the teacher. Failing to understand, students' reactions went from rejection (don't want to hear) to frustration and withdrawal. Moreover, the students also expressed their interests in certain types of activities in the interviews, but they were not explicitly given the chance to negotiate and did not proactively raise their voice. The students' passive reaction did not bring about any visible effect since the teacher did not seem to notice. One stated reason for this passive reaction was that the student was 'afraid to ask the teacher' (Duong), which was related to the power distance between teachers and students. There can, of course, be other reasons such as the constraints of the learning program and textbook, or students' passivity due to the cultural norms. It can be seen that the students had negative and passive reactions instead of proactive constructions, not just because of students' 'natural' and 'cultural' passivity, but also because of the possible negative effects of the power distribution between teachers and students. Hence, besides other factors not observed here, the power distance between teachers and students in which the teacher is the one who initiates and controls classroom activities, might have played a part in constraining students' voices.

When these students were either momentarily excluded from the classroom interaction or chose to exclude themselves by passive reactions, they did not participate in the learning activities and could not learn. If learning is the result of comprehensible input (Krashen 1985), there was no learning happening here since the students did not understand what the teachers said. In other words, if learning is the result of active participation in communicative activities (Savignon 1997), the students here seemed to be excluded from the learning process.

Teachers' Differential Treatment of Students

The power in the classroom rested almost entirely with the teachers. It was noticeable that during the lessons the same students were repeatedly invited to read the text or to answer the questions while some others were not invited at all. Retrospective interviews with both students who were often invited and students who were not reveal that the teachers tended to select those students who often give correct answers in each lesson. Those who answered correctly several times were invited more, and those who were not able to answer or generally answered incorrectly were mostly ignored. This was consistently observed in all three teachers' lessons, and students of all three classes commented that: 'The teacher only called on good/better students' (Phuong, Huong, Duong, Thuy); 'They study English well so the teacher calls on them only' (Phuong, Huong); 'the teacher knew I often could not answer questions correctly so I knew she would not call on me' (Huong). From the students' perspectives, the teachers distributed the opportunities for practice and for contributing to the lesson unequally among students. At the same time, they also recognised that the teachers' distribution of opportunities to participate was based on the ranking of students' academic ability.

The big-fish-little-pond-effect (BFLPE) (Marsh 1987) can be referred to here since these students used comparative wording to describe their peers as more capable learners. According to the BFLPE theory (Marsh 1987), the stronger peers are taken as a frame of reference, the lower the self-concept of other students. The performance of the other students who were perceived as being better coupled with the teacher's unequal distribution of participating opportunities reinforced lower self-concept of the less active ones and positioned them at the lower end of the competence hierarchy. Low self-concept has been found to negatively affect students' learning aspiration (Marsh 1987) and learning interest (Marsh et al. 2005), which can also help explain the students' passive reaction and withdrawal, as reported in the previous section.

In class C, the teacher invited students to read a text in the following way:

> Teacher C: Now read the text please. I would like some of you to stand up and read. Thang, đọc to cho cô hai đoạn [read aloud two paragraphs for me]

> Thang: [Read the two paragraphs]

> Teacher C: Can you continue? *Bạn đọc tiếp có được không? Đọc hay đọc tiếp.* [Can you continue to read the rest, please. You read well, so continue to read.]

> Students: [laughing]. [Some students turn around, looking at Thang, laughing].

Contradicting her own stated intention from the beginning to call on several students to read the text aloud, the teacher only asked Thang, the one who had fluent and clear pronunciation, to read the whole text rather than inviting others, because Thang 'read well'. The laughter that followed could indicate that the students might not have expected what the teacher did.

It was also one way students exercised power by expressing their reaction to the teachers' action, indicating that it was not the way it should be. In this case, the other students might have been waiting for their chance to read aloud the rest of the text but the teacher seemed not to notice. The laughter of the students did not change the teacher's action. Besides, when the teacher explicitly said that Thang 'read well, so continue to read', she unconsciously sent the message to the other students that they are less competent than Thang. As a result, they have no chance to read aloud. This finding suggests that the teacher unintentionally taught hierarchy and reinforced inequality among students. During the retrospective interviews, students also voluntarily commented on that episode:

> When the teacher invites students to read the text, she often only invites those who read well. She should invite those who do not read well to help them improve their competence instead, but she doesn't. I don't like it that way. Her repeated action like that gradually discourages students from reading. They don't want to show their ability. She usually invites Thang; he reads the entire lesson, not leaving any chance for others to read. (Thuy)

Through the teacher's explicit comments on more capable students and the more chances she offered them, the students recognised their academic positions ascribed by the teacher on a hierarchy of superior and weaker students. Thuy used such words as 'those who read well' and 'those who do not read well' to describe students in the class, which indicated her acceptance of the positions ascribed. However, she did not see such positions as stable or fixed but fluid and changeable as she believed students could 'improve their competence' when they are given more chances, and they have 'ability' which they were discouraged from showing.

Whether reading the text aloud facilitates learning or not is not the focus of this paper. However, it is seen as a learning opportunity by students. By giving this chance only to Thang, the teacher also positioned Thang on a higher rank in the hierarchy of competence. Nonetheless, instead of being perceived as providing input for the class, he was believed to rob the other students of learning opportunities as 'he read the entire lesson, not leaving any chance for others to read.' In this case, the teacher's unfair distribution of chances for practice limited students' access to language learning opportunities and to more powerful positions.

Students' Reactions

The students saw that teachers' choice of students to participate was based on the ranking of students' abilities. While some students expressed resentment and silently protested the unfair distribution of learning opportunities by the teacher, some other students left the task for others and chose to withdraw and remain passive, and 'just sat at the back and watched' (Quynh). The duty and opportunities of learning are shifted to the ones who 'study better' (Quynh). However, Hue, the one who was called on more often, did not always see being invited as being given learning opportunities and was not always satisfied with being constrained by the pressure to be accurate. She said:

> I didn't want to speak out loud because *I am afraid if it was wrong it would be funny* … At first, I suddenly found no one raised their hands, I knew I would be called, and I was called. I stood up thinking 'Oh, why do you call me, I don't know what to say'. I was standing trembling and startling because of fear. I was so nervous that I even said 'I like apricot blossom because it's yellow, and I like peach blossom because it's pink', but in fact, I don't like pink at all. When I sat down my friends asked me 'When did you start to like pink?' I felt pressured standing there. …. They all let me be gun-fodder. (Hue)

In this instance, being invited to answer by the teacher was not seen as an opportunity any more but as the duty to find the correct answer and to report the product of learning. At certain times in the classroom interaction, the teachers' frequent calls on better students made them fear being called on and even caused them to tremble and startle when standing up. The chance for Hue to speak out more often, even when she was not ready, was seen by her as being 'gun-fodder' for her peers, standing up to protect her friends from the threat of being called on by the teacher. With the war metaphor, 'gun-fodder' (Hue), the class activities, especially when the teacher invited students to answer questions, were seen as a 'battle' between teachers and students rather than a facilitative learning environment. At this point, the wish to call on students who are more likely to provide a correct answer was pushed to an extreme and no longer seen as a chance to practice or contribute to the process of learning.

Despite being positioned as more capable and given more opportunities to participate, Hue did not seem to happily accept such positioning by the teacher. She did not actively choose to tremble or startle with fear or nervousness because her fear was real. Her fear also caused her to make mistakes in saying that her favourite colour was pink, which was found to be strange by her peers. By using the metaphor 'gun-fodder' and blaming her friends for putting her there, Hue seemed to want to negotiate a less stressful position. She might have wished the teacher would call her less often, especially when she was not confident enough. However, the way the student negotiated for such a position was rather passive and might have been noticed by her peers but not by the teacher.

While Hue was called on more often than she needed, others were not invited as frequently as they wished:

> At that time, I was sure that the teacher would not call me. *Many other times she called me, and I could not read, so she knew. That's why she almost never called me to read again.* Even though I thought I would read that time but she pointed at some others at the back. … With this we could see the answers in the book, but we didn't raise our hands to answer. I was also discouraged because I thought she knew when she called me I couldn't say it right. *Every time she calls someone to read, she won't call me.* She only calls those who learn well to answer. (Huong)

Huong recognised that because she failed to answer the teacher's question 'many other times' before, she was 'never called again'. She recognised that she seemed to be fixedly positioned by the teacher as incapable after some failures. However, Huong twice reported on cases in which she knew the answer, or she would be ready to read the lesson. By doing this, she seemed to see positioning as fluid rather than fixed and stable but she was not given further chances, which discouraged her from continuing to negotiate for participating opportunities and repositioning herself to a more desirable identity.

Besides, some other students who were invited less also tried to negotiate chances to participate by actively and explicitly raising hands (e.g., Vu) while some others chose to passively withdraw (e.g., Quynh, Huong and Duong). While the students who were frequently called on were not ready to answer, the other students who wanted to raise their voice were not given much attention or were even ignored by the teacher. Nevertheless, none of these efforts achieved any significant effects in terms of changing the teachers' ways of distributing participation opportunities. Such attempts at agency (Norton and Toohey 2011) failed to contest the decision made by the teacher after some of the students' failures.

In this case, we can see the picture of agentive and active students, struggling to negotiate different positions from those ascribed to them by the teachers. The students seem to view positioning as a process, as fluid and changeable, and want to negotiate chances to change. In contrast, the positions the teachers ascribe to them seemed to be fixed and stable. Possibly due to the higher power distance, the struggle of the students was less obvious and mostly went unnoticed by the teachers. The teachers' positioning not only hinders learning and negatively influences students' self-concept, but it is also rigid and defies negotiation.

In the end, both those who were assigned higher positions and those who were assigned lower positions were dissatisfied with their positions or the distributed learning opportunities. However, due to the higher power distance between teachers and students, the students' attempts to negotiate more flexible and powerful positions almost passed unnoticed by the teacher.

Hierarchy in Student–Student Interaction

The distribution of learning opportunities based on the ranking of competence in teacher–student interaction was also seen to be reproduced in student–student interaction in student group work, which was also mediated by the need to pursue accurate answers.

> The group task is equally divided to the members of the group according to their ability. The competent one is in charge of the *more difficult task* and has responsibility for assisting other members. (Duong)

When asked how they distributed responsibilities in group tasks, students reported that the tasks would mostly be allocated to those 'who study well' (Tan), 'study English better' (Tram) or 'the group leader will do all the tasks of the group' (Hoang Anh). They seemed to accept this option because they thought that those who studied well would have a 'more accurate answer' (Manh). The hierarchical positioning of the students, coupled with the big-fish-little-pond effect, continued to be seen in the student–student interaction where those with low self-concept when compared with their peers maintained a low view of their ability and participated less in group work. Interestingly, Duong saw such distribution where the more capable would not only do more challenging tasks but also be in charge of assisting others in the process as 'equally divided'. This means the teachers' practice not only makes students position and be positioned in a hierarchy of competence but also helps form a *distorted* concept of equality among students.

This distribution of responsibilities among students in group work can be seen as the reproduction of the teachers' distribution of learning opportunities. While seeking convergent answers, this practice of dividing group task responsibilities may be seen as acceptable by students. Such practices in creative group tasks, where students need to contribute different ideas, as in Hoang's (2013) study, make the more capable learners dissatisfied when their ideas are not immediately accepted and the less capable resentful when their ideas are not valued. The unequal division of task responsibilities based on ranking of students by teachers, when reproduced in group tasks, especially in activities requiring creativity, hinders effective and satisfactory group work. Consequently, the teachers' practice hinders the process of promoting equity and developing group work skills. This is in line with the argument proposed by Mantle-Bromley and Foster (2005), that sometimes the embedded conventions of schooling get in the way of helping students gain the necessary skills.

Discussion and Conclusion

Taking into consideration the potential of English language teaching practice to (re)produce inequality (Bright and Phan 2011, Pennycook 2001), the study problematises the classroom practices in three high school English classrooms in the Vietnam context, which is described by Hofstede as a higher power distance culture. By drawing on students' voices, the study unpacks certain classroom practices to see how power relations play out in positioning students, and how such positioning impacts the distribution of learning opportunities. It investigates what happens inside classrooms as teachers and students manage and interpret power that shapes their interactions.

The study found that the teachers' practices did reflect the power distance between teachers and students as well as among students themselves in classrooms, where teachers make almost all the decisions in class including initiating learning activities and distributing learning opportunities, while students position themselves and others based on a hierarchical academic order. This is in line with the description of high power distance classrooms made by Hofstede (1986) and Hadley (2001).

However, while Hofstede and Hadley only describe the different patterns of interaction in the classroom and suggest conforming to such patterns, this study problematises such patterns by analysing their possible effects on students' learning opportunities. It found that by consistently inviting certain students to participate in class activities and ignoring others, the teachers make students recognise unequal distribution of learning opportunities based on a hierarchy of competence. The findings also add nuances to the complex picture, indicating that by passively withdrawing, students are actively resisting practices in which they occupy unequal power of negotiation rather than expecting and accepting power differences, as in Hofstede's study (1986). English teachers need to be aware of the subtle reactions by students in order to adjust their teaching methods, develop a more culturally appropriate model and avoid reproducing existing power relations.

In line with Kayi-Aydar's (2013, 2014) studies, the classroom interactions in this study also play an important role in determining positions of the students in class, and this has effects on the students' access to participation in class activities. However, unlike in Kayi-Aydar's studies where students actively assign different positions for themselves and their peers, in this study of classrooms in a high power distance context, the teacher plays an important role in assigning positions to students, and the students recognis their ascribed positions. While those in higher positions of the hierarchy of competence were constantly given more chances to participate in the language learning activities, those in lower positions were rarely given this chance. Consequently, those who were not given the chance were unlikely to learn the language because participating in the language learning practice is essential to the language acquisition process (van Lier 2001; Norton and Toohey 2011). Such practices promote the reproduction of unequal power distribution not only between teachers and students but also among students themselves and reinforce students' lower self-concept, which has been found to negatively affect students' learning aspiration and interest (Marsh 1987; Marsh et al. 2005). The study also found that the distribution of responsibilities in group tasks in student–student interaction was also based on the assumed hierarchy of competence, which can be considered as the reproduction of unequal distribution of power and responsibility.

The students recognised their assigned positions in a hierarchy of competence relative to their peers. At the same time, they also saw their positions as fluid and changeable. At times, both those in the higher and lower ends of the hierarchy were dissatisfied and frustrated with such power relations and distribution of learning opportunities and wanted to negotiate changes in the positioning. The dissatisfaction, frustration and resistance were reported indirectly; however, such resistance did not turn into agency that helps students negotiate for change. The power distance between teachers and students may have hindered such a negotiation process.

The hierarchical ranking of competence among peers coupled with the power distance between teachers and students not only constrains opportunities for weaker learners to engage in learning activities, but also limits their chance of negotiating more powerful positions. Such limited and limiting social positioning of the students in this context is in line with Lee's (2008) and Menard-Warwick's (2008) findings, where teachers' instructions play an important role in positioning students. The distribution of learning opportunities based on an assumed hierarchy of competence by teachers in this study is among the customary classroom activities and societal discourses that, according to Menard-Warwick (2008), constrain students' possibilities for claiming more desirable identities.

The findings of this research offer some implications for teachers. First, a culturally sensitive pedagogy does not simply mean conforming to the observed practices found in the classroom without considering how power relations influence social positioning, distribution of learning opportunities and social justice. In such a context where power belongs to the teacher, teachers could exercise their power in order to help students exercise their power (Gore 1992). As classroom power relations that promote learning are essential (Pace and Hemmings 2007), it is necessary for teachers to empower students, and lower the power distance between them and their students. For instance, they could encourage students to speak up or voice their opinion during class and allow more chances for learners to discuss learning activities. They could adjust their ways of controlling classroom activities and use more appropriate pedagogical practices by being more sensitive to certain students' non-verbal cues indicating their withdrawal or resistance during classroom interaction.

The findings also indicate that teachers' tendency to give more chance to talk to certain students can limit others' access to learning opportunities and affect the way students position themselves and others; as Kayi-Aydar (2014) stated, 'teacher talk and behaviours might shape how students position their peers' (pp. 24-25). Thus, instead of focusing on more competent learners, teachers could *redistribute* learning chances among students more equally to allow students to negotiate more desirable positions and to have access to more learning opportunities. Moreover, more research into power dynamics of classroom interaction is necessary to find suitable pedagogical practices that could offer students more powerful positions, or more enhanced sets of possibilities for social interaction and agency.

References

Ahearn, L.M. (2001). Language and agency. *Annual Review of Anthropology*, 30, 109-137.

Black, L. (2004). Teacher–pupil talk in whole-class discussions and processes of social positioning within the primary school classroom. *Language and Education*, 18(5), 347-360.

Bright, D., and Phan, L.H. (2011). Learning to speak like us: Identity, discourse and teaching English in Vietnam. In L.J. Zhang, R. Rubdy and L. Alsagoff (eds.), *Asian Englishes: Changing perspectives in a globalised world* (pp. 121-140). Singapore: Pearson.

Canagarajah, S. (1999). *Resisting linguistic imperialism in English teaching*. Oxford: Oxford University Press.

Duff, P.A. (2002). The discursive co-construction of knowledge, identity, and difference: An ethnography of communication in the high school mainstream. *Applied Linguistics*, 23(3), 289-322.

Gee, J.P. (2011). *An introduction to discourse analysis: Theory and method* (3rd edition). New York and London: Routledge.

Gore, J. (1992). What we can do for you! What can 'we' do for 'you'? Struggling over empowerment in critical and feminist pedagogy. In C. Luke and J. Gore, *Feminisms and critical pedagogy* (pp. 54-73). New York: Routledge.

Hadley, H. (2001). *Power distance: Implications for English language teaching*. Niigata University of International and Information Studies. Retrieved 28 February 2016 from http://www.nuis.ac.jp/~hadley/publication/powerdistance/hadpower.htm

Hoang, T.H. (2013). *Collaborative interaction and the cultural values underlying group work satisfaction: A case study of Vietnamese students of English*. PhD Thesis, The University of Queensland, Brisbane.

Hofstede, G. (1986). Cultural differences in teaching and learning. *International Journal of Intercultural Relations*, 10(3), 301-320.

Hofstede, G., Hofstede, G.J., and Minkov, M. (2010). *Cultures and organisations: Software of the mind: Intercultural cooperation and its importance for survival* (3rd edition). New York: McGraw-Hill.

Holliday, A., Hyde, M., and Kullman, J. (2010). *Intercultural communication: An advanced resource book for students*. New York: Routledge.

Kayi-Aydar, H. (2013). 'No, Rolanda, completely wrong!' Positioning, classroom participation and ESL learning. *Classroom Discourse*, 4(2), 130-150.

Kayi-Aydar, H. (2014). Social positioning, participation, and second language learning: Talkative students in an academic ESL classroom. *TESOL Quarterly*, 48(4), 686-714.

Krashen, S. (1985). *The input hypothesis: Issues and implications*. New York: Longman.

Lee, E. (2008). The 'other(ing)' costs of ESL: A Canadian case study. *Journal of Asian Pacific Communication*, 18(1), 91-108.

Lin, A.M.Y. (1999). Doing-English-lessons in the reproduction or transformation of social worlds. *TESOL Quarterly,* 23(3), 392-412.

Mantle-Bromley, C., and Foster, A.M. (2005). Educating for democracy: The vital role of the language arts teacher. *The English Journal*, 94(5), 70-74.

Martin-Beltrán, M. (2010). Positioning proficiency: How students and teachers (de)construct language proficiency at school. *Linguistics and Education*, 21(4), 257-281.

Marsh, H.W. (1987). The big-fish-little-pond effect on academic self-concept. *Journal of Educational Psychology*, 79, 280-295.

Marsh, H.W., Trautwein, U., Ludtke, O., Koller, O., and Baumert, J. (2005). Academic self-concept, interest, grades, and standardized test scores: Reciprocal effects models of causal ordering. *Child Development*, 76(2), 397-394

Menard-Warwick, J. (2008). 'Because she made beds. Every day'. Social positioning, classroom discourse, and language learning. *Applied Linguistics*, 29(2), 267-289.

Norton, B., and Toohey, K. (2001). Changing perspectives on good language learners. *TESOL Quarterly*, 35(2), 307-322.

Norton, B., and Toohey, K. (2011). State-of-the-art article. Identity, language learning, and social change. *Language Teaching*, 44, 412-446.

Pace, J.L., and Hemmings, A. (2007). Understanding authority in classrooms: A review of theory, ideology, and research. *Review of Educational Research*, 77(1), 4-27.

Parrot, W. (2003). Positioning and the emotions. In R. Harré and F. Moghaddam (eds.), *The self and others: Positioning individuals and groups in personal, political, and cultural contexts* (pp. 29-43). Westport, CT: Praeger Publishers.

Pavlenko, A., and Lantolf, J.P. (2000). Second language learning as participation and the (re)construction of selves. In J. P. Lantolf (ed.), *Sociocultural theory and second language learning* (pp. 155-177). Oxford: Oxford University Press.

Pennycook, A. (2001). *Critical applied linguistics: A critical introduction.* Mahwah, New Jersey: Lawrence Erlbaum Associates.

Savignon, S. (1997). *Communicative competence: Theory and classroom practice.* New York: McGraw-Hill.

Talmy, S. (2009). Forever FOB? Resisting and reproducing the other in high school ESL. In A. Reyes and A. Lo (eds.), *Beyond Yellow English: Toward a linguistic anthropology of Asian Pacific America* (pp. 347-365). Oxford: Oxford University Press.

van Lier, L. (2001). Constraints and resources in class room talk: Issues in equality and symmetry. In C.N. Candlin and N. Mercer (eds.), *English language teaching in its social context: A reader* (pp. 90-107). New York: Routledge.

CHAPTER 10

AGENDAS, ASPIRATIONS, EDUCATION AND ENGLISH LANGUAGE TEACHING IN KIRIBATI

Indika Liyanage

Abstract

Economic liberalisation along with privatisation of services and institutions, of which education is one, is the precursor to aid-dependent economies where policy decisions are often influenced by conditions associated with aid. Countries that rely on regular monetary aid from wealthy donors for sustenance usually succumb their economic, social and educational policies to donor agendas. Kiribati, a Pacific Island state, is no exception. For example, pressures exerted by the donors have accelerated the structural adjustment policies in Kiribati and other Pacific Island states which suggests that economic liberalisation of these countries is currently on the agenda. In the field of education, these adjustments, among other initiatives, strive to prioritise the use of English over the vernacular where proficiency in English is becoming an increasingly important criterion for employment. Locals (i-Kiribati – People of Kiribati), however, tend to show strong resistance due to powerful attachments to their local community values. In this chapter, I highlight these issues in relation to the tensions experienced by the i-Kiribati in their efforts to keep local aspirations afloat.

Keywords: English education, employment, donor, economic liberalisation

Introduction

Processes of globalisation, with the interests, cultures, ideologies and language (English) of global superpowers, are pervasive and hegemonic in developing countries. These nation states, irrespective of their size or geographic location, are involved in processes of globalisation, succumbing their economic, social and educational policies to a capitalist agenda (Phillipson 2001). Pacific Islands, of which the Republic of Kiribati (Pronounced *keer-ah-bhass*) is one, are no exception. Under pressure from peripheral agencies such as the World Bank (WB), International Monetary Fund (IMF), Asian Development Bank (ADB), and regional donors like Australia and New Zealand, structural adjustment policies in Kiribati and other Pacific Island states have accelerated (Firth 2005; Tisdel 2000, 2002). A review of reports and policy documents (Asian Development Bank 2008a, 2008b; Purfield 2005; World Bank 2006) suggests that currently economic liberalisation of these countries is on the agenda. Economic liberalisation along with privatisation of services and institutions is the precursor to competitive, aid-dependent economies in these countries where policy decisions are influenced by the conditions associated with various forms of aid and expertise. In terms of education, privatisation of educational institutions and prioritisation of English as the medium of instruction are unavoidable results in such economies.

The case of Sri Lanka in terms of the processes of globalisation and English language teaching is one example of this. Sri Lanka's economic liberalisation began with the introduction of the 'Free Trade Policy' in 1977 (Kelegama 2006; Lakshman 1985) and since then the socioeconomic, sociopolitical and sociocultural effects of globalisation have resulted in Sri Lanka's dependence on global agents for sustenance. The financial assistance from global agents comes with conditions for loan recovery, which in turn impact heavily on government policies. Among other things, the impact on policy and practice has been immense in education and the teaching and learning of English in the country. In education, attempts are being made to replace the 'Policy of Free Education' through privatisation of educational establishments in which English language is the medium of instruction (Punchi 2001). In English language teaching, especially teacher education, material development and pedagogic applications are done mostly to serve the interests of the donors and without much regard for socially situated practices of teaching and learning (Liyanage 2010; Perera and Canagarajah 2010).

In this chapter, I highlight these issues in relation to the tensions experienced by the i-Kiribati (People of Kiribati) in their efforts to keep local aspirations afloat. The chapter begins with a brief description of Kiribati and its educational system, and draws on my experiences as an English language teaching consultant between 2006 and 2009. As part of this in-country consultancy, educational establishments and their practices had to be observed. Observations included teaching and learning activities at the Kiribati Teachers' College, Senior and Junior Secondary Schools, and use of and attitudes to the use of English in the community. In addition to this, numerous consultations were conducted with educational professionals at all levels of employment and community members representing the Kiribati society. Observations and interview data gathered from a practising teacher of English during this consultancy are used as evidence to highlight the issues in this chapter. The interview participant (referred to as ATE) had over 12 years of teaching experience in a Senior Secondary School, and had graduated from an overseas university.

Education in Kiribati

Kiribati comprises a landmass of just over 800 kilometres spreading across 33 atoll islands which lie from east of Nauru to French Polynesia and is situated in the Central Pacific Ocean. These atolls were colonised and administered under Gilbert and Ellice Islands by the British until they gained independence and became a republic in 1979. I-Kiribati, the people of Kiribati, number about 90,000 and more than half of these people live in the capital Tarawa (Asian Development Bank 2007). Kiribati is currently a member of the United Nations, Pacific Islands Forum, the Commonwealth, the Pacific Community, ADB, IMF, and the WB (US Department of States 2008) and is one of the poorest countries in the Asia Pacific region (Asian Development Bank 2008b; Tisdel 2000). Tisdel (2000, 76) comments: 'the smallest of these nations, the atoll economies of Kiribati and Tuvalu, have little land mass, extremely poor soils and little diversity of natural resources – fish is their main natural resource.' Given the limitations associated with production in-country, almost all food items need to be imported from overseas. Kiribati receives its main income through remittances from the i-Kiribati employed overseas, licences for fishing in their waters and development assistance.

Formal education in Kiribati commences in primary schools for children aged six years and continues for six years. Secondary education follows primary education and is organised under three categories of school: Junior Secondary Schools for three years up to Form 3, Senior Secondary Schools for three years up to Form 6 or, for a very small number, for four years up to Form 7, and Combined Junior Secondary Schools and Senior Secondary Schools. Primary Schools and Junior Secondary Schools are run by the government and students gain automatic entry into Junior Secondary Schools which operate in each island. At the end of Junior Secondary School, students sit competitive examinations to secure places at higher Forms. There are currently 16 registered Senior Secondary Schools in Kiribati and two combined Junior Secondary Schools and Senior Secondary Schools. Of these, only three Senior Secondary Schools are run by the government. All others are operated by churches (Republic of Kiribati Ministry of Education 2007). Postsecondary education is available in Tarawa at the University of the South Pacific (USP) Extension Centre, the Kiribati Teachers' College, Kiribati Technical Institute, the Marine Training Centre, and Kiribati School of Nursing.

Throughout Kiribati, the quality of formal education is generally low due to a widespread shortage of teachers, teaching resources, and standard infrastructure (Liyanage and Walker 2013). Kiribati Government authorities require that teachers complete Form 5 for Primary Teachers, and Form 7 for Junior and Senior Secondary, as academic qualifications. The minimum required teacher qualification is a two year certificate program offered by the Kiribati Teachers' College. There is a severe shortage of teachers with nationally required academic qualifications or professional training. For example, in Senior Secondary Schools only 56 per cent of employed teachers have completed Form 7 while only 30 per cent have completed the two year certificate program at the Kiribati Teachers' College (Republic of Kiribati Ministry of Education 2007). Apart from a very few volunteer teachers who are associated with religious missions, the schools do not attract qualified teachers from overseas.

English Language Teaching

English language is a subject in the country's formal education system, but the outcomes of its instruction have suffered due to many reasons. As in education generally, there are insufficient teachers, who are either poorly trained or not trained at all, with the exception of a very few who have completed their studies in English speaking countries. English teachers are inequitably distributed among Kiribati's various islands and the scarcity of available resources and infrastructure is in serious need of improvement. For example, there are only 14 libraries for 87 Primary Schools in the country (see Republic of Kiribati Ministry of Education 2007 for statistics).

The English language teaching curriculum is old; it follows the curriculum that the British had during colonial times with a very heavy focus on English literature. My observations of English language teaching practices in Senior Secondary Schools indicated that in most lessons students are taught answers to a set of pre-identified examination questions, such as the differences between novels and short-stories, types of drama, as well as formal and informal writing. Some lessons do include cloze and reading comprehension exercises. Except for reading and writing, there is very little focus on speaking and listening. Observations of Kiribati Teachers' College lectures and workshops indicated that teachers are trained to provide specific answers to students' final examination questions. Observations also revealed that, more often than not, English language teaching in Senior Secondary Schools and English language teacher education at Kiribati Teachers' College occur in the local vernacular.

There are many reasons for the use of the vernacular in English language teaching in Kiribati. According to my observations, the small expatriate community in Kiribati is of the opinion that teachers' lack of proficiency in the language is the apparent reason for using the vernacular. However, these teachers were adequately capable of participating in conversations conducted in English and articulating themselves to me as those who did not have any proficiency in the vernacular. The English teachers explained that the communal ethic strongly expects them to use the vernacular in society and the same is expected of them in the English classes. The idea was corroborated by a senior official of a tertiary educational institution in Tarawa who had gained a doctoral qualification from an English speaking country. According to this official's version, he had to abandon lecturing in English mainly due to the communal ethic referred to above and partly also due to students' lack of proficiency. Additionally, my observations of English language teacher-trainees who had come to Kiribati Teachers' College after 20 years of teaching to upgrade their skills confirmed that they also found it difficult to talk to one another in English during training activities because of this social norm.

Unlike most of their postcolonial counterparts, where eagerness to use English to achieve elevation to a higher pedestal of elitism and kinship is the norm (see Liyanage 2012 and Samarakkody and Braine 2005 for Sri Lanka and other examples), the i-Kiribati generally shun English for fear of being attached to a different class. Although the situation is not pedagogically conducive to producing better outcomes in English language teaching, i-Kiribati's wariness to communicate orally in English is perhaps a result of the unique culture in Pacific islands which 'is to some extent in conflict with the Western ethic promoting competition and the pursuance of self-interest' (Tisdel 2000, 80).

Donor Agendas and Medium of Instruction Policy

The objective of donor aid agencies and nations to position independent postcolonial Kiribati as a participant in regional and global affairs and activities hinges upon acceptance of the imperative for development of a local professional and administrative class highly literate in English. However, English as medium of instruction, an education policy embraced in similar settings and for similar reasons across the Asia Pacific region (see, e.g., Lamb and Coleman 2008), has encountered resistance in Kiribati classrooms, as the local teacher participant explains: 'They do understand English. There's a saying that you understand more but you can't say it. That is quite true. When we explain things in English they understand it. But unfortunately they cannot answer back fluently' (ATE).

If we wish to understand not being able to *answer back fluently* in Kiribati classrooms, we need to look beyond mere competence to scrutinise what amounts to a pervasive reluctance to use English in classrooms that perplexes the few overseas volunteer teachers, and frustrates teachers of English attempting to implement language teaching approaches that rely on participation in socially meaningful interaction.

Reluctance to use a target language - in this case English - is not unique to Kiribati; learners everywhere believe speaking English in class is the greatest challenge they face (Aragão 2011) and language teachers are familiar with variations in learner preparedness to use a second language in particular contexts, and the concept of 'willingness to communicate' (WTC) (McCroskey, Richmond, McCroskey and Daly 1987). WTC was initially regarded as an individual trait closely linked to anxiety stemming from shyness and the fear of shame or rejection, although variations in predisposition to WTC have since been associated with cultural groups (McCroskey and Richmond 1990); for example, as reported frequently in settings such as foreign language classrooms in Japan (Doyon 2000). These instances are considered to originate in the fear experienced by individuals of negative social evaluation and/or 'a keen sensitivity to cues of being rejected' (Doyon 2000, 2). Reports (e.g., Garrett and Young 2009; Imai 2010; Miccoli 1997, 2003; Price 1991; So and Dominguez 2005) of learner embarrassment and fears of judgment related to attempts to use a target language attribute reluctance to learners' perceptions that teachers and other learners possess superior knowledge (Aragão 2011; Bailey 1983), and language teachers associate learners' experiences of these fears with *actual* effects that impact on performance, both physiological and psychological, such as 'disturbances in speech and … derangements in the processes of attention, reflection, volition and memory' (Platt, Ruch, Hofmann and Proyer 2012, 87).

However, Cao (2014, 810) argues that WTC, as manifested in language classrooms, is characterised also by 'fluctuation and dynamism due to variations in its … environmental, and linguistic antecedents, which interdependently exert facilitative and inhibitive effects on it.' Investigations of WTC among learners in Kiribati classrooms need to consider mediation of language use by conditions that are less to do with specific instances of communication, but instead attempt to encompass intergroup dynamics (Cao 2014) that situate WTC in relation to broader social contexts experienced by individuals. Aragão (2011, 311) argues that core beliefs, in this case deeply imbued shared cultural beliefs, play a central role in how students behave in learning environments. In the case of Kiribati learners of English, psychological and situated WTC are mediated by powerful attachment to the values of their local community and its negative social evaluations within these parameters, rather than any shyness or embarrassment eventuating from their knowledge of or performance using the target language. This shapes the observed reluctance to participate in English medium of instruction classrooms because:

> … when someone speaks in another language, then the people around him will mock him saying that he is from that island, he is from that country, you should go there and live there and why should he come here and live with us when he is not speaking in our language. … the place of English in our culture is not as important as our own language. … If you speak English, you cannot survive outside. What I mean by this is that Kiribati is very important because they … when you speak … when you communicate with Kiribati, everyone understands you and then cooperates with you, can give you everything. Whereas, if you speak in English, no one will understand you… (ATE, Lines)

The threatened mockery of Kiribati learners of English, and students in English medium classrooms more generally, reveals a misalignment between the norms and values of the community and the policy of English medium of instruction in educational institutions. The social power exerted upon individuals by these threats requires a reassessment of the complex relations between situated responses of learners and contexts of classroom teaching and learning. If we accept that classroom experiences are important in broader socialisation of individuals through the reproduction of cultural norms and values (Holodynski and Kronast 2009), English medium of instruction situates learners at a collision of local aspirations and global impositions certain to generate conflict for individuals who adopt or embrace English.

The context of teaching and learning and performance extends beyond classroom walls adding a potent feature to the emotional dimension of learning, the threat of mockery that, according to the senior official of a tertiary educational institution in Tarawa, amounts to the insult of aspiring to be a 'foreigner'. In such an environment, generally accepted explanations of learner behaviour are turned on their head; rather than being motivated to learn to avoid feelings of shame because of fear of misunderstandings or miscommunications (Torres 1992), fear of ridicule of demonstrated success as a learner inhibits learning. Explanations of learning based on models of social-comparison orientation (Micari and Pazos 2014) rely on individuals' perceptions of superiority or inferiority in relation to others considered similar, but, in the context of Kiribati, beliefs widely held in the community about knowledge and use of English mediate perceptions of superiority or inferiority and shape performance-goal orientations (Micari and Pazos 2014) of English learners and users.

In responding to external demands to develop an administrative and business class of individuals fluent in English, policy makers in Kiribati have assumed that classrooms alone define 'a public forum for some to be recognised and rewarded while others are shamed and sanctioned' (Dagenais, Day and Toohey 2006, 214) sufficient to motivate learners to work to achieve the goal of English proficiency. This reflects the Western focus of societies on individuals rather than on relationships, and on self-reliant and self-contained individualism within relationships (Scheff and Retzinger 2000). Expectations that learner self-concept and self-worth will lead to English being embraced for the apparent personal advantages and advancement have failed to account for social and self-evaluations based on norms other than those of the institution.

In Kiribati, however, the power of esteem and the fear of shame believed to underpin success or failure to learn, to progress or to meet goals (Holodynski and Kronast 2009) operates so much more powerfully in the broader community outside the classroom, that institutional learning objectives are severely compromised. Shame is avoided and esteem garnered through rejection of an achievement orientation in order to align with local norms. De-emphasis of the relational that Scheff and Retzinger (2000) identify as a defining characteristic of the modern world suggests that, to understand the reluctance to embrace English as the medium of instruction in Kiribati, researchers and educators can no longer ignore that 'in a traditional society, there is NOTHING more important than one's relationships' (Scheff and Retzinger 2000, 4, emphasis in the original).

Conclusion

Education in general and English language teaching in particular need help and assistance from developed countries and their donors for the republic of Kiribati and other poor nations in the region to re-build and reorganise their infrastructure, resources and expertise to meet the knowledge demands of the modern world. However, there is an acute need for such assistance to be placed within frameworks that respect and honour the tenets of local cultures and educational traditions. Additionally, the response in Kiribati to a policy of English as medium of instruction emphasises the necessity for a comprehensive body of research of socially situated and preferred practices of learning and teaching in these countries prior to training teachers, teacher-trainers and curriculum restructure in education and English language teaching. As I have discussed elsewhere (Liyanage 2003, 2010, 2012; Liyanage and Bartlett 2008), without such knowledge the implementation of pedagogic practices and curricula will be untenable and counterproductive. Given the example of Sri Lanka discussed earlier in this paper, what remains unanswered is how far the nation states in the region in general and Kiribati in particular will be capable of negotiating the interests based on and around their primordial ties in receiving and repaying the loans from global donors.

References

Aragão, R. (2011). Beliefs and emotions in foreign language learning. *System, 39*(3), 302-313.

Asian Development Bank (2007). *Priorities of the people: Hardship in Kiribati.* Manila: Asian Development Bank.

Asian Development Bank (2008a). *Annual report 2007* (Vol. 1). Manila: Asian Development Bank.

Asian Development Bank (2008b). *Asian Development Bank & Kiribati 2008.* Suva: Asian Development Bank.

Bailey, K.M. (1983). Competitiveness and anxiety in adult second language learning: Looking at and through the diary studies. In H.W. Seliger and M.H. Long (eds.), *Classroom oriented research* (pp. 67-103). Rowley, MA: Newbury House.

Canagarajah, A.S. (1999). *Resisting linguistic imperialism in English teaching.* Oxford: Oxford University Press.

Cao, Y. (2014). A sociocognitive perspective on second language classroom willingness to communicate. *TESOL Quarterly, 48*(4), 789-814. doi:10.1002/tesq.155.

Dagenais, D., Day, E., and Toohey, K. (2006). A multilingual child's literacy practices and contrasting identities in the figured worlds of French immersion classrooms. *International Journal of Bilingual Education and Bilingualism, 9*(2), 205-218. doi:10.1080/13670050608668641.

Doyon, P. (2000). Shyness in the Japanese EFL class. *Language Teacher – Kyoto – JALT, 24*(1), 11-16.

Firth, S.G. (2005, April 5-8). *Globalization on the Pacific Islands.* Paper presented at the 2nd South-east Asia and the Pacific subregional tripartite forum on decent work, Melbourne, Australia.

Garrett, P., and Young, R.F. (2009). Theorizing affect in foreign language learning: An analysis of one learner's responses to a communicative Portuguese course. *The Modern Language Journal, 93*(2), 209-226.

Holodynski, M., and Kronast, S. (2009). Shame and pride: Invisible emotions in classroom research. In B. Röttger-Rössler and H.J. Markowitsch (eds.), *Emotions as bio-cultural processes* (pp. 371-394). New York: Springer.

Imai, Y. (2010). Emotions in SLA: New insights from collaborative learning for an EFL classroom. *The Modern Language Journal, 94*(2), 278-292.

Kelegama, S. (2006). *Development under stress: Sri Lankan economy in transition.* London: Sage.

Lakshman, W.D. (1985). IMF–World Bank intervention in Sri Lankan economic policy: Historical trends and patterns. *Social Scientist, 13*(141), 3-29.

Lamb, M., and Coleman, H. (2008). Literacy in English and the transformation of self and society in post-Soeharto Indonesia. *International Journal of Bilingual Education and Bilingualism, 11*(2), 189-205. doi:10.2167/beb493.0.

Liyanage, I. (2003). Is importing ELT pedagogies viable anymore? The case of Sri Lanka. In B. Bartlett, F. Bryer and R. Roebuck (eds.), *Reimagining practice: Researching change* (Vol. 2, pp. 163-174). Brisbane, Australia Griffith University, School of Cognition, Language, and Special Education.

Liyanage, I. (2010). Globalisation: Medium-of-instruction policy, indigenous educational systems and ELT in Sri Lanka. In V. Vaish (ed.), *Globalization of language and culture in Asia* (pp. 209-232). London: Continuum.

Liyanage, I. (2012). Critical pedagogy in ESL/EFL teaching in South-east Asia: Practices and challenges with examples from Sri Lanka. In K. Sung and R. Pederson (eds.), *Critical ELT practices in Asia: Key issues, practices, and possibilities* (pp. 137-152). Rotterdam, The Netherlands: Sense Publishers.

Liyanage, I., and Bartlett, B. (2008). Contextually responsive transfer: Perceptions of NNES on an ESL/EFL teacher training programme. *Teaching and Teacher Education, 24*(7), 1827–1836.

Liyanage, I., and Walker, T. (2013). Cultural concepts and EIL: The case of the Republic of Kiribati. In N.T. Zacharias and C. Manara (eds.), *Contextualizing the pedagogy of English as an international language: Issues and tensions* (pp. 119-133). Newcastle. UK: Cambridge Scholars Publishing.

McCroskey, J.C., and Richmond, V.P. (1990). Willingness to communicate: Differing cultural perspectives. *Southern Communication Journal, 56*(1), 72-77. doi:10.1080/10417949009372817.

McCroskey, J.C., Richmond, V.P., McCroskey, J.C., and Daly, J.A. (1987). Willingness to communicate. *Personality and Interpersonal Communication, 6,* 1-11.

Micari, M., and Pazos, P. (2014). Worrying about what others think: A social-comparison concern intervention in small learning groups. *Active Learning in Higher Education, 15*(3), 249-262. doi:10.1177/1469787414544874.

Miccoli, L.S. (1997). Learning English as a foreign language in Brazil: A joint investigation of learners' experiences in a university classroom, or, going to the depths of learners' classroom experiences.

Miccoli, L.S. (2003). Individual classroom experiences: A socio-cultural comparison for understanding EFL classroom learning. *Ilha do Desterro, 41*(1), 61-91.

Perera, K., and Canagarajah, S. (2010). Globalisation and English teaching in Sri Lanka: Foreign resources and local responses. In V. Vaish (ed.), *Globalization of language and culture in Asia* (pp. 106-119). London: Continuum.

Phillipson, R. (2001). English for globalisation or for the world's People? *International Review of Education, 47*(3-4), 185-200.

Platt, T., Ruch, W., Hofmann, J., and Proyer, R.T. (2012). Extreme fear of being laughed at: Components of gelotophobia. *The Israeli Journal of Humor Research: An International Journal*, 1, 86-106.

Price, M.L. (1991). The subjective experience of foreign language anxiety: Interviews with highly anxious students. In E.K. Horwitz (ed.), *Language anxiety: From theory and research to classroom implications* (pp. 101-108). Englewood Cliffs: Prentice Hall.

Punchi, L. (2001). Resistance towards the language of globalisation – the case of Sri Lanka. *International review of education, 47*(3-4), 361–378.

Purfield, C. (2005). *Managing revenue volatility in a small island economy: The case of Kiribati. IMF working paper* (WP/05/154). Retrieved from Asia and Pacific Department:

Republic of Kiribati Ministry of Education. (2007). *Digest of education statistics*. Tarawa: Republic of Kiribati Ministry of Education.

Samarakkody, M., and Braine, G. (2005). Teaching English in Sri Lanka: From colonial roots to Lankan English. In G. Braine (ed.), *Teaching English to the world: History, curriculum, and practice* (pp. 147-157). Mahwah, NJ: Lawrence Erlbaum.

Scheff, T.J., and Retzinger, S.M. (2000). Shame as the master emotion of everyday life. *Journal of Mundane Behavior, 1*(3), 303-324.

So, S., and Dominguez, R. (2005). Emotion processes in second language acquisition. In P. Benson and D. Nunan (eds.), *Learners' stories: Difference and diversity in language learning* (pp. 42-55). Cambridge: Cambridge Universtiy Press.

Tisdel, C. (2000). Poverty in the Pacific Islands. *International Journal of Sociology and Social Policy, 20*(11/12), 74-102.

Tisdel, C. (2002). Globalisation, development and poverty in the Pacific Islands. *International Journal of Socio Economics, 29*(11/12), 902-922.

Torres, L. (1992). Code-mixing as a narrative strategy in a bilingual community. *World Englishes, 11*(2–3), 183-193. doi:10.1111/j.1467-971X.1992.tb00063.x.

United Nations (2002). *United Nations common country assessment: Kiribati*. Suva: Office of the United Nations resident coordinator.

US Department of States (2008). Background note: Kiribati. Retrieved from http://www.state.gov/r/pa/ei/bgn/1836.htm

World Bank (2006). *Opportunities to improve social services: Human development in the Pacific Islands* (39778). Retrieved from Human Development Sector Unit, East Asia and Pacific Region.

CHAPTER 11

ISSUES OF EQUITY IN KOREAN HIGHER EDUCATION

Academic Deans' Stances on the Three-No's Policy

Dong Kwang Kim

Abstract

Since its introduction in 1999, the Three-No's policy (Sambul Jeongchaek) has been the principle governing university admissions in Korea. Designed to promote equity and fairness, this policy enjoins three prohibitions: universities cannot give their own entrance exams; they cannot prefer particular high schools over others, and they cannot admit students on the basis of their parents' monetary contributions to the institution. These three no's are sensitive political issues not only among universities but in Korean society at large because they are directly linked to social class. This paper seeks to examine a group of Korean academic deans' understanding of equity issues in Korea as they relate to the Three-No's policy and the increasing performance gap between Seoul/metropolitan area universities and universities located in regional provinces. Taking a phenomenological approach, this qualitative study involves interviews with 26 academic deans and senior professors at flagship national and private universities to explore the challenges as subjectively experienced by them. The study finds that Seoul area university deans generally regard the Three-No's policy with disfavour whereas regional university deans tend to support it. The study also finds that Korean academic leaders are torn between the values of competition and academic excellence on the one hand and educational equity and social justice on the other; and that hard piecemeal choices must be made in favouring one value over another.

Keywords: equity, Three-No's policy, Korean education, social class, social justice, university ranking

Introduction

One of the most serious issues that Korean higher education faces at present is determining the best criteria and methods for university admissions. The future of students – their jobs, incomes, marriage prospects, etc. – depends, to a great extent, on whether or not they enter prestigious universities (Kim and Lee 2006; Lee 2008). Since the system of university admission is mainly based on a competitive exam, Koreans generally consider universities to be rankable on a monotonic scale, with Seoul National University at the head of the list. College graduates, too, inherit the social prestige of the university they attend (Sorensen 1994). Consequently, there has been intense competition for admittance to prestigious institutions. Studying in a top ranked university significantly influences the later success of graduates as the alumni become a strong support network (Shin 2012). To ensure equity in university access, as well as to address the issue of huge financial and social costs stemming from the private tutoring that students use to gain entry to top ranked universities, the Three No's policy (*Sambul Jeongchaek*) has been in place from the mid-1990s.

In this paper, I will examine Korean academic deans' outlook on the current university admission system, and the increasing pressures on it. Being academics as well as administrators or managers, academic deans, arguably, understand the institutional realities of Korean higher education better than anyone else. I will first examine their stance on the Three-No's policy, often regarded as an attempt to prevent the wealthy from monopolising access to the top universities. I will then examine the increasing performance gap between Seoul/metropolitan area universities and the universities located in regional provinces, and the social/economic consequences of that gap. Some scholars (Grubb, Sweet, Gallagher and Tuomi 2009; Kim and Lee 2005; Shin 2009) note the gap, but they do not discuss the Three-No's policy as a response to it.

By way of introduction, I will make a few observations on the Three-No's policy. The policy enjoins three prohibitions: universities cannot give their own entrance exams; they cannot prefer some high schools over others; and they cannot admit students on the basis of their parents' monetary contributions to the institution. Based on Article 32 of the Higher Education Act, the Ministry of Education (MOE) establishes and announces every year 'The Basic Plan for Admission Screening to Universities or Colleges'. The plan or rule applies to universities, colleges, teachers' colleges and industrial colleges. The earliest document indicating what is now known as the

Three-No's policy is 'The Revised Basic Plan for Admission Screening to Universities or Colleges for the Academic Year 2004' released on 31 March 2003. This document states:

> The criteria and methods for university admissions may be determined and implemented autonomously by universities, but essays and written examinations, admissions for monetary contributions, and distinctions of high schools are to be limited to 'the minimum' for normalisation of primary and secondary educations and for fair and rational selections of students. ... when the minimum requirement is breached, cooperation will be induced through the demand for rectification and the exercise of administrative and financial measures. (Revised Basic Plan for Admission Screening to Universities or Colleges for the Academic Year 2004, p. 7)

The prohibition of university-specific exams (essays and written examinations) was already in place in 'The Basic Plan for Admission Screening to Universities or Colleges for the Academic Year 1997'. As the 2004 document includes the ban on distinctions of high schools, the Three-No's policy took full shape and has been in place since, despite often heated contestations by some quarters – mostly prominent private universities and well-to-do students and their parents. The MOE's attempt to legislate the policy has not yet been successful; the ministry, nonetheless, enforces it through reduction of the budget (or financial assistance) and the number of students recruited for non-complying universities, as well as comprehensive audits of the universities.

The Three No's policy is hotly contested because it presents a tension between equity and competition. As such, its efficacy has been compromised. The Three No's is the MOE's policy to ensure equity in student access to higher education. This equity is important because access to higher education is widely viewed as the starting point of social class differentiation in Korea. At the same time, competition is a real concern for academic deans. Often, the presumed competitiveness of universities is shown in the form of university rankings. The university rankings are determined in no small measure by students securing employment upon graduation, as well as by the financial conditions of the universities to which students' tuition monies contribute a great deal. If that is the case, it is understandable why academic deans seem so keen on recruiting wealthy and well-connected students. Before proceeding further, let us look at some facts of Korean higher education.

Context

Korea is a country of about 50 million people. As of 2010, the number of Korean higher education institutions was 411. Eighty-two of these are based in the capital city of Seoul while 329 are in the provinces. Traditionally, Seoul National University is most highly regarded of all Korean institutions of higher education, followed by some private universities in Seoul such as Yonsei University and Korea University. National universities in Busan (Pusan National University), Daegu (Kyungpook National University), and some other universities in major cities are also highly regarded. However, the differences between the top universities and the rest are not so great as to undercut the value of education and experience at the 'lesser' universities. Along with other international rankings by the Times Higher Education, Shanghai Jiaotong University, and QS Apple (Asia), the *JoongAng Daily* ranking, published in Korea, is often consulted and is particularly influential on Korean parents. The validity and reliability of the procedures taken by US News and World Report for American universities have been widely criticised as they have enabled universities to 'game' the system by exaggerating the numbers that affect the final rankings (Grubb, Sweet, Gallagher and Tuomi 2009). For the same reasons, the JoongAng Daily ranking may be considered unsound.

While universities may be widely distributed throughout Korea, the same cannot be said for its other resources. Korea suffers from concentration of virtually all enterprises in the capital area — Seoul and the surrounding Gyeonggi province. Approximately 55 per cent of manufacturing firms, 66 per cent of regular four-year universities, 73 per cent of R&D institutions, 77 per cent of venture businesses, and 84 per cent of government agencies are located in the capital area (Lee 2014). As we shall see, this over-concentration of political and economic power has had a decisive impact in altering the traditional ranking and value of universities throughout the country. This in turn has induced a strong preference among many Koreans for moving to Seoul, with its variety of employment and cultural options, thus creating the issue of equitable access to quality education and all the goods associated with it.

In the decades immediately following the Korean war (25 June 1950 – 27 July 1953), higher education was a means of creating social mobility and overcoming class barriers by increasing opportunities for lower class families. In recent decades, however, the growth of the Korean economy has slowed (Heritage Foundation 2017), thereby decreasing opportunities for advancement. Whereas formerly there were many opportunities for all college graduates, now there are good opportunities for graduates only from the top ranked universities.

At the same time, the wealthy have also become better at 'gaming' the university recruitment system, thereby monopolising access to the best universities. One example of this may be found by examining Korea's hagwons (cram schools for the country-wide university exam, the College Scholastic Aptitude Test). While many Koreans send their children to hagwons, the wealthy have access to better ones. Elite hagwons have, in many cases, accumulated vast amounts of data on the university exam system (Lee 2005; Sorensen 1994; Sung 2011). This superior test preparation gives the wealthy much better access to elite schools. As a result of the increasing monopoly of the best schools by the wealthy, social mobility through education has become more restricted, and education has become a mechanism for class reproduction rather than for social mobility (Koo 2007). All this has resulted in a sharp polarisation in social classes in Korea that did not exist 20 to 30 years ago (see, for example, Koo 2007).

A final feature of the Korean educational landscape that we need to consider for this study is the new neo-liberal performance regime that has been imposed by the government. The regime's emphasis on outcomes and performance has seen the proliferation of performance indicators and league tables compiled according to performance measures over the last two decades or so. This phenomenon has been called 'policy as numbers' (Rizvi and Lingard 2010; Rose 2010). The performative policy as numbers approach entails a form of accountability at national level, closely aligned with the new public management, which emphasises efficiency and effectiveness. This performance regime, which ties performance indicators to funding, has become a major driver of university policy.

Research Methodology

This paper aims at describing the challenges to Korean higher education as subjectively experienced by academic deans rather than as objective and quantifiable social phenomena such as those that could be statistically established. Korean academic deans are in a unique position to witness first-hand the important issues of Korean higher education as they play out in institutional settings. On the one hand, being academics, they understand the academic side of the mission of the university; and on the other hand, as administrators or managers, they interact with the major actors of the university and understand their points of view on policy. Therefore, it is arguable that no one is in a better position than academic deans to understand the institutional reality of Korean higher education, especially when it comes to the interaction of policy, economics and their impact on equity, student access and participation.

This paper takes a phenomenological approach to research, which emphasises the meaning of lived experiences. I borrow other people's experiences because through them we can become more experienced ourselves. Interviews were designed and conducted in which the deans were asked to talk about their experiences and feelings about the most pressing issues facing Korean higher education today. As I was interested in gathering and recording the lived experiences of Korean academic deans, I mainly used interviews as a means to collect data. Each interview lasted for an hour on average. Of the six universities that were chosen for investigation, three are national universities: Seoul National University (SNU), Pusan National University (PNU), and Kyungpook National University (KNU). These national universities are 'flagship' universities that represent the provinces of their locations and have long been standard-bearers of Korean higher education. The other three universities chosen for this study are private universities – Korea University (KU), Yonsei University (Yonsei), and Sungkyunkwan University (SKKU) – which have served as models for other private universities in Korea. Altogether 26 interviews – 23 with academic deans and three with senior professors – were conducted. The interview data have been analysed on the assumption that deans have to perform duties or tasks that involve contrasting, sometimes even competing challenges or values – in the case of this study, competition and equity.

Contextualising the Three-No's

Since 1999, the Three-No's policy has governed university admissions in Korea. This policy prohibits universities from offering institution-specific entrance exams, making distinctions among high schools, and granting admissions based on donations. The primary objective of the Three-No's policy is to prevent the wealthy from monopolising the best universities and becoming a self-perpetuating caste, thereby destroying all hope of social mobility for the rest of society. To understand how the Three-No's policy addresses the issue of equity, it will be useful to examine each 'No' in the policy.

The first 'No' addresses the issue of university-specific entrance exams. Currently, the College Scholastic Ability Test (CSAT) is the only examination used for student selection. All Korean students therefore can study for one exam, secure in the knowledge that all Koreans compete in the same field and have at least some chance at gaining entrance into an 'elite' university.

It is argued that, if university-specific examinations were revived, it would increase the unfair advantage that rich students have over poor ones. Cram schools and tutoring services focused on the entrance exams of elite universities will proliferate, intensifying – much more than now – the competition for entry into these universities. Students from privileged social classes would increase their chances of getting into prestigious universities by employing private tutoring services tailored to the elite universities (Kim and Kim 2013; Sung 2011). Less wealthy students, on the other hand, would not dare to spend their time studying to get into elite schools, a gamble that might not pay off. Rather, they will focus on studying for the 'lower' ranked schools where they feel they have a better chance.

The second 'No' bans the practice of distinguishing among high schools based on their perceived quality (Park 2007; Sung 2011). It is easy in Korea to distinguish rich cities and districts from poor ones; rich areas have a higher concentration of population, professionals, facilities, government offices, major firms, and schools, particularly hagwons. Students from schools located in rich areas tend to perform better (Lee and Brinton 1996). Growing class differences in educational opportunities are most distinguishably expressed in geographic locations with Seoul's Gangnam (south of the Han River) areas being surrounded by top-ranking private institutions and cram schools, while Gangbuk (north of the Han River) was falling far behind in these private as well as public educational opportunities (Koo 2007).

According to the Blue House (presidential palace) homepage (16 March 2006), for example, students from Gangnam district had a rate of entrance to SNU nine times higher than that of Gangbuk students in 2005. The statistics showed that 25.4 students per 1,000 applicants from Gangnam district entered SNU compared to 2.8 students per 1,000 from Mapo district or 3.8 students from Guro district in Seoul. A similar ratio of difference was found between Gangnam and Gangbuk students in their success in entering Yonsei and KU (Koo 2007, 17-18). Although a stark difference may exist between Gangnam and Gangbuk areas in Seoul, the really uncomfortable truth lies in the fact that districts in regional cities and provinces are falling far behind even Gangbuk.

Universities are keen on recruiting students from rich districts, either because they tend to perform better or because they can be more helpful financially in the form of parent donations. As a result, universities would prefer to distinguish between schools in rich districts and those in less affluent areas. This practice would lead to the further solidification of social class and an increased polarisation of society in Korea.

The third 'No' bans university admissions based on donations. The reason for this 'No' is obvious. If it were allowed, students from rich family backgrounds would be able to study at the most prestigious universities even if they were less academically qualified than other students from poor backgrounds. This 'money-for-admission system' sets up a 'scandalously unjust advantage for wealthy families not able to gain merit-based admission' (Sung 2011, 529).

New Pressures on Universities

As recent neo-liberal reforms in education inexorably proceed, universities are increasingly placed under a performance regime (Rizvi and Lingard 2010, 2011). In this new performance regime, state funding is dependent on a university achieving measurable standards of success. Measurable success therefore becomes a financial necessity for universities.

This struggle for measurable success is intensified by the fact that the Korean student pool is shrinking due to the decline in the general population. In fact, it is expected that many universities will be closed within the next several decades (Kim and Kim 2013; Kim and Lee 2006). Thus, Korean universities are not just competing for increased status and funding; they are competing for sheer survival.

With these pressures in the background, it is not surprising that Korean academic deans show great interest in recruiting top students. Strong students tend to have a better chance at getting jobs upon graduation and passing the important examinations for becoming civil servants, lawyers, certified public accountants and doctors. The success of students in securing employment is directly linked to the reputation and the ranking of their universities.

A great many deans complain about the government dictating what methods of selection universities should use, taking issue with both the Three-No's policy and the MOE's way of enforcing it. Their displeasure is expressed in the remarks of a national university dean: 'The MOE [Ministry of Education] keeps taking issue with universities on admission policies and student quotas' (Dean B). Another national university dean says: 'The MOE imposes too uniform a standard for universities on many issues, including methods of student recruitment' (Dean S).

But understandably the bitterest complaints about the government's control over student recruitment criteria come from private universities: 'Despite its pretensions, the state is not giving autonomy – this should change. … For example, even in student recruitment, the government dictates what methods of selection should be used' (Dean K2). The dean's wish for greater autonomy in student recruitment is echoed by another private university academic, who says: 'The so-called SKY [Seoul National, Korea, Yonsei] universities demand autonomy in admission policy – in selecting students in any way they want, including the use of university-specific entrance examinations' (Professor S).

Universities are always in need of greater revenue. The government itself is pushing national and private universities alike to embrace a mode of governance that favours a market approach to higher education (Kim and Kim 2013; Marginson and Considine 2000; Park 2007; Rizvi and Lingard 2010, 2011; Sung 2011). It is therefore understandable that universities would want to have autonomy in areas currently governed by the Three-No's policy. Thus, the neo-liberal funding system which rewards high rankings and high employment rates, along with the threat of university closure due to a shrinking student pool, have eroded support among many university deans for the Three-No's policy and have, in fact, created opposition to it.

Disparity between Seoul Area Universities and Regional Universities

One result of this extreme competition for the best students is that the rankings of many national universities are falling. This phenomenon mainly affects national universities in the regions while the ranking of 'Seoul National University is kept alive' by its unique and privileged status, as some private university deans have observed as part of this study. The falling rankings of national universities in the regions are tied to the employment rate of their graduates. The fact is that almost all of the big firms in Korea, such as Samsung, Hyundai, SK, LG, Doosan, etc., are located in Seoul and they prefer to hire graduates of universities from the capital area – Seoul and the surrounding Gyeonggi province. The reasons for the preference are various: the perceived quality of education at Seoul-based universities, the graduating students' familiarity with the geography of the city, the use or adoption of the Seoul accent, the easy access to venues of interview, etc. All of these contribute to a preference for graduates of Seoul-based universities.

The perceived higher quality of education at Seoul-based universities was initially a reflection of the Seoul-centric view of everything in Korea, a country, which has historically had a highly centralised administration. Under the influence of the 'normative' Seoul-centric view, the recruiters in the big firms have preferred to hire graduates of Seoul-based universities. Not surprisingly, Seoul-based universities can now boast of the high rate of student employment and retention. Of course, Seoul area universities claim that this fact reflects a higher quality of education. To their repertoire of presumed educational excellence, they are adding new research capabilities. It is this perception (accurate or not) of the quality of education and research at these universities that induces evaluation agencies to rank them higher vis-à-vis the universities in the regions.

Whatever the validity of university rankings, they have great significance with regard to educational equity (Clarke 2007; Morphew and Swanson 2011). University rankings, particularly domestic ones, are tied to the rate of student employment; and universities in the regions are suffering from the consequences of these rankings. A national university academic put his thoughts and feelings about the slipping of national universities in the regions as follows:

> This, ultimately, is linked to the problem of unemployment. The problem of university rankings – the yawning gap, in substance or reputation, between the universities in Seoul and those in the regions – is that universities in the regions are dying. (Professor K)

In this way, a kind of vicious circle has been created in which graduates from regional universities have a harder time finding employment than those from Seoul universities. Therefore, many students graduating from regional universities or colleges want to move to Seoul, depriving regional areas of skilled labour (Grubb, Sweet, Gallagher and Tuomi 2009).

Two national university deans also reported the declining competitiveness and rankings of their institutions with a tone of chagrin: 'My college at KNU has, traditionally in the past, enjoyed the prestige of being the best college south of the Han River. However, these days, the gap between universities in Seoul and in the regions is getting bigger' (Dean L, KNU); 'PNU is the "king of the hill". This is the best university in south-eastern Korea, but its competitiveness, compared to that of universities in the capital area, is increasingly falling' (Dean KNU).

The MOE's policy of competitiveness enhancement, declared in comprehensive reform plans named the The National University Advancement

Plan and The National University Advancement Plan Step Two finalised in 2012, contains such ideas as national university incorporation, and the introduction of the annual performance-based salary system. To push for its business-inspired neo-liberal reform agendas, the government has used as justification the seemingly unsatisfactory performance by national universities.

Echoing the feelings of many deans at national universities in the regions and unconvinced that the criteria employed are fair or reasonable, another national university dean comments on what passes for university rankings with an expression of incredulity and anguish:

> If you go to deans' meetings, you hear KNU ranks 18th or 19th in the whole of Korea. It's just a matter of time before KNU falls below 20th. The reason for it is that universities in Seoul will occupy 1st through 20th; those small-to-medium-sized universities – four-year universities – will be ranked among top 20. The next is two universities: PNU and KNU. Chonnam National University (CNU) is a borderline case. The future rankings are already out there; people are saying this in a self-mocking sort of way. (Dean R)

For a long time, the pecking order of higher education institutions in Korea has been that Seoul National University and the more established private universities – Korea University and Yonsei University – formed the top tier, followed by national universities in the regions. But according to the University League Table, published by the *JoongAng Daily*, for the last 12 years, an average of eight out of the top 10 universities have been private institutions in Korea (Kim 2008). Of these eight private institutions, except for the two small but very-well-endowed science and engineering universities (POSTECH [Pohang University of Science and Technology] and KAIST [Korea Advanced Institute of Science and Technology]), all – Korea, Yonsei, Sungkyunkwan, Hanyang, Seogang, Ewha Womens and Kyunghee – are located in Seoul. This state of affairs, which exacerbates the issue of equity surrounding quality higher education and all the goods associated with it, prompted the government to respond with the Three No's policy.

Noting both the increasing gap between universities in Seoul and universities in the regions on the one hand and the tendency to fixate on this gap on the other, Professor K proposes a more relaxed approach to the issue of university rankings:

> Once a ranking of universities has been established, it gets fixed and the gap between the groups ahead and the groups behind is getting bigger and bigger. So there's a need to approach university rankings from a more relaxed point of view. But private universities are playing this game hard with a policy of selection and concentration. (Professor K)

A national university dean warns of the ever-increasing disparity between the universities in the capital area and the universities in the regions, which he seems to suggest is an anomalous development of higher education in Korea: 'If the current situation continues, in the end, private universities in Seoul will have increasingly superior prestige, and national universities in the regions will fall behind and keep declining in the future' (Dean C).

In fact, this state of affairs has already materialised in the last 10 to 20 years (Kim and Lee 2006), although its most serious consequences are only now beginning to be felt. That is, the better reputation of the private universities in Seoul, initially based on the dubious criteria mentioned earlier, is actually translating into substance due to the increased revenue resulting from this reputation causing a real gap between them and national universities in the regions. The gap is even bigger, of course, between the private universities in Seoul and the private universities in the regions, which are in most cases far 'worse' than national universities in the regions.

SNU, the national university in Seoul, has been spared the rankings decline that the national universities in the regions have experienced. One dean explains its advantages, saying 'SNU is located in Seoul, and has a good infrastructure. Its legal basis is a decree by the President of the Republic of Korea … As such, it is unlike the national universities in the regions whose legal basis is a decree by the Prime Minister' (Dean C). This dean further laments that regional universities, such as his own, do not have the advantages that SNU possesses when competing with Seoul-based private universities, saying 'When we compare PNU with Yonsei, KU, and SKKU, we don't have much of an advantage over them, unlike SNU' (Dean C).

Many academic deans at national universities in the regions are making efforts to address the disparity in educational quality and reputation between the universities in the capital area and those in the regions. For example, a national university dean says that he had been concerned more than anything else with raising the stature of his institution: 'My college at KNU used to be held in high esteem but it keeps falling now. So how do I raise its stature – that's what demanded most of my attention' (Dean R). Another national university dean is proposing the formation of a consortium of national universities in a wide region comprising a province and two special cities to compete with universities in the capital area:

> I think the south-eastern region, more narrowly Busan, Ulsan and Gyeongnam Province, can form its own consortium to compete with the greater Seoul area. A precondition for the prosperity of this region is that it establishes an educational system, which can compete with that of the greater Seoul area. (Dean C)

Clearly aware of the disadvantages that their regional institutions are suffering, academic deans at regional universities nonetheless think that 'a university's own effort is most important' (Dean K). At the same time, they call loudly for a more balanced approach to education and the economy throughout the country. Their logic is simple, but persuasive - if the whole is going to develop, the parts should come along; without the parts' contribution, there can be no prosperity of the whole. 'If Korea is to prosper, shouldn't residents of Busan be able to get their education in Busan?' (Dean S).

> I believe that Korea can't prosper with Seoul as the only axis. ... If we keep going on the single axis, what we'll see is not the effect of economy of scale but that of 'non-economy' or 'inefficiency of scale', and it'll be bad for the prosperity of our society. (Dean C)

Thus in the comments of these deans, we can discern that there is a causal cycle set up which pushes the reputation and funding of Seoul area universities upwards and regional universities downwards. The initial high status and other advantages of Seoul area universities lead to better graduate employability and high rankings. These results lead to increased funding and increased student competition to get into Seoul area universities. The increased funding allows Seoul area universities to finance reputation-increasing 'luxuries' such as research; the increased competition for admission allows them to recruit the best and best-connected students in the country. These increases in the amount of research and the quality of their students further increase the reputation and graduate employment rate of Seoul universities, thereby leading to further increases in funding and rankings. This process seems to repeat itself with an ever-increasing intensity, raising rankings of Seoul area universities even higher.

For the regional universities, it is just the opposite – lower rankings lead to recruiting poorer students and less funding, which lead to even lower rankings. A downward cycle is thereby created that also repeats itself with ever-increasing intensity. If not arrested, it is feared that this cycle will lead to the extinction of many regional universities (Kim and Kim 2013). It will also be an unhappy state of affairs for students who go to regional universities. As the reputation of their universities sinks lower and lower, they will become more and more unemployable.

The increasing disparity in quality and status between Seoul-area universities and regional universities will, in turn, reinforce the unequal economic class system that is already a problem in South Korea. This is because socioeconomic status plays a substantial role in the college choice process. Lower-income students, constrained by their socioeconomic status, are inevitably less likely to choose a selective, more expensive institution than their more privileged peers (Steinberg et al. 2009). Lower-income students are also more likely than their peers, controlling for other factors, to choose to attend a university close to home (McDonough 1997; St John et al. 2001; Pryor, et al. 2008). Therefore, if the regional universities of South Korea suffer, so will poor and middle class students throughout the country. The Three No's policy safeguarding the regional universities also safeguards poor and middle class students throughout the country.

Discussion – Implications of the Policy

In the comments of the Korean deans, we see the impact of the various factors affecting Korean higher education. The increasing gulf between Seoul and the provinces, the impact of the *hagwons* and the elite monopolising of the best universities, the shrinking student pool, and the neo-liberal performance regime – all of these contribute to a sense that there is a fierce competition for survival among the Korean colleges, a competition that manifests itself in a desperate scramble to recruit the wealthiest, best connected and most promising students. As one dean from this study put it, it is extremely important to recruit excellent students from the very beginning. Students from privileged social classes may have a greater chance to get into prestigious universities, which in turn will give them an advantage in social life. This practice leads to the solidification of social class and the polarisation of society in Korea.

The responses of the deans to this hyper-competitive environment fall into three categories. The first is expressions of anxiety – even despair – over the growing gulf between the Seoul-based universities and the universities in the provinces. Even the Seoul-based universities seem to display great anxiety. Perhaps they sense that they too are not immune to the forces that are plaguing the provincial universities, after all.

The second response of the deans is to question the criteria by which the universities are judged. Many of the rankings are popular and unscientific, and their validity may justly be questioned (Bruni 2016; Marszal 2012; Pusser and Marginson 2013). Prior to the neo-liberal regime such rankings could be shrugged off, but in the current environment deans are forced to obsess about them.

Finally, many of the deans respond to the new competitive environment by opposing the Three No's policy. This policy represents the government's efforts to ensure equity in student access to education. However, under the pressure of the new neo-liberal performance regime that the government has initiated, it has drawn bitter complaints from many university deans as being no longer appropriate. Universities, particularly private universities, are always in need of greater revenue. Also, the government itself is leading national and private universities alike to the mode of governance that favours the market approach to higher education. Therefore, academic deans, particularly those at private universities, want to have autonomy in the areas under the grip of the Three-No's policy. Academic deans, especially those from universities located in the Seoul area, find these policies curtailing their freedom to act within the new competitive norms set by the government. On the other hand, regional university deans tend to support the Three-No's policy as a check, albeit inadequate, on the increasing disparity between Seoul-based universities and regional ones.

Concluding Remarks

Ultimately, the controversy over the Three No's policy reflects a conflict between the equity that Korean society at large wants and needs on the one hand, and the new competition-based reforms that the government is implementing on the other. There will be no simple answers, no clear right and wrong on this conflict. Both competition and equity are good and necessary, but they are inherently in tension. In the end, Korean university admission policies must be developed in an interplay between the needs of the various universities, the ideals of academia, and the needs and ideals of the Korean people.

References

Bruni, F. (2016). Why college rankings are a joke. *The New York Times*, 17 September 2016.

Clarke, M. (2007). The impact of higher education rankings on student access, choice, and opportunity. *Higher Education in Europe, 32*(1), 59-70.

Grubb, W.N., Sweet, R., Gallagher, M., and Tuomi, O. (2009). *OECD reviews of tertiary education: Korea.* Paris: OECD.

Heritage Foundation (2017). *Index of Economic Freedom: South Korea.* Retrieved 12 October 2017 from http://www.heritage.org/index/pdf/2017/countries/southkorea.pdf

Kim, J., and Kim, H.S. (2013). Globalization and access to higher education in Korea. In H.-D. Meyer, E.P. St. John, M. Chankseliani and L. Uribe (eds.), *Fairness in access to higher education in a global perspective: Reconciling excellence, efficiency, and justice* (pp. 129-151). Rotterdam: Sense Publishers.

Kim, S., and Lee, J.H. (2006). Changing facets of Korean higher education: Market competition and the role of the state. *Higher Education, 52*(3), 557-587.

Kim, T. (2008). Higher education reforms in South Korea: Public–private problems in internationalising and incorporating universities. *Policy Futures in Education, 6*(5), 558-568.

Koo, H. (2007). Changing faces of inequality in South Korea in the age of globalization. *Korean Studies, 31*, 1-18.

Korean Ministry of Education (2003). The Revised Basic Plan for Admission Screening to Universities or Colleges for the academic year 2004. 31 March 2003.

Lee, C.J. (2005). Korean education fever and private tutoring. *KEDI Journal of Educational Policy, 2*(1), 99-107.

Lee, M.H. (2008). The 'public' and the 'private' in Korean higher education: One private dominating system. *Journal of Asian Public Policy, 1*(2), 199-210.

Lee, S, and Brinton, M.C. (1996). Elite education and social capital: The case of South Korea. *Sociology of Education, 69*(July), 177-192.

Lee, S.C. (2014). *Challenges in regional college collaboration: Cases of Japan, the U.S., and Korea.* Retrieved 16 October 2017 from UNESCO–WTA Cooperative Projects website: http://uw.wtanet.org/ds_imgs/sub02/uw01/05.pdf

Marszal, A. (2012). University rankings: Which world university rankings should we trust? *The Telegraph*, 4 October 2012.

McDonough, P.M., Antonio, A.L., Walpole, M.B., and Pérez, L.X. (1998). College rankings: Democratized college knowledge for whom? *Research in Higher Education, 39*(5), 513–537.

Marginson, S., and Considine, M. (2000). *The enterprise university: Power, governance and reinvention in Australia.* Cambridge/Melbourne: Cambridge University Press.

Meek, V.L., Goedegebuure, L., and Swanson, C. (2010). The changing nature of academic middle management: A framework for analysis. In V.L. Meek, L. Goedegebuure, R. Santiago and T. Carvalho (eds.), *The changing dynamics of higher education middle management* (pp. 229-241). Dordrecht/New York: Springer.

Morphew, C.C., and Swanson, C. (2011). On the efficacy of raising your university's ranking. In J.C. Shin, R.K. Toutkoushian, and U. Teichler (eds.), *University rankings: Theoretical basis, methodology and impacts on global higher education* (pp. 185-199). Dordrecht/New York: Springer.

Park, H.-Y. (2007). Emerging consumerism and the accelerated 'education divide': The case of specialised high schools in South Korea. *Journal for Critical Education Policy Studies, 5*(2). Retrieved 22 September 2015 from http://www.jceps.com/wp-content/uploads/PDFs/05-2-14.pdf

Pusser. B., and Marginson, S. (2013). University rankings in critical perspective. *The Journal of Higher Education, 84*(4), 544-568.

Pryor, J.H., Hurtado, S., DeAngelo, L., Palucki, L., Tran, B., and Tran, S. (2008). *The American freshman: National norms for fall 2009*. Berkeley: University of California Press.

Rizvi, F., and Lingard, B. (2010). *Globalizing education policy*. Abingdon, Oxon/New York: Routledge.

Rizvi, F., and Lingard, B. (2011). Social equity and the assemblage of values in Australian higher education. *Cambridge Journal of Education, 41*(1), 5-22.

Rose, N.S. (2010). *Powers of freedom: Reframing political thought*. Cambridge, UK/New York: Cambridge University Press.

Shin, J.C. (2009). Classifying higher education institutions in Korea: A performance-based approach. *Higher Education, 57*, 247-266.

Shin, J.C. (2012). Higher education development in Korea: Western university ideas, Confucian tradition, and economic development. *Higher Education, 64*, 59-72.

Sorensen, C.W. (1994). Success and education in South Korea. *Comparative Education Review, 38*(1), 10-35.

St John, E.P., Asker, E., and Hu, S. (2001). The role of finances in student choice: A review of theory and research. In M.B. Paulsen and J.C. Smart (eds.), *The finance of higher education: Theory, research, policy, and practice*. New York: Agathon.

Steinberg, M.P., Piraino, P., and Haveman, R. (2009). Access to higher education: Exploring the variation in Pell Grant prevalence among U.S. colleges and universities. *The Review of Higher Education., 32*(2), 235–270.

Sung, C.J. (2011). Cultivating borrowed futures: The politics of neo-liberal loanwords in South Korean cross-national policy borrowing. *Comparative Education, 47*(4), 523-538.

CONTRIBUTORS

Dr Taghreed Jamal Al-deen is an Associate Research Fellow for the UNESCO Chair, Cultural Diversity and Social Justice, at the Alfred Deakin Institute for Citizenship and Globalisation. Taghreed holds a PhD from Monash University. Her doctoral research examined migrant mothers' involvement in children's education. In this research, she looked at issues of education, migration, ethnicity, class, gender, motherhood in Islam and multiculturalism.

Ms Zahra Ali is a PhD student at Monash University. Zahra has taught English as an International Language (EIL) units in the Faculty of Arts at Monash University and the Monash English Bridging (MEB) course at Monash College. Her research interest includes TESOL, language, culture and identity, and intercultural communication.

Dr Raqib Chowdhury taught at Dhaka University from 1997 to 2004, and since 2008 has been teaching at Monash University. He holds Masters degrees in English Literature and Education and has published in the areas of TESOL, international education and identity. He is the author of *Desiring TESOL and International Education: Market Abuse and Exploitation*, and the editor of *Enacting English Across Borders: A Critical Study in the Asia Pacific*.

Dr Venesser Fernandes is an Educational Leadership Studies Lecturer in the Faculty of Education, Monash University. Her areas of teaching and research interests include: Leadership and Organisational Studies; School Leadership; School Accountability and Improvement Systems; Data-Driven Decision-making Processes; Evidence-based School Improvement Systems; and Educational Policy Analysis and Development.

Dr Ram A. Giri was a reader at Tribhuvan University, Nepal, from 1990 to 1999. Before joining the English Language Centre of Monash University he taught EIL units in the Faculty of Arts. He has published journal articles, book chapters and co-edited books. His research interests include languages education policy, language and culture, and academic writing.

Dr Hoang Thi Hanh is a Lecturer at the University of Languages and International Studies, Vietnam National University Hanoi. She completed both MA-TESOL and PhD degrees at the University of Queensland. Her research interests include intercultural communication and EFL methodology.

Mr Alireza Fard Kashani is a PhD candidate at Deakin University, Australia. He obtained his BA and Master's in English Literature and Applied Linguistics, respectively, from Isfahan University and the University of Science and Technology, Iran. His areas of research are language, culture and identity.

Dr Farzana Khan completed her doctorate from the Faculty of Education, Monash University, Australia. She is a hermeneutic phenomenologist who researched the impact of purdah (veiling), globalisation and tradition on Muslim female graduates in Bangladesh. Her research interests include inclusive education, teaching for diversity and gender studies.

Dr Dong Kwang Kim is currently Professor at the Institute of Global Human Resource Development at Okayama University. He was trained both in education and philosophy. His current academic and practical interests lie in the field of higher education with a particular focus on preserving humanistic values in the higher education curriculum.

Dr Melinda Kong is currently a Senior Lecturer and Course Director of MA TESOL at Swinburne University of Technology, Sarawak, Malaysia. She has presented in leading international conferences, and has published in the areas of teacher education, identity, and curriculum and pedagogy.

Associate Professor Indika Liyanage is Associate Head of School (International Partnerships) and Discipline Leader of TESOL/LOTE in the School of Education, Faculty of Arts and Education at Deakin University. His current research interests include issues in second language teacher education, language teacher professional development, teacher agency, and contextually responsive knowledge transfer of language teachers across socio-cultural boundaries.

Ms Kaoru Matsunaga had worked as an English instructor at Nagoya University of Foreign Studies and Aichi Shukutoku University after obtaining a Master of Education (TESOL) degree from Monash University in Australia. She is currently undertaking a PhD at Monash University. Her research interests are EFL teaching and learning and identity construction.

Ms Lavanya Raj is a psychologist, educator and social worker. People development is her core area of strength. She works in multiple capacities in educational institutions, through organisational consultancy and non-governmental grassroots projects through which she works for women's development in underrepresented communities. Currently she is completing a PhD in Leadership and Quality in Higher education in Australia.

Dr Hossein Shokouhi is a Senior Lecturer at Deakin University and has published in *Lingua, Discourse Studies, Australian Journal of Linguistics,* two co-authored books, and has been a visiting scholar at Potsdam University in Germany, Deusto University in Spain, and La Trobe University in Australia, from where he received his PhD.

Ms Pham Thi Ngoc Thanh has been a Lecturer at the Faculty of Foreign Studies at Vietnam Maritime University since 2015. She was trained in English Teacher Education. Her research interests include intercultural communication, ICT in EFL, and second language teaching and learning.

Dr Shashinie Thenabadu commenced her teaching at Peradeniya University in 1996 and then joined the University of Colombo, Sri Lanka, in 2003 where she currently teaches as a Senior Lecturer in ELT. She holds Masters degrees in Linguistics and TESOL and engages in research in areas such as EMI and ESL.

Dr Joel Windle is Assistant Professor at the Institute of Modern Languages at the Fluminense Federal University (Brazil) and Senior Adjunct Research Fellow at the Faculty of Education, Monash University (Australia). His research, drawing on the fields of sociology of education and applied linguistics, focuses on educational inequalities.

Dr Lilly K. Yazdanpanah teaches in the Faculty of Education at Monash University. Her research centres on the construction of teacher and student identity, emotions, and cultural diversity in English language classrooms. She also serves as the Submissions Editor of *TESL-EJ* and is a member of the Advisory Board of the *Journal of Studies in Learning and Teaching English* and the Nepal English Language Teachers' Association (NELTA).

CPSIA information can be obtained
at www.ICGtesting.com
Printed in the USA
BVHW090345081118
532492BV00001B/4/P